# EPHESIOLOGY

I have personally been enlightened by Michael's insights in regards to what it takes to start a movement like the early church that spanned much of the known world with the Gospel. Though I have earned multiple theological degrees, this is the first time I have heard the insights Michael has given in this book. It has motivated me to the point that I am having him train my staff and board of elders and deacons—hoping to light the fire for evangelism in their hearts as well.

REV. STEVE GIBSON
lead pastor, Wellspring Church, Hudsonville, Michigan

Despite the fact that the modern missiological use of the phrase "church planting movements" is quite recent (in terms of over 2,000 years of church history), the phenomenon of the rapid multiplication of house churches was clearly birthed and evolved almost two millennia ago in Ephesus and other early Apostolic church plants. I love the concept of a book that examines the multiplication and growth of the early church in Ephesus while also integrating that study with an examination of relevant passages in the Epistles, Acts, and Revelation. Michael intertwines illustrations of contemporary church planting movements with the study of the biblical theology of the church and early church multiplication movements. The Book of Ephesians' clear focus on the believer's intimacy with God, the centrality of the gospel of grace, the Holy Spirit empowerment for service and requisite holistic integrity of the life and family of a follower of Jesus make it the perfect New Testament book—and early church movement—to study in order to understand the explosion of the gospel that began in Ephesus almost 2,000 years ago! I recommend this strategic book to others in order to motivate the global church to sprint towards the finish line of the Great Commission!

DR. KURT NELSON
president and CEO, East West Ministries International
author of *Finishing Well: Encouraging Pastors to Persevere under Persecution*

Dr. Cooper's proposal is creative, and the book will make a good contribution to existing literature on the theology of church planting movements. Among its merits is the fact that the book combines research in New Testament with current issues and realities in church planting movements worldwide, drawing upon Dr. Cooper's extensive experience in this area. I think the book will be welcomed by missiologists and church planters and it should find its place as a text in Bible colleges and seminaries.

DR. HAROLD A. NETLAND
professor of Philosophy of Religion and Intercultural Studies,
Trinity Evangelical Divinity School
author of *Christianity and Religious Diversity*

Masterfully handling the book of Ephesians and using its content as a definitive guide, Michael T. Cooper lays a theologically strong foundation that is both corrective and directive to disciple making movements. The principles he gleans from the book of Ephesians and related texts help to ensure the ongoing multiplication and maturation of a movement. Because these are supra-cultural principles, they are applicable anywhere in the world.

MARVIN J. NEWELL
staff missiologist, Missio Nexus

A century ago, Roland Allen demonstrated how far nineteenth century missionary practice had departed from the example of the Apostle Paul. His work is still in print, used by many and needed to be used by more. Michael Cooper is accomplishing the same task of calling the church back to the Biblical foundation of missions and church planting. In Allen's day, missions was married to the spirit of progress and colonialism. In our day, it is married to the vagaries of contemporary culture and the gimmicks of modernity. What is needed is exactly what Dr. Cooper is proposing, namely a reexamination of the Biblical methodology of Paul. It is applicable to the church planting around the world just as Allen's work, written for the mission field, has been used by churches and para-church ministries in North America.

DR. JAMES STAMOOLIS
missiologist and educational consultant
author of *Eastern Orthodox Mission Theology Today*

Wow—GREAT resource! Far too often we forget the basics in church planting and church multiplication movements. *Ephesiology* gives a solid biblical understanding to the original church planting movement, and provides a healthy DNA understanding for local congregations, denominations, and ministries to grow effectively. Dr. Cooper has made a significant contribution to the Kingdom here. I'm adding this book to our recommended resource tool kit for GACX (Global Alliance for Church Multiplication) team.

NATE VANDER STELT
executive vice president, Global Alliance for Church Multiplication

"What will it take?" This is one of the questions that keep me awake at night, and I believe Michael too. He and I share an irresistible curiosity and zeal for a gospel-movement in our communities, country, continent, and world. With stories of such movements exploding in the hardest to reach places around the globe, the church in North America (along with other places where the church has plateaued or is in decline) would do well to learn from what has now become known as church planting movements (CPMs). I have benefited greatly from Michael's experience and insights detailed in this book, both theologically and practically. I highly recommend this book to every pastor, church planter, Christian leader, and academic who needs permission to embrace a radical paradigm that originated in first-century Ephesus and answers the question, "What will it take?"

MATTHEW TILL
lead pastor, Restoration Church, Lake Zurich, Illinois
adjunct professor of Biblical Studies, Trinity International University

I am really excited about Michael's new book, *Ephesiology*. Using the Ephesian church as a model for understanding church planting movements better is brilliant. I have generally separated out the various passages and books that relate to the Ephesians and, at times, may have missed some important emphases and principles that all of us who are engaged in church planting need to consider in our strategies.

DR. JOE L. WALL
professor of Systematic Theology, Grace School of Theology
author of *Going of Gold*

# EPHESIOLOGY

*A Study of the Ephesian Movement*

MICHAEL T. COOPER

WILLIAM
CAREY
PUBLISHING

Published by William Carey Publishing
10 W. Dry Creek Cir
Littleton, CO 80120 | www.missionbooks.org

William Carey Publishing is a ministry of Frontier Ventures
Pasadena, CA 91104 | www.frontierventures.org

Mike Riester, cover and interior design
Rory Clark, Indexing
Andrew Sloan, copyeditor
Melissa Hicks, managing editor

ISBNs: 978-1-64508-276-7 (paperback),
        978-1-64508-278-1 (mobi),
        978-1-64508-279-8 (epub)

Printed Worldwide

24 23 22 21 20   1 2 3 4 5

Library of Congress data on file with publisher.

# CONTENTS

133920

# FOREWORD

I first met Michael in the spring of 2018. My wife, Mary, and I were in the thick of planting a new church in the suburbs of Chicago with a heart to serve the community and share the gospel of hope and restorative grace in Jesus Christ. We were filled with the Spirit, driven by our faith, and ambitious about what the Lord might do through our new ministry. Even our sending organization was optimistic in our vision, experience, and the possibilities of what might come of starting a new evangelistic community of faith. But optimism gave way to discouragement, confusion, and deep theological questioning.

I understand this is common among new church planters. Regardless of their training or experience, many become deeply burdened and often succumb to mounting pressure or discouragement. However, being on the vulnerable and unprotected frontlines of an impending cultural collapse of postmodernism, growing secularization, and the declining trust in anything related or affiliated with "church," we knew God was helping us see that something had to change. It was becoming clear to us that the North American "Evangelical Exile" was well underway, and if we had any hope to be part of God's mission and plan for his future church, we needed to lay down our ways and follow his ways.

Mary is a former student of Michael's—"Dr. Cooper" to her. In God's undeniable timing and perfect orchestration, Mary had reconnected with Dr. Cooper earlier in 2017 and the dialogue began. He shared about his experiences studying church planting movements around the globe. He was actively equipping and training hundreds of church planters in both open and closed countries. As a missiologist, Michael was seeing the Great Commission at work in explosive and miraculous ways. Stories like his often left me pondering, "Why not here?"

Michael happened to be traveling through Chicago later that spring and we eagerly set up a meeting. We sat down for the first time at the Panera Bread where I'm presently writing the foreword to this book. It was at this meeting that we shared our concerns with contemporary forms of evangelicalism, discussed the findings of mass rates of conversions to Christianity taking place in other parts of the world such as Asia and the Middle East, and explored the implications for the church in the West.

Michael also shared some early thoughts he had been working on regarding the Apostle Paul's ministry in Ephesus. His thesis was centered on this influential pagan city in the first century that saw an incredible church multiplication movement focused on a single goal—the glorification of God in all things. No programs, no central funding, no cathedrals, no professional clergy, and no evangelistic events. Just the Word of God, the Holy Spirit, and faithful believers in Christ living to glorify the Father against all odds.

If these were the pieces to a missiological puzzle that led to a multiplication movement recorded in the New Testament church, then shouldn't we expect to see evidence of similar movements today? As it turns out, we do.

Backed by research and robust missiological exegesis, *Ephesiology* explores this tension between the first Christian movement and modern movements or the lack thereof in Western contexts. What *Ephesiology* has sought to do is what few have attempted—let alone succeed in. *Ephesiology* seeks to stand in the gap of the broad spectrum of Christian ecclesiology, explore its roots in the New Testament, remain committed to historic orthodoxy, and apply a missiological-theism as a foundational practice and underpinning to the purpose and mission of every disciple of Jesus Christ.

*Ephesiology* is not another methodology or attempt to re-contextualize evangelicalism to a growing secularized West. *Ephesiology* is the re-examination of the ancient gospel message given to us in the New Testament with the goal for every believer to participate in God's plan—to unite all things in Christ (Eph 1:10).

*Ephesiology* and the ideas contained within this book have the potential to disrupt the majority of existing institutional and historical traditions of the faith over the millennia. Such a disruption is ultimately necessary and bound to come that have emerged upon Western Christianity. Will we purposefully seek to restore the church and what has been lost on our own, or will we be forced to re-examine ourselves in exile? It's in this light that I believe *Ephesiology* is part of the answer (if not the answer) to what God hopes to accomplish through his children in the rapidly evolving twenty-first century.

I'm deeply thankful for Michael's friendship, his invitation to allow people like Andrew Johnson and myself to speak into and help shape his work, and most importantly, his commitment to the world-changing gospel message given to us in Jesus Christ for the whole world. For any reader who takes seriously what is written on the pages that follow, I trust you will be deeply challenged and awakened to the heart of God's mission for the world.

MATT TILL
lead pastor, Restoration Church, Chicago, IL
Co-host, Ephesiology Podcast

# PREFACE

In 1989 I was wrestling with my place in missions and especially with the relationship between the church and parachurch organizations. Having come to Christ through the high school ministry of Cru in 1980, all I really knew was the parachurch. As a new Christian, I started attending Spring Branch Community Church. Joe Wall was the pastor in those days, and although I did not get to know him then, he has become a dear colleague where I serve now.

While I attended church in high school and throughout college, I was not really thinking about its relevance in my life, nor did I think I needed to, as I later joined the staff of Cru. Then, in 1990, as the walls of communism continued to collapse and changes to ministry paradigms were shifting, I picked up Bob Logan's *Beyond Church Growth: Actions Plans for Developing a Dynamic Church* and learned there might be a more strategic ministry in church planting. The book was revolutionary, so much so that I stepped away from reading it with a clear vision for going to seminary and becoming a church planter. Well, as it turned out, things did not quite happen in that way, for which I am very thankful. Church planting came first, and in the summer of 1990 we launched a new work in former communist Romania that continues to help me understand the positives and negatives of church planting movements.

Ronnie Stevens was the pastor of Munich International Community Church at the time I worked with Cru's Eastern Europe/ Soviet Union ministry, and he helped me muster the courage to step away from the parachurch and apply what I had learned about multiplying disciples in the context of a new church plant. With his encouragement and one of his systematic theology books, I headed off to be among the first Western church planters in Romania. I was young and ambitious, and admittedly naïve. But I had great ministry role models in Ronnie and the Cru staff working in Eastern Europe and the Soviet Union. I understood how to multiply disciples, thanks to Mike Crandall, Tom Atchison, and Ray Anderson. I knew how to put together a strategy to win the lost, build them in the faith, and send them to make disciples. So over the next five years seven church planting streams began in the unreached area of south-central Romania.

Later, my wife, Loré, and I did attend seminary, where we focused on sharpening our understanding of church planting and leadership development. Eventually, I graduated with an MA in missions. However, not satisfied with unanswered questions regarding the legitimacy of taking people out of the Orthodox Church, we decided to head to Illinois to continue studies focused on the early Church Fathers and the growth of the church after the New Testament. About a year and a half into my PhD program, I encountered a new religious movement that successfully revived an ancient traditional religion which had connections to Asia as well as to Saint Patrick and the Irish missionary monks. I had come to the point of satisfactorily answering the questions about the Orthodox Church and now concentrated on why religious movements grow. It was no accident that the Lord directed me to focus my doctoral work and academic research on these religious movements, as their growth pattern was similar to the growth we see in church planting movements around the world today.

During my seminary studies, and especially while church planting in Romania, the church in Ephesus became a source of inspiration. While in seminary, I learned that if I wanted to understand the church, a good place to start was with the letter to the Ephesians. Additionally, since leadership for a church is a vital part of church planting, I needed to master 1 Timothy. Similarly, to multiply disciples, I needed to understand 2 Timothy. Paul's letter to the Ephesians and his second letter to Timothy occupied much of my study, discipleship, and preaching in Romania, as our church leaders in Curtea de Argeş and Bucureşti had to suffer through my early attempts to learn from that New Testament movement. After completing my Greek studies, Ephesians and 2 Timothy were the next two texts I translated into English. Not that translating Greek makes me an expert, but it was important to see and read what that church and those leaders saw and read.

It is not an exaggeration to say that this book was twenty-five years in the making. I don't think that taking twenty-five years to write a book on the movement in Ephesus makes it all the worthier to read. However, it is a topic that I have thought about for quite some time. *Ephesiology* [n. i-fē-zē-ă-lə-jē]: *The Study of the Ephesian Movement* is the product of a life lived on the mission field, then in the academic world, and now back on the mission field. It has been a joy to write, not because I am finally putting my thoughts on paper, but because of the countless interactions I have had with people all over the world on this topic. It has led me to believe that maybe there is something to be said for a comprehensive look at what happened in Ephesus. After all, this was a movement that shaped our past theological ideas and continues to impact Christianity today.

I believe the movement that began in Ephesus is the most significant movement in the history of Christianity. More New Testament books are directly tied to Ephesus than any other church. Outside of Jerusalem, more apostles are associated with Ephesus than any other city. The movement that spread throughout Asia is mentioned more often than that of any other region in the New Testament. God did something incredible through those faithful saints who knew that their adoption in Christ led them to join with God in his mission.

This book is indeed an exercise of doing theology in community. So many people have spoken into my life and have impacted what I have written. They are in no way to blame for what you will read. I take sole responsibility. Nevertheless, this book would not be what it is if not for how the Lord used others to help give it shape.

Of special note are two dear brothers in Christ, Andrew Johnson, associate pastor at Neartown Church in Houston, and Matt Till, lead pastor and church planter at Restoration Church outside of Chicago. They have spent countless hours engaging the material through texts, video calls, and the Ephesiology podcast. I appreciate these guys more than I can express.

Mark Anderson originally gave me the idea for the neologism Ephesiology. Like Matt and Andrew, Mark and I have exchanged numerous texts, emails and phone calls wrestling through what was really happening in Ephesus and when it all happened.

Our pastor, Steve Gibson, has been gracious enough to allow me to take the staff at Wellspring Community Church in Hudsonville, Michigan, through several chapters to help me make sure I am connecting with church leaders. I am grateful for their encouragement around the conference table, as well as through numerous outside conversations.

Heath Haynes and the Bridge at Montrose in Houston, Texas, were early testers of the material in the form of a seminar. They are now developing their Movement Action Plan to engage their community with the gospel.

Devlin Scott has offered keen insights and encouragement, as he and Katie are engaging their community in Boston.

Dr. Neal Brower's courage to discuss Ephesiology with his district's pastors has given me hope that maybe God can use the principles to ignite a movement in a denomination.

Dr. Jim Stamoolis graciously read early chapters and offered keen missiological insights and encouragement, as he always does.

Dr. Dudley Brown lent his early Church Fathers and New Testament expertise to help sharpen the chapter on Paul's letter to the Ephesians.

The team at William Carey Publishing—Denise, Melissa, Katie, Andy, Mike—have been a true joy to work with. Their commitment to excellence in publishing and their care to ensure the book faithfully communicates its thesis went beyond my expectations.

Our kids, now adults, have spent many hours listening to me talk about Ephesus and the missiologically theocentric nature of the movement at the dinner table, in the car, while playing pool or tennis, or while cycling. I have enjoyed our theological discussions beyond expression. They continue to be just as rich and insightful as they were when they attended elementary school.

Loré, of course, is really responsible for making this book happen. Without her prayers, encouragement, courage, and sacrifice I would not have been able to meet the people I have met or see their work around the world.

I need to mention that there are so many people on this planet who have been an inspiration to me. These are dear brothers and sisters who daily risk their well-being for the gospel. Whether it was on the dusty roads traveling to Karamoja, trekking to villages on the Great Himalayan Trail, hiking through the dense jungle of Colombia, or fellowshipping at a conference center in Manila, the times with Christian leaders have been thrilling and stimulating. I cannot begin to fathom what some of these dear brothers and sisters face daily, and I am so grateful for the opportunity to have seen their service to the Lord. Many of the people I write about live in countries where persecution is real. Their names have been changed in order to protect them.

Finally, I pray for you, the reader, in much the same way that Paul prayed for the group of disciples who first read Ephesians:

> For this reason I bow my knees before the Father, from whom every family in heaven and on earth is named, that according to the riches of his glory he may grant you to be strengthened with power through his Spirit in your inner being, so that Christ may dwell in your hearts through faith—that you, being rooted and grounded in love, may have strength to comprehend with all the saints what is the breadth and length and height and depth, and to know the love of Christ that surpasses knowledge, that you may be filled with all the fullness of God. (Eph 3:14–19)

If God were to be so gracious and answer that prayer, I know you will be transformed by the missiologically theocentric movement he began almost two thousand years ago.

## Using the QR Codes

At the end of each chapter, you will find a QR code. Simply scan the code with your smartphone and you will be directed to the Ephesiology website (https://ephesiology.com), which contains video lessons and discussion guides for each chapter as they relate to this remarkable New Testament movement. My sincere gratitude to Andrew Johnson for developing the discussion guides and spending countless hours thinking about how to effectively engage people in an urban context. We trust that these guides will help you wrestle with the New Testament movement that began in Ephesus and with what might be applicable to your ministry.

# CHAPTER 1

# Introducing Ephesiology

I met Juan in the jungle of the Sierra Nevada de Santa Marta Mountains on the northeastern coast of Colombia. The snowcapped mountains are the highest elevation along the Caribbean Sea. Somewhere around thirteen thousand Kogi live in twenty-nine communities spread out along that range. They are a traditional animistic people who do not want to have contact with those they call "younger brother."

Juan grew up in one of the Kogi communities, and when he was a boy he met two missionaries who shared the gospel with him. This had a transformational impact on Juan's life, and everyone in the community recognized it. Later Juan attended a school in Bogota, where he decided to become a pastor so that he could take the gospel back to his people. After completing his education, he returned to the mountain. People noticed the difference Jesus made in his life. Slowly others began to desire the peace of Christ Juan experienced, and eventually sixty Kogi converted to Christianity.

Not long after these conversions, community leaders began to feel threatened by this new group. The lifestyle they had observed among the predominately Catholic Colombians who called themselves Christians brought deep fear that their traditions would be impacted. They began to persecute the new Kogi believers and finally gave them an ultimatum: either renounce their faith or be killed! Juan and the other Christians fled their homes. They left everything—fathers and mothers, brothers and sisters, and all their earthly possessions—to start a new community whose hope is to reach back to their people with the gospel.

Over the years since their exile, they have dubbed *The Jesus Film* into the Kogi language, committed their language to writing, translated the New Testament, and are presently working on translating the Old Testament. Their vision is to see an indigenous movement in the jungles of Colombia proclaiming the good news of Jesus Christ. Their dream began with a cost. No doubt it will cost more. But it is a cost that we all need to assess if we desire to be a part of a movement of God like we see in the New Testament. Perhaps there is no better New Testament movement to study than the one that began in Ephesus in AD 51.

## Ephesiology: A Study of the Ephesian Movement

If you are looking for a commentary on Ephesians, you have picked up the wrong book. This book is about the fantastic work of the Holy Spirit that resulted in all of the Roman province of Asia hearing the gospel.[1] Like commentaries, however, I offer plenty of interpretation of Paul's letter bearing the title "Ephesians," as well as other texts associated with the city. This is not a biblical theology of missions, either, although we will see timeless principles that ensured the movement would become indigenous. Rather, the book is a missiological theology of the Bible.

You might wonder about the distinction between a biblical theology and a missiological theology. The former makes missions a subset of biblical theology, something that is one among many different biblical theologies—of the church, of leadership, of God, etc. The latter puts missions at the core of the Bible. Missions is the Bible's purpose, as missions seeks God's glorification by the proclamation of his will to every people, nation, tribe, and tongue. As the South African missiologist David Bosch said, "God's very nature is missionary" (1991, 390), so we should clearly see his missionary activity through the disciples and what they wrote.

Unlike commentaries and biblical theologies, my interest is in the missiologically theocentric movement that began in the great city of Ephesus and lasted for the next generation. How did the movement start? What did its adherents believe? Who were its leaders? How did it multiply? What sustained its growth? Those are the questions I hope to answer in this book, appropriately titled *Ephesiology: A Study of the Ephesian Movement.*

---

1. The Roman province of Asia extended from the eastern coast of the Aegean Sea to the border of Galatia in central Asia. Asia is generally used in reference to the Anatolian peninsula of modern-day Turkey.

I am also interested in what happened in the movement that led many to embrace false teaching and return to pagan practices. Much of my academic career focused on researching religious movements in Western society (Cooper 2010). The one common denominator in most of these movements is that they are made up of disillusioned Christians who decided to walk away from their faith in pursuit of another. Why does this happen? It is not uncommon for sure. Paul knew many who walked away from the faith. In fact, he would write to Timothy that everyone in Asia had left him (2 Tim 1:15).

I am interested in how to prevent people from walking away from the faith. This topic cannot be left to the theological gymnastics of our modern interpretations about the doctrines of election and predestination, which are often misunderstood in Paul's writings. Neither can it rely on the altruistic acts of social justice in hopes that one can prove the merit of Christianity.

My goal, ultimately, is for us to come away with a deeper appreciation for God's mission in the world through church planting movements (CPMs). A few years ago we could only count a handful of CPMs. Today we are tracking more than 708![2] One CPM organization alone has seen God work through a reported planting of an average of 815 house churches each week and the baptism of one thousand new believers every day.

The same kind of fantastic events that we see in the book of Acts between AD 33 and 63 and in the city of Ephesus between AD 51 and 96 are still happening all around the world: imprisonments, riots, and beatings, as well as visions, miracles, and martyrdom. On the backs of many brothers and sisters in Christ are borne the scars of suffering for the Lord and the fruit of thousands coming to Christ every day. It is not their theology or acts of justice that bring people to Christ. It is their faithful dedication to fulfilling God's will to his praise and glory.

---

2. The Global Alliance for Church Multiplication reports there are 2,912 reports of active CPM engagement and 708 stage 5 CPMs that have grown to four-plus generations. The result is more than 69 million believers and 4.5 million churches with approximately 96,000 believers in each stage 5 CPM. The average church size is 15 (see https://vimeo.com/325214876 for the video report). As of the January/February 2020 issue of Missions Frontiers, there are a reported 1,035 known kingdom movements (see http://www.missionfrontiers.org). There is a lack of precision in these reports due to the dynamic nature of movements.

**Movements by People Cluster in Country**

- 1 Movement
- 2 - 3 Movements
- 4 - 6 Movements
- 7 - 10 Movements
- 11 - 14 Movements

"The gospel of the kingdom will be preached as a testimony to all nations, and then the end will come."
MATTHEW 24:14

**24:14**

FIGURE 1: CHURCH PLANTING MOVEMENTS AROUND THE WORLD (COURTESY OF 24:14)

I have the awesome privilege of traveling around a good part of the globe. I have been introduced to the most committed Christians I have ever met. I have sat with many of our brothers and sisters to hear their stories, some of which are told in this text. Those stories are at times tragic, even fatal, but all of them honor God, who is in pursuit of people.

I often wonder what we are missing in the West. I am not advocating for persecution or praying for the church in the West to experience affliction. Instead, I am encouraging a missiologically theocentric movement that will joyfully risk everything for the glory of God and the advancement of the gospel. This is what we see in the church of Ephesus. This is the example of Juan and the courageous Kogi Christians. These are not counter-cultural movements. Rather, they are movements that appropriately engage their cultures with the good news. They are not extravagant, but they are costly.

## The Life Cycle of a Movement

Some argue that CPMs are simply the latest craze. On the contrary, I will argue that CPMs were Spirit-empowered movements in the first century and that God is still at work in similar ways in the twenty-first century. The term *CPM* is certainly anachronistic, but that is not new. We tend to put new labels on old principles to package them for the modern consumer of the latest ministry fads. To some degree, I came to CPM as a skeptic. In some ways, I am still a skeptic when I hear CPM used as a strategy since it is more likely the result of disciples multiplying. Like you, perhaps, I have heard amazing stories of movements, whether after the fall of communism in 1989 or the mass conversion of Dalits in 2002. These short-lived "movements" were similar to others we see in history and in our day.

"Movement" is a repeatedly used term these days. We have the civil rights movement and women's liberation movement that live on today in new movements like #MeToo and Black Lives Matter, and probably in a hundred similar "movements." The reality is that many of these so-called movements are a flash in a pan. The Time's Up movement is one of many examples. After initial outrage instigated by the Harvey Weinstein sexual assault allegations, criticism of its leaders quickly stymied any further momentum. "Occupy" is another example of a movement that began with great energy, as hundreds gathered to occupy Wall Street, Chicago, and Washington, but we hardly hear anything about the "movement" today.

The movement we thought we started in post-communist Romania essentially died a slow death as the country discovered the materialistic pleasures of the West. I wish I could blame the failure entirely on these pleasures, but the uncomfortable fact is that we applied a Western institutional method and essentially squelched what the Holy Spirit was doing. Where appropriate, I will unpack this experience more as we look at the New Testament movement.

Movements have a so-called life cycle.[3] Nearly five decades ago Herbert Blumer (1969) outlined this life cycle in four stages. First, a movement commonly emerges out of concerns that initially grab the attention of a few but then become widespread. In the beginning, the participants are not necessarily well organized and might not be clear on their ultimate objectives, but they are passionate about a cause. Second, as the movement grows and matures in its identity, its adherents become increasingly organized and solidified around a strategy. Third, the movement's staff are trained and a formal organization begins to enact the strategy. Finally, the movement begins to decline, most often seen in terms of its struggle to mobilize others to its cause.

Decline, however, does not necessarily mean that the movement fades from society, although that can certainly happen. Instead, several outcomes are possible (Miller 1999). One outcome could be that opponents of the movement attempt to divert pressure away from the movement by rewarding its leaders, thereby creating hypocrisy at worst and compromise at best as the leaders become distracted. Repression and persecution can also dissuade movement leaders from continuing. Government pressure or violence against a movement can test the leaders' resolve. A movement might decline due to the successful

---

3. In chapter 10 I'll suggest that causes have a life cycle while movements have a rhythm.

accomplishment of its goal. Similarly, a movement could decline as a result of its ideals becoming mainstream in society (Macionis 2001).

Some religious movements exemplify these outcomes, such as the Shakers, Heaven's Gate, Branch Davidians, and Peoples Temple, in which decline manifested in the movement's fading from society. Others amplify the mainstreaming of a movement. Islam, for example, began in the mid 600s and is on pace to be approximately the same size as Christianity by 2050. Mormonism's rapid growth, which initially caused alarm in a majority Christian environment in the 1800s, has now plateaued, indicating the movement's mainstreaming, as it is no longer seen as a threat. Mainline and evangelical Christianity, both once movements and then mainstream, are in decline, forecasting the potential for their future demise.

| Religion | 2007 Percentage | 2014 Percentage | Change |
|---|---|---|---|
| Christian | 78.4 | 70.6 | -7.8 |
| Protestant | 51.3 | 46.5 | -4.8 |
| Evangelical | 26.3 | 25.4 | -0.9 |
| Mainline | 18.1 | 14.7 | -3.4 |
| Catholic | 23.9 | 20.8 | -3.1 |
| Orthodox | 0.6 | 0.5 | – |
| Mormon | 1.7 | 1.6 | – |
| Jehovah's Witnesses | 0.7 | 0.8 | – |
| Non-Christian Faiths | 4.7 | 5.9 | +1.2 |
| Jewish | 1.7 | 1.9 | – |
| Muslim | 0.4 | 0.9 | +0.5 |
| Buddhist | 0.7 | 0.7 | – |
| Hindu | 0.4 | 0.7 | +0.3 |
| Unaffiliated | 16.1 | 22.8 | +6.7 |
| Atheist | 1.6 | 3.1 | +1.5 |
| Agnostic | 2.4 | 4.0 | +1.6 |
| Nones | 12.1 | 15.8 | +3.7 |

TABLE 1: RELIGIOUS LANDSCAPE OF THE UNITED STATES (PEW RESEARCH CENTER)

The key to the ongoing success of a movement is its maturation process. At this critical juncture, leaders can decide to take the movement toward an exponential growth model that will see a percentage of population gain over time or to an addition model that cannot keep pace with population rates. An addition model will grow in numbers but will not grow in influence. The bureaucratization stage will lead to an institution, but not necessarily to social transformation. An exponential growth model, on the other hand, will multiply more followers and will begin to see change in the culture.

The early church represented an exponential growth model that lasted for nearly a hundred years. There were definitely hints of institutionalization along the way. As the church grew at phenomenal rates in the first decades, organizational structures, like the addition of "deacons" in Acts 6 to care for certain populations in the movement, could have had an institutionalizing effect. Providentially, persecution propelled the movement into more growth. The council of Jerusalem in Acts 15 could have derailed the movement if it had taken a rigid stance on particular cultural issues. Thankfully, freedom and grace in the ongoing maturation process overcame legalism. Even in the church of Ephesus, we see early hints of an institution, which we will discuss later in this book. For now, the question is whether we want to be a movement or an institution—or perhaps some combination of the two.

| Movements | Institutions |
| --- | --- |
| Mobilizing members for the cause | Teaching an audience content |
| Exponential growth of disciples | Addition of new members |
| Transformational leadership | Authoritarian leadership |
| Frontiers | Boundaries |
| "What's on the other side of the mountain?" | "How do we get to the top?" |
| Pushing the limits | Setting the limits |
| Risk taking | Risk avoiding |
| Theocentric—"It's about God" | Anthropocentric—"It's about us" |
| People-minded—equipping others for ministry | Program-minded—doing the ministry ourselves |
| "Let's go get them" | "Build it and they will come" |

TABLE 2: COMPARISON OF MOVEMENTS AND INSTITUTIONS

Both the church in the United States and the global church face challenges as we move forward in the third decade of the twenty-first century. After years of growth that forecasted the completion of the Great Commission, there are now more people outside the reach of the gospel than ever before. In addition to challenges confronting the advancement of the gospel, we confront internal challenges as well, in a world of social media where it is so easy to criticize what is different.

## The Challenge in the United States

We face a serious issue in our country. Christianity in the United States is not keeping up with population growth. In 1990, 86.2 percent of the US population identified as Christian. In 2014, that number decreased to 70.6 percent. Today, only 65 percent of the US adult population identifies as Christian. Perhaps even more alarming is that 30.5 million US adults have completely left the church, but at least not Christianity, and another 34.5 million have not only left the church but no longer identifying with any faith (Packard 2015). That amounts to 30 percent of the US adult population who had once associated with a church and now no longer do. In one of the most "Christian" parts of the country—Michigan's "Bible Belt"—the number of those no longer associating with Christianity is only two percentage points from outnumbering those who continue to identify as Christian.

In spite of this, evangelicals continue to grow in sheer numbers, yet less in influence as well as in percentage of the population. The word "evangelical" in our culture, for example, has become associated with political and social institutions that have little to do with sharing the good news of Jesus Christ. If you tell someone you are "evangelical," they will be more inclined to believe you voted for Donald Trump than experienced new life in Christ (Weber 2017).

What we are doing in our gospel activity is simply not working. The evangelistic events that draw extreme sports athletes, well-known Christian musicians, and helicopters dropping Easter eggs from the sky are not multiplying the numbers of the redeemed. No matter how many billions of dollars we spend each year on church renovations or new buildings—worldwide we spend about $8 billion (Johnson and Zurlo 2020)—Christianity in this country is regressing.

This regression has caused me to wonder if we have lost the vision of multiplying disciples (2 Tim 2:2) and have focused on our own legacy that borrows believers, constructs buildings, creates programs, and divides churches. In recent years we have seen the downfall of spiritual leaders who have been placed on a platform that they have not been able to handle. From extramarital affairs and homosexual relationships to heretical teaching and exploitation of givers, the reputation of pastors in America is increasingly characterized as unethical (Zylstra 2018).[4] In fact, I would say that the church in the US has become like the forty-year-old church of Ephesus we meet in Revelation 2:1–7, as she abandoned her vision for the work of her first love.

This book is not a rant against the American church. It is not coming from a disillusioned missionary who has reified the persecuted church. As we will see, some of the persecution the church faces overseas is self-afflicted. Neither am I blind to the institutionalization that occurs shortly after the New Testament era. Instead, I agree with the late churchman John R. W. Stott:

> Every church in every place at every time is in need of reform and renewal. But we need to beware lest we despise the church of God, and are blind to his work in history. We may safely say that God has not abandoned his church, however displeased with it he may be. He is still building and refining it. And if God has not abandoned it, how can we? It has a central place in his plan. (1979, 73)

God continues to use the church in the United States. We still send more missionaries around the world than any country on the planet. However, very few of those missionaries go to places where the gospel has never been. Nevertheless, we still give more money to missions than any other country, even though only 1 percent actually goes to spread the gospel in places it has never been (Johnson and Zurlo 2020). People are still coming to Christ every day in the United States. People are still being discipled. However, Thom Rainer (2018) estimates that between six and ten thousand churches in the US closed their doors in 2018. That is about one to two hundred every week, and the future does not look any brighter.

Many are raising the question of what is next for the American church, and many are attempting to provide answers. I hope this book contributes to the answers. *Ephesiology: A Study of the Ephesian Movement* journeys from the launch of the church in Ephesus to her sustainment as a movement whose heart to glorify God focused on reaching more people with the gospel. In the intervening forty years, the church was grounded in God's mission and led by those who multiplied generations of disciples. This is the story of Paul's missiological theology situated in the grand narrative of God's will and made accessible for the church today.

---

4. Zylstra reports the findings of a Gallup Poll showed that 48 percent of Christians trust the clergy, while only 25 percent of non-Christians trust the clergy.

## The Challenge for the Global Church

Global Christianity faces similar challenges. According to the Center for the Study of Global Christianity, between 2000 and 2010 Islam grew at 1.86 percent annually, while Christianity grew at 1.32 percent. In 1910, Christianity made up 34.8 percent of the global population. In 2010, that percentage declined to 32.8. Kent Parks (2017) estimated that in 2017 29 percent of the global population was outside of the reach of the gospel, a number that has grown from 24 percent in 1990. Today there are more people than ever who will not have an opportunity to hear the gospel of Jesus Christ. In 1900, there were only 880 million people to reach with the gospel. Today there are 2.1 billion who do not have a chance of hearing the good news that is intended for them because no one is going to them.

| Religion | Percentage in 1910 | Percentage in 2010 |
|---|---|---|
| Christians | 34.8 | 32.8 |
| Muslims | 12.6 | 22.5 |
| Hindus | 12.7 | 13.8 |
| Agnostics | 0.2 | 9.8 |
| Chinese folk-religionists | 22.2 | 6.3 |
| Buddhists | 7.9 | 7.2 |
| Ethnoreligionists | 7.7 | 3.5 |
| Atheists | 0.0 | 2.0 |
| New Religionists | 0.4 | 0.9 |

TABLE 3: WORLD RELIGIONS BY ADHERENTS (WORLD RELIGION DATABASE)

Alongside of the sheer numbers of people who do not know Christ, global Christianity is challenged with resourcing missionaries to go to where the gospel has never been. Johnson and Zurlo (2020) estimated that $56 billion was given to foreign missions in 2018, which is an average of about $24 a year per Christian, up from $12 per year in 2010. Less than 2 percent of all money given for missions is spent reaching the 2.1 billion who are unevangelized.

Not only is resourcing missionaries a challenge, recruiting missionaries willing to go to where the gospel has never been is equally challenging. In 2001, there were 416,000 foreign missionaries. That missionary force grew to 468,000 in 2006, but declined by 17 percent to 400,000 in 2010.

Despite what seems to be a large missionary force, most missionaries are deployed to majority Christian countries (Johnson and Zurlo, 2020). Alongside of the shrinking numbers of missionaries, in the United States we are confronted with a millennial generation who are more confident that they are gifted to share their faith than past generations, but yet increasingly believe they should not share their faith with others if the goal is the other person's conversion (Barna Group 2019).

Resourcing and recruiting missionaries is only overshadowed by the exporting of a Western theology and ecclesiastical structure that believes it is the correct model for all of Christianity. Roland Allen reminded us over a century ago that the Holy Spirit who guides the Westerner is the same who guides believers in other countries (1912). We should fully expect the theology and church polity that emerge from various cultures to look different than the West. Just like the cultural issues in Ephesus were different than those in Corinth, resulting in theological expressions that made sense in those places, so the cultural differences between Dallas and Dehli are different and we should expect to see unique expressions of theology emerging in both places.

My hope is that *Ephesiology* will help to address some of these issues. I have become convinced that if we read the text with the eyes of the original hearers we will see God's movement in the world in a different light. This type of missiological reading tells the story of God's mission and how we are to join with his mission in presenting the gospel in ways that make sense to others. *Ephesiology* is about what God is doing in the world. While there are definitely instructions for us to follow, Paul's primary concern was to complete the mission he was given by Christ himself. The instructions we read in the Ephesian corpus were not a list of didactic pedagogical decrees written by a prominent first-century educator. Rather, the Ephesian corpus is a missionary mandate that demands our participation as followers of Christ.

## How to Read This Book

We are not exactly certain when Paul wrote Ephesians, nor are we certain from where it was written. Some even question whether it was actually written by Paul—I am not among those. We are fairly certain that the events of Acts 19 took place between AD 52 and 56. It seems likely that Paul did not stay in Ephesus for that entire period, as he made a "painful visit" to Corinth (2 Cor 2:1), but would ultimately return to Ephesus discouraged by what he learned and then write the "severe letter" (2 Cor 2:4). All this to say, there were many challenges facing the Christianity of Paul's world, and those challenges add color to the movement in Asia. He genuinely bore the daily burden for all the churches in Achaia, Macedonia, and Galatia, as well as the new movement of churches in Asia. As you read this book, remember that the events are not isolated. As much as is possible, I will weave some of those events into the story.

To do Ephesiology, it is essential to get to know the texts of the movement in Ephesus, so I would suggest that you listen to or read them for yourself. Start with Acts 18:18–20:38 for a picture of the launching of the movement. Next, read Ephesians. Paul's letter dates as early as AD 53, which would place it as being written from a prison in the Roman province of Asia, to as late as AD 63, placing its provenance from a prison in Rome. No matter where it was written, Paul was in prison for certain (Eph 3:1).[5] He writes a letter to another church in the Asian city of Colossae that is very similar to Ephesians. Due to space considerations, we will not look at this epistle in detail. Paul's first letter to Timothy could have been written as early as AD 55 while Paul was either on his way to or in Macedonia (Acts 20:1–3), or as late as after his release from imprisonment in Rome in AD 64.[6] Second Timothy is likely to have been Paul's last letter, or at least the last we have, and probably written around AD 67 from Rome. Nevertheless, these two epistles follow the events in Acts and Ephesians, so read them accordingly.

Other texts associated with Ephesus will also add color to the story. In fact, nearly 40 percent of the New Testament books have some connection with Ephesus and Asia. John's Gospel, for example, was written while the apostle lived in the city. It seems probable that his three epistles were also written from the same place. Revelation contains a letter to the church of Ephesus, as well as to six other churches in Asia. These letters from the ascended Jesus provide more information about the challenges the churches faced in sustaining the movement. John's corpus, written between AD 63 and 96, will help us understand more of the events during the gap between Paul's death and Jesus' revelation to John. Finally, 1 and 2 Peter are addressed to churches in Asia and highlight some of the cultural issues early Christians confronted. I will briefly touch on these when pertinent.

---

5. There is ample textual evidence in the epistle entitled "Ephesians" for early dating: 1) The fact that Paul does not mention any Ephesian elders by name suggests it was written before the movement was firmly established and/or to a broader audience in Asia. 2) No major theological heresies are addressed, indicating a young movement. 3) Unlike the other Prison Epistles (Colossians, Philemon, Philippians), Ephesians is not coauthored by Timothy, which indicates Timothy was not with Paul during this imprisonment (Acts 19:21-22). 4) There was a clear issue between Jews and Gentiles in Paul's early ministry in Ephesus (Acts 19:9), which could have landed him in prison.

6. I lean toward an early date for 1 Timothy for the following reasons: 1) Paul is in Macedonia when he writes (1 Tim 1:3; Acts 20:1-2); 2) Timothy is still considered young (1 Tim 4:12); 3) Timothy was to appoint an overseer (τὸν ἐπίσκοπον) in Ephesus, who had not been appointed by the time of the Ephesian elder meeting (1 Tim 3:1; Acts 20:17ff). More will be discussed in chapter 7, "Leading a Movement."

Since there were no printing presses at this point in history, and due to the oral nature of Roman and Greek learning, the texts were intended to be heard rather than read. It seems that oral learning was much preferred in the early church. Papias writes in his *Exposition of the Sayings of the Lord* (ca. 110), "I did not suppose that information from books would help me so much as the word of a living and surviving voice" (In Irenaeus, *Against Heresies* 3.39.3–4). So, I want to encourage you to listen to the texts, especially after you read chapters 3, 4, and 5 on "Launching a Movement." These chapters will give you a bit of the historical and cultural flavor of Ephesus and will, hopefully, enrich the texts as you listen to them. It will also help you process what the early movement in Asia learned from the Apostle Paul. In our day and age, you can listen to the texts through an audio Bible app, some of which are free. Another way you can listen to the texts is by gathering a roomful of believers together and reading the texts aloud, just like what would have happened when they were originally heard.

Our goal in listening to or reading the texts is to hear with the ears of the Ephesians. There are very specific issues Paul addresses that are directly tied to the culture. We have to first understand these issues if we have any hope for properly applying the text today. For the most part, we can discover the cultural issues from within the actual texts if we read attentively.

One of the challenges we face as modern interpreters of ancient texts is that we tend to complicate their understanding with complex exegesis and expository preaching. While there is value to both proper exegesis and preaching, we have to be very careful to not read our contemporary culture into the text. I am as susceptible to my own personal biases seeping into interpretation as anyone. So, with that tidbit of advice, save your commentary reading, indeed even the reading of this book, until after you have thought about, heard, and read the biblical accounts of the movement in Ephesus for yourself.

When I teach this material, I often gather with a small group of believers somewhere in the world, explain the culture of Asia and events in Acts, and then we simply open the texts together, asking the Holy Spirit to guide our understanding. It is such a rich time that you might actually find that you have wasted your money on the purchase of this book. Still, I will have felt that I have done my duty in contributing to the writing of the book, and you will have helped equip national leaders around the world by purchasing it. That is a good thing, for which I thank you.

God began a movement when Jesus ascended and the Holy Spirit filled the disciples. The new believers were committed to sharing the love of Christ with all, and they were willing to risk all—just like Juan and his band of new disciples in the jungles of Colombia. Will you take that risk, knowing that Jesus will always be with you and the Holy Spirit will empower you to declare the glory of God everywhere you go? I hope *Ephesiology* will inspire you to do just that.

## Timeline for the Movement in Ephesus

One final thought is merited. A book could be written just on the challenges of trying to date the writing of the various texts related to God's movement in Asia. As much as is possible, I will address some of the dating issues in the book. For now, here is my timeline for the events that took place in Asia during Paul's second and third missionary journeys.

| Date | Acts | Event | Significance |
|------|------|-------|--------------|
| AD 51 | 18:18-20 | Paul, Priscilla, and Aquila go to Ephesus | |
| | | Paul writes the first letter to Corinth | Letter is lost, but deals with sexually immoral people (1 Cor 5:9). |
| | 18:22-23 | Paul goes to Antioch | Paul spends some time there; encourages churches in Galatia and Phrygia. |
| | 18:24-26 | Apollos arrives in Ephesus | Priscilla and Aquilla accurately explain Jesus; Apollos is from Alexandria, Egypt. Tradition holds that Mark started the church in Alexandria. |
| | 18:27-28 | Apollos goes to Corinth | See 1 Cor 1:12; 3:4. |
| AD 52 | 19:1-2 | Paul returns to Ephesus | Paul makes a 1,500-mile journey to encourage the churches in Galatia before returning to Ephesus, and could have visited the cities of the other six Asia churches of Revelation (walking eight hours a day, it would take forty-six days to travel this area); Nero becomes emperor at age sixteen. |
| | 19:2-7 | Paul encounters some of John the Baptist's disciples | Holy Spirit comes on them and they speak in tongues and prophesy. |
| | 19:8-9a | Teaching in synagogue | Paul teaches for three months in the synagogue. |
| | 19:9b-10 | Teaching in school of Tyrannus | Paul teaches for two years in the school. |

| Date | Acts | Event | Significance |
|------|------|-------|--------------|
| AD 52 | 19:11-17 | Miracles performed; Jewish exorcists incident | |
| | 19:18-20 | Book-burning | |
| | 19:21-22 | Paul travels throughout Asia | Paul meets many of the leaders (Asiarchs) in Asia during his travels throughout the region (perhaps travelling sporadically for the nine-month gap between the synagogue and school teaching, and his remarks to the Ephesian elders); churches in Colossae, Philadelphia, Smyrna, Pergamum, Laodicea, Sardis, and Thyatira, which was most likely already started by Lydia. |
| AD 55 | 19:22 | Timothy and Erastus go to Macedonia | Most likely they also go to Corinth. Erastus stays and becomes the city treasurer. See 1 Cor 4:17. |
| | | Paul writes 1 Corinthians | Leadership conflict in Corinth, along with pagan practices creeping into the church. |
| | | Paul writes Ephesians/ Laodecians (debated) | Sends letter with Tychicus the Asian (Eph 6:21); was not co-authored with Timothy like the other prison epistles; Paul is in chains when he writes (Eph 3:1; 6:20); earliest manuscripts address the letter to the Laodecians. |
| | 19:23-41 | Riot | Idol-makers of Artemis; temple of Artemis is one of the wonders of the ancient world; practices associated with Artemis are addressed in Ephesians and 1 Timothy. |
| | 19:31-34 | Asiarchs and Alexander | Asiarchs intervene to prevent Paul from going into the crowd; Paul knowing some of the Asiarchs, members of a provincial council made up of representatives from major cities, suggests that Paul traveled around Asia prior to the Artemis event. See 1 Tim 1:20; 2 Tim 4:14 for references to Alexander. |

| Date | Acts | Event | Significance |
|---|---|---|---|
| AD 55 | 19:35-41 | Town clerk's testimony about the Christians | Gaius and Aristarchus are detained |
| AD 56 | 20:1-3 | Timothy returns to Ephesus (debated) | See 1 Cor 16:11; Paul anticipates Timothy's return to Ephesus. |
| | | Paul goes to Macedonia | See 1 Tim 1:3; Paul leaves Timothy in Ephesus. |
| | | Paul writes 1 Timothy (debated) | Written from Philippi; see 1 Tim 1:3; additional layer of church leadership due to the phenomenal growth in Asia—see Ignatius' letter to Ephesus. Paul warns Timothy about irreverent babble—a possible reference to Euodia and Syntyche (Phil 4:2). |
| AD 57 | | Mark writes Gospel (debated) | 7Q5 fragment from Qumran. Mark is known by the churches in Asia (see Col 4:10). |
| | | Paul in Greece | Paul spends three months in Greece. |
| | | Paul writes Romans | Written from Corinth—see Rom 16:23; Prisca (aka Priscilla) and Aquila have left Ephesus and are back in Rome. |
| | 20:3b-5 | Paul returns to Macedonia | Timothy joins Paul in Philippi, along with several others. |
| | | Paul writes 2 Corinthians | Written with Timothy from Philippi. |
| | 20:6-16 | Paul in Troas | Paul spends seven days in Troas after the days of Unleavened Bread. |
| AD 57 | | | Eutychus falls out of window. |
| | 20:17-38 | Paul in Miletus | Paul meets with Ephesian elders; he would not see these elders again, Acts 20:38. |

TABLE 4: TIMELINE FOR THE MOVEMENT IN EPHESUS BETWEEN AD 51 AND 57

# CHAPTER 2

## Church Planting Movements in the Book of Acts

In the fall of 1990 I sat in a football stadium in Craiova, Romania, listening to an American evangelist present a persuasive message. The audience enthusiastically listened to the gospel, as they continued to experience their first tastes of freedom from the brutal dictator Nicolae Ceaușescu. Fantastic reports of the event appeared in a popular Christian magazine a few months later, claiming the breakout of a revival in this city of more than a quarter million people as thousands prayed to receive Christ. Perhaps unknown to the author of the magazine article, the offer of a prayer to receive Christ in a majority Orthodox Christian country was always met by a willing response, as an Orthodox believer would never reject such an opportunity. While hands went up around the stadium and crowds began to flood the pitch for a free New Testament, the three evangelical churches in the city did not see any substantial growth.

Missionaries often embellish stories to report on the work of God. Perhaps due to the excitement of the moment or the desire to demonstrate to donors that their financial gifts are bearing fruit, hyperbole has always been a part of telling the Christian story. As we will see, Luke demonstrates similar tendencies. The reporting is not malicious; rather, in Luke's case it is a rhetorical device utilized to communicate something significant taking place that can only be explained as a movement of the Holy Spirit. Nevertheless, we can verify the data and see that God used faithful followers of Christ to birth a fantastic movement of churches around the Roman Empire. Indeed, as Luke records, these were people "who have turned the world upside down" (Acts 17:6).

Today, some missions strategists refer to the remarkable growth of Christianity in the first century as the initial example of a church planting movement (CPM). Steve Smith, who witnessed the birth of a CPM in China, defines it as "the Spirit-empowered rapid multiplication of disciples and churches generation by generation" (Smith and Kai 2011, 19).

David Garrison, a leading advocate of CPM strategy, lays out three general components of a movement. First, there is rapid growth as new disciples are immediately encouraged to share their faith within their network and ultimately start new churches. Second, the growth is exponential, following Paul's model of discipleship to entrust what he had taught to faithful people who will do likewise (2 Tim 2:2). According to Garrison, a CPM occurs when there are three generations of believers faithfully reaching a population. The final component of a CPM is indigeneity; the new churches emerge out of the culture without the trappings of Western Christianity (Garrison 1999, 2004).

Smith and Garrison are not without their critics—i.e., those who contend that CPMs did not exist in the era of the New Testament.[7] In 2014, the *Southwestern Journal of Theology* dedicated an issue to examine claims made by Smith, Garrison, and others, as well as the CPM initiative of the International Mission Board of the Southern Baptist Convention (IMB). In the spirit of academic pursuit and concern, the consensus of the issue was that some of the practices of contemporary advocates of CPMs, especially those promoting training for trainers (T4T), could lead to churches weak in faith and doctrine. Among the leading concerns of contributors to the journal were a de-emphasis on theological education, early appointment of new believers as leaders of new churches, under-emphasis on areas considered reached by the gospel, and potential insider movement compromises (Wilder 2014).

Unlike the critics, I would suggest that we can indeed identify CPMs in Luke's account of the early missionary efforts of Jesus' disciples, especially in Paul's efforts and definitely in the Roman province of Asia. The components of rapidity, multiplication, and indigeneity seem evident in what the writer communicated as a movement of the Holy Spirit in the early history of the church. The rapid spread and growth of the Christian movement was remarkable, as Paul testified to those in Rome that he no longer had any work from Jerusalem all the way around to Illyricum (Rom 15:23). By the time he wrote Romans in AD 57, the movement in Asia was exceptionally large.

---

7. Among other critics, see Jackson Wu, "There Are No Church Planting Movements in the Bible: Why Biblical Exegesis and Missiological Methods Cannot Be Separated," *Global Missiology* 1, no. 12 (2014); and Aubrey Sequeira, "A Plea for Gospel Sanity in Missions," available at https://www.9marks.org/article/a-plea-for-gospel-sanity-in-missions/.

Around AD 53–54, about a year into the ministry in Asia, Paul's closing remarks to the believers in Corinth indicates that there were already several churches (1 Cor 16:19). He saw that "a wide door for effective work" had opened up to him in Asia (1 Cor 16:8–9). In just a two-year period, Luke tells us that "all the residents of Asia heard the word of the Lord" (Acts 19:10). Hyperbole? Perhaps—yet it expresses the heart of a Holy Spirit movement in spreading the gospel and making disciples that results in Christians gathering together in house churches.

As we get into *Ephesiology* and the study of a New Testament movement, we want to start at the beginning to put the movement in the context of what the Holy Spirit did on the day of Pentecost and how that impacted first-century Christianity. So, in this chapter we will examine the growth of the early church by utilizing population data of selected first-century cities that had been reached by the early missionaries alongside of contemporary conversion-rate data for unreached people groups. The evidence in Acts, as well as in Paul's epistles, suggests that there were indeed indigenous church planting movements characterized by rapid expansion and multiplication. Rather than a strategy for the expansion of the gospel, however, the CPMs in Acts were the result of faithful follwers of Christ empowered by movement leaders to make more disciples, who assembled together in the homes of believers.

## Measuring the Growth of Christianity in AD 33–AD 67

The Acts of the Apostles (Acts) provides a glimpse into the first thirty-four or so years of the Christian movement. Among the book's purposes was documenting evidence to combat the charges of subversion to the Roman Empire brought against the movement. Its author, Luke, was a physician (Col 4:14) and likely a Gentile, perhaps even Greek. He was an early disciple, probably from the region of Troas in Asia (Acts 16:8–10), perhaps the city of Alexandria (the main Roman port of transportation to Europe), from where the Acts narrative includes his personal eyewitness account. We know that a church formed in the region (Acts 20:6), presumably by Paul or his disciples. It could have been formed as early as Acts 16:8–10, before his first journey to Macedonia in AD 48. We know Paul had an ongoing ministry in Troas, as he mentions it while waiting for Titus before departing for Macedonia (Acts 16:8; 2 Cor 2:12–13). Almost a decade later, around AD 57, he returned for seven days on his way to Jerusalem prior to meeting the Ephesian elders (Acts 20:6). Luke, therefore, most likely came to Christ in Paul's ministry and joined him in AD 48 as he continued on his second missionary journey.

There is little doubt that Luke used hyperbolic language in communicating the results of the gospel. For example, in regard to the day of Pentecost in AD 30, Luke writes, "Now there were dwelling in Jerusalem Jews, devout men from every nation under heaven" (Acts 2:5). We know that this was simply a rhetorical device indicating that many people were in the city. It is apparent that the population of the city grew during times of festivals and declined over subsequent weeks as people returned to their homes. However, it does not seem plausible that "every nation under heaven" was in Jerusalem at that time. Nevertheless, Luke reports that there were people from the world he knew: "Parthians and Medes and Elamites and residents of Mesopotamia, Judea and Cappadocia, Pontus and Asia, Phrygia and Pamphylia, Egypt and the parts of Libya belonging to Cyrene, and visitors from Rome, both Jews and proselytes, Cretans and Arabians—we hear them telling in our own tongues the mighty works of God" (Acts 2:9–11).

Luke records that at the end of Peter's proclamation of the gospel, about 3,000 people believed and were baptized (Acts 2:41). Not too long afterward, another 5,000 men believed (Acts 4:4). As their numbers continued to increase (Acts 5:14), in a relatively short period of time, the church grew from 120 to nearly 14,000 men, women, and children in the city of Jerusalem alone.[8]

These data present a challenge, however. Estimates of the population of Jerusalem in the first century put the number of inhabitants of the city at around 10,000 at the time of Herod (Russell 1958, 82). Considering the fact that there were additional people attending the *Shavout* (Feast of Weeks) from "every nation under heaven," as Luke suggests, and the fact that Jewish men were required by law to attend the pilgrimage feasts (Deut 16:16), we can easily assume that the population swelled significantly, as Josephus suggested on one occasion during the reign of Nero (AD 53–68):

> And that this city could contain so many people in it is manifest by that number of them which was taken under Cestius, who being desirous of informing Nero of the power of the city, who otherwise was disposed to condemn that nation, entreated the high priests, if the thing were possible, to take the number of their whole multitude. So these high priests, upon the coming of their feast which is called the Passover, when they slay their sacrifices, from the ninth hour to the eleventh, but so that a company not less than ten belong to every sacrifice, (for it is not lawful for them to feast singly

---

8. There are New Testament scholars on both sides of the notion that the 5,000 men in Acts 4:4 were in addition to or included the 3,000 people who believed and were baptized in Acts 2:41. See Schnabel (2004, 3) who asserts that the community grew to 5,000 people and Larkin (1995, 70) who maintained the number of new believers at 10,000 men, women, and children. One core issue is the population of Jerusalem. However, neither Schnabel or Larkin recognize the possibility of a sizeable influx of Jews attending the Feast of Weeks. It seems to me that it is plausible to suggest a total of 14,000 men, women, and children since Jewish men were required to travel to Jerusalem and attend feasts.

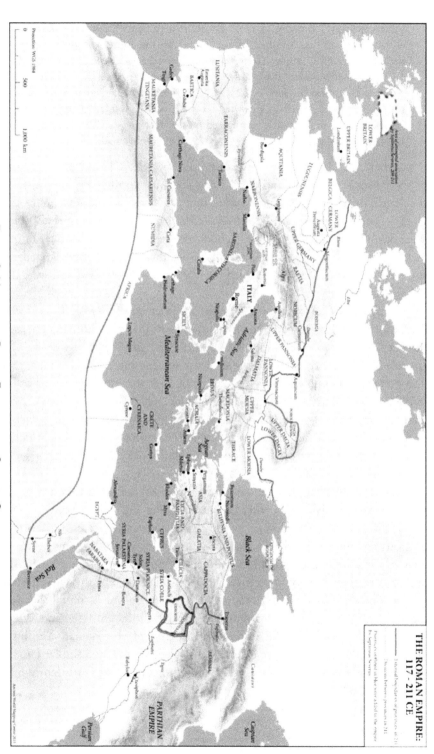

FIGURE 2: MAP OF THE ROMAN EMPIRE IN THE SECOND CENTURY

by themselves) and many of us are twenty in a company, found the number of sacrifices was two hundred fifty-six thousand five hundred; which, upon the allowance of no more than ten that feast together, *amounts to two million seven hundred thousand two hundred persons that were pure and holy;* for as to those that have the leprosy, or the gonorrhea, or women that have their monthly courses, or such as are otherwise polluted, it is not lawful for them to be partakers of this sacrifice; nor indeed for any foreigners neither, who come hither to worship. (*The War of the Jews,* VI, 9, 3; emphasis added.)

If there were 2.7 million "pure and holy" people in Jerusalem at the time of the Passover in AD 30 and every male Jew was required to "appear before the Lord" during the Feast of Weeks, then it is easy to see how more than 10,000 people could respond positively to the message of the gospel, especially since devout Jews were hearing the good news of the awaited Messiah in their own languages. We might conclude that even though descriptive language of the events was used, Luke's recorded numbers could be verified and were thus accurately documented.

Using data on the growth of new religious movements (NRMs), Rodney Stark, the Baylor University sociologist of religion, suggests that the Christian population was not as numerous as Luke leads us to believe. Stark admittedly begins with a low estimate of 1,000 Christians in Jerusalem in AD 40, ignoring Luke's account of more than 8,000 (see footnote 2). His basis for doing so is the population of Christians in the Roman Empire at the time of Constantine, relying on a range between von Hertling's estimate of 7.5 million and MacMullen's lower estimate of 5 million. Stark does not believe precision is necessary in these estimates and is simply looking for what might be the most plausible explanation for a majority Christian population in the empire by AD 350.

Additionally, Stark based the growth rate of early Christianity on his study of Mormonism in its first century. During the period between 1830 and 1930, Mormonism grew at a 3.42 annual percentage rate in a favorable religious environment—that is, an environment in which differing beliefs are relatively free from discrimination. While Mormons were certainly persecuted at points in their history, the general religious landscape of the United States in the nineteenth century was increasingly characterized as pluralistic, with many competing—albeit Christian and mostly Protestant—religious views. Consequently, based on the imprecise estimates of the Roman Empire in AD 300 and the assumption that Christianity would grow at a similar rate as a modern religion, Stark suggests table 5 as representative of Christianity in its first three hundred years.[9]

9. Others have used Adolph von Harnack's estimate of 6 million Christians in AD 300, which represented 10 percent of the population. Keith Hopkins, like Stark, uses an arbitrary starting point of 1,000 Christians in AD 40. See Keith Hopkins, "Christian Number and Its Implication," *Journal of Early Christian Studies* 6, no. 2 (1998): 185-226.

| Year | Estimated Number of Christians | Percentage of Population |
|------|-------------------------------|--------------------------|
| 40 | 1,000 | 0.0017 |
| 50 | 1,400 | 0.0023 |
| 100 | 7,530 | 0.0126 |
| 150 | 40,496 | 0.07 |
| 200 | 217,795 | 0.36 |
| 250 | 1,171,356 | 1.9 |
| 300 | 6,299,832 | 10.5 |
| 350 | 33,882,008 | 56.5 |

TABLE 5: CHRISTIAN GROWTH PROJECTED AT 40 PERCENT PER DECADE (STARK 1996, 7)

While the interest of this chapter is not the size of Christianity at the time of Constantine, it is important to make some observations regarding Stark's analysis. First, Stark does not factor in the element of an amazing event occurring on the day of Pentecost in AD 30. The Holy Spirit descended on the 120 disciples, and potentially hundreds of thousands of people heard the gospel for the first time. Second, Stark does not allow for the accuracy of Luke's account in Acts. It is interesting that he will permit his own imprecision in estimates but does not extend the same courtesy to the ancient writer who recounts in the first of his two-volume set, "It seemed good to me also, having followed all things closely for some time past, to write an orderly account for you, most excellent Theophilus, that you may have certainty concerning the things you have been taught" (Luke 1:3–4).

Third, Stark is not allowing for the potential downward trend of Christianity during times of persecution and plague, nor does he consider the nominalism of churches as we see in some of the seven churches of Asia (Rev 2:1–3:22). John's transmission of the seven letters from Jesus Christ to the seven churches was clearly motivated by Jesus' desire for the churches to understand that every nation, people, tribe, and language would one day be present before God's throne and John was not to grow weary of this prophecy (Rev 10:11). Finally, Stark looks at the total population of the Roman Empire instead of looking specifically at the population of the cities and regions of the empire. We might assume that the gospel was received more readily in some cities, like Philippi, than in others, like Athens.

In light of these observations, I suggest that a more fruitful pursuit of estimating the Christian population in the first century will consider several key factors. The first key factor takes into consideration the populations of cities where we know of missionary activity in the first century. Second is the allowance for a degree of trust in Luke's hyperbolic references. Third is the utilization of contemporary data that is more in line with the context of the Roman Empire and an unfavorable religious context than data based on Mormon growth in a favorable context. Namely, looking at modern conversion rates among people groups who have had little or no access to the gospel would better correspond to the situation in the first century.

## A Model for Estimated Growth Rates in Acts

Bearing in mind the population estimates of selected cities in Acts, we can assume a degree of responsiveness to the gospel and arrive at some preliminary conclusions regarding the growth of early Christianity. Based upon what we know today concerning the likelihood of someone without access to the gospel responding positively to the good news of great joy when engaged by missionaries, it might be likely that the early church had a similar response rate. This cannot be an exact determination, as we do not have sufficient statistical data from the first century. Nevertheless, Luke's references to the spread of the gospel and the attention Christians garnered from government and religious officials indicates a movement that had some level of influence across the empire.

To help provide a point of reference for the potential growth of an early Christian movement, it might be beneficial to consider the growth of a CPM-focused agency, especially in light of Stark's assumptive data based on early Mormonism. CPM agencies are typically mission organizations focused on taking the gospel to difficult-to-reach places, including places where people have little or no access to the gospel and where there is hostility toward Christianity. For example, between January of 2013 and December of 2017 East West Ministries International (EWMI) presented the gospel to 120.4 million people, with the result of just over 9.4 million indicating professions of faith. That amounts to about one out of every thirteen individuals responding positively to the Christian message.[10] The organization, however, is interested in seeing disciples made, not simply professions of faith. According to EWMI, a disciple constitutes a person who makes a profession of faith, is baptized, and participates in a community of believers.[11] In the same time period, EWMI reported 1.28 million new disciples. In other words, 13.67 percent of those who profess faith become disciples, while 1.06 percent of those who hear the gospel become disciples (see table 6). Utilizing this data, we will begin to construct a plausible explanation for the rapid growth of the early Christian movement.

---

10. Information available from https://www.eastwest.org/impact/. Accessed February 14, 2019. Methods of outreach have varied over the history of the church so it is difficult if not impossible to make a one-to-one correspondence. Nevertheless, faith in Christ as a necessity for salvation has not changed and that is my interest in doing a comparison between the early Christian movement and a contemporary missions agency.

11. See more at https://www.eastwest.org/unreached/.

**Growth of Christianity in Jerusalem**

Looking specifically at Jerusalem around AD 14, the city had an estimated population of 10,000 (Russell 1958, 83). Allowing for a measure of growth, by AD 30 the population could have been around 12,000. Luke tells us that 120 disciples were gathered in Jerusalem waiting for the promised Holy Spirit (Acts 2:1). After asking about the kingdom, Jesus redirected their attention to the assignment of taking the gospel to all parts of the world. So they were waiting for the power to be Jesus' witnesses (Acts 1:8). As they were gathered together, the Holy Spirit came like the rush of wind, with tongues of fire appearing on the disciples. At once the disciples began to share the gospel in other languages to the people who were gathered for the Feast of Weeks. Scholars debate what exactly happened—whether the disciples actually spoke in different languages or whether those hearing the gospel heard it in their languages. Whatever the case, after Peter explained what was happening, Luke records that about 3,000 people believed and were baptized.

Miraculous occurrences continued over the course of the next months. In Acts 3, a lame beggar was healed. In Acts 4, Peter and John were arrested, and Luke writes, "But many of those who had heard the word believed, and the number of the men came to about five thousand" (4:4). After their release, the believers gathered and prayed for boldness to continue the mission (Acts 4:23–31). There was an amazing unity among the believers, and "great grace was upon them all" (Acts 4:33). After the instance with Ananias and Sapphira lying about their wealth, the church continued to grow: "And more than ever believers were added to the Lord, multitudes of both men and women" (Acts 5:14). There is, by this time, an estimated 14,000 men, women, and children in Jerusalem who put their faith in Christ.

The challenge in calculating how a first-century group of people would respond to the gospel lies in the fact that we do not know exactly how many people heard the message. In the case of the day of Pentecost (also known as the Feast of Weeks), we know the response numbered about 3,000. However, how many people actually heard Peter's sermon is unknown. Peter and the other 119 disciples were gathered together in a house in Jerusalem. Wherever the house was located in the city, people heard the 120 speaking in as many as 16 languages and likely even more. It seems improbable that all 2.7 million "pure and holy" Jewish persons who might have been gathered for the Passover fifty days prior and stayed for the Feast of Weeks heard the gospel on that day. Nevertheless, over the course of the following weeks and months the number of believers grew significantly as the disciples continued to share their faith and the news spread among the population.

With this in mind, here are four assumptions related to the first-century movement and data from EWMI. First, if 3,000 people responded to the disciples' message and days later another 5,000 men responded, we might assume that there were as many as 14,000 new converts, including women and children. Second, these 14,000 people could easily be considered disciples because they were baptized and began to gather in homes to study, fellowship, worship, and pray together. Third, if we assume the 1.06 percent "disciple rate" we observed in EWMI, then there could have been as many as 1.32 million people who heard the gospel from Peter and the others. Fourth, if Josephus were correct that 2.7 million ceremonially clean men attended the Passover on the occasion he reported during Nero's reign, it is easy to accept that many of the men also came with their wives and perhaps children. It is hardly possible to accurately estimate how many people were in the city during the Feast of Weeks. Nevertheless, if we reason that during the fifty days between Passover and the Feast of Weeks some people returned home and also maintain that there were women and children present, as well as those who would have been considered ceremonially unclean, as we observe when Peter and John healed the man at the Beautiful Gate (Acts 3:2), then we might reasonably claim that there were still as many as 2 million people in the city during the events that led to Acts 2–5.

| Organization | Gospel Exposures | Disciples Made | Rate |
|---|---|---|---|
| EWMI | 120.4 million | 1.28 million | 1.06% |
| Acts 2-5 | 1.32 million | 14,000 | 1.06% |

TABLE 6: CONVERSION COMPARISON

The amazing growth we observe in Jerusalem propelled the church to become a phenomenal movement around the empire. Undoubtedly, many of those who were gathered for the Feast of Weeks returned to their homes and carried the gospel with them. Many others stayed in Jerusalem, and their numbers were large enough for the apostles to recognize the necessity for additional leaders to help meet the needs of the saints. Luke tells us, "And the word of God continued to increase, and the number of disciples multiplied greatly in Jerusalem, and a great many of the priests became obedient to the faith" (Acts 6:7). A rapidly growing movement began, largely due to the sense of responsibility of the disciples, by the empowering Holy Spirit, to boldly speak the word of God.

## The Gathering Place of the Early Church

It would be an amazing story even if it stopped there, but it did not. The believers in Jerusalem were ultimately dispersed around Judea and Samaria after Stephen's stoning. By the time Saul (aka Paul) is on the scene, house churches were well established, as he "was ravaging the church, and entering house after house, he dragged off men and women and committed them to prison" (Acts 8:3). Luke writes that the early Christians gathered together in the houses of believers. And believers certainly assembled at the temple in Jerusalem on occasion. However, the focal point of disciple-making took place among the networks of Christ-followers, which resulted in their gathering together in homes.

With most houses in the Roman Empire ranging between one thousand and three thousand square feet (Fu 2016), we can see that a home could easily accommodate a gathering of believers. With the average family size during the Roman Empire being four people (Monfort 1996), multiple families would gather in one location to hear God's Word, pray, fellowship, and worship. We see this explicitly in Jerusalem, where the disciples practiced "breaking bread in their homes" (Acts 2:46). In Philippi, the believers gathered in the home of Lydia (Acts 16:15, 40). In Ephesus, Paul taught from house to house (Acts 20:20). In Troas, the believers were gathered in an upper room of a house (Acts 20:8).

The significance of the house as a gathering place for the early church cannot be understated. While there were certainly times when large numbers of believers gathered together, as at the temple in Jerusalem (Acts 2:46), a dedicated structure for such a gathering was not the norm. In fact, the first undisputed archeological evidence for a church structure is not recorded until AD 241 in Syria. Even here, the structure was a home with a dedicated room for worship (Silver 2010).

The New Testament provides several additional examples of house churches. In Corinth, there seem to be at least three groups meetings in homes (1 Cor 1:11–16). Similarly, in Rome there were at least three groups, perhaps more, meeting in the homes of believers (Rom 16:3–5, 14–15). The idea of the home or household as a place of spiritual practice in the Roman Empire was well known. Paul and his band of missionaries would have naturally encouraged early believers, especially Gentiles, to meet in homes, as this was a culturally appropriate practice. These households were networks of personal relationships in a patron-client culture in which the head of the household was also the head of cultic practices as well as a family business. It comes as no surprise that one requirement for a church leader was someone who managed his household well (1 Tim 3:5, 12).

Meeting in houses could easily accommodate the rapid growth of the early church. Equally significant is the fact that these house churches were spread throughout a city, allowing members of the movement to interact effortlessly with friends, neighbors, and others in their social network. While it is difficult to determine the average size of a social network in the first century and therefore the potential size of a house church, such a sphere of influence would contribute to the Christian impact on the empire (McClure 2016).[12] Nevertheless, based on the estimate of early Christian growth (see tables 5 and 6), table 7 represents a reasonable estimation of the number of house churches by AD 67.

| City | Estimated Population in First Century | Estimated Growth of Disciples by AD 67 | Estimated Number of House Churches |
|---|---|---|---|
| Rome | 350,000 | 35,000 | 2,333 |
| Alexandria | 216,000 | 21,600 | 1,440 |
| Damascus | 31,000 | 3,100 | 207 |
| Tyre | 20,000 | 2,000 | 133 |
| Sidon | 12,000 | 1,200 | 80 |
| Cyrene | 8,000 | 800 | 53 |
| Antioch (Syria) | 90,000 | 9,000 | 600 |
| Antioch Pisidia | 17,000 | 1,700 | 113 |
| Perga | 3,600 | 360 | 24 |
| Corinth | 50,000 | 5,000 | 333 |
| Thessalonica | 35,000 | 3,500 | 233 |
| Athens | 28,000 | 2,800 | 187 |
| Ephesus | 51,000 | 5,100 | 340 |
| Mitylene | 23,000 | 2,300 | 153 |
| Miletus | 15,000 | 1,500 | 100 |
| Rhodes | 7,500 | 750 | 50 |
| Total | 957,100 | 95,710 | 6,381 |

TABLE 7: ESTIMATED NUMBER OF HOUSE CHURCHES IN MAJOR CITIES OF THE ROMAN EMPIRE

---

12. McClure's interesting study of Jesus' social network estimates a sphere of influence of 121 people among his family, religious and civil authorities, and stigmatized people.

## Christian Impact on the Roman Empire

There is little doubt that Christianity became a formidable social movement. Sociologists today know that a social movement in which 10 percent of the population is committed to its cause represents the tipping point in influencing the greater society (Xie et al. 2011). This would explain the amount of attention Christianity was receiving as the numbers of believers grew all over the empire. For instance, Paul tells us that the faith of the Thessalonians was known all over Macedonia and Achaia to such an extent that he no longer needed to say anything (1 Thess 1:8). Paul told the believers in Rome that their faith was known "in all the world" (Rom 1:8). Paul attracted the attention of government officials and local religious leaders, as we see him imprisoned in Philippi and most likely in Asia, and later in Jerusalem, Caesarea, and Rome. The fact that Paul developed a relationship with the Asiarchs in Asia speaks volumes to the type of impact Christianity had in many cities. Claudius' expulsion of Jews and Christians from Rome sometime between AD 41 and 53 and Nero's persecution of Christians in AD 64 after the great fire in Rome were not random acts but deliberate attempts to extinguish God's movement, as Christianity had grown in popularity and influence.

Rome's attempts to extinguish the movement continued into the second century. Pliny, the governor of Bithynia and Pontus, acknowledged the significant growth of Christianity while maintaining hope that Christians could be reformed to Roman religious customs. In his letter to Emperor Trajan (ca. AD 112), he recounts:

> I therefore postponed the investigation and hastened to consult you. For the matter seemed to me to warrant consulting you, especially because of the number involved. For many persons of every age, every rank, and also of both sexes are and will be endangered. For the contagion of this [Christian] superstition has spread not only to the cities but also to the villages and farms. But it seems possible to check and cure it. It is certainly quite clear that the temples, which had been almost deserted, have begun to be frequented, that the established religious rites, long neglected, are being resumed, and that from everywhere sacrificial animals are coming, for which until now very few purchasers could be found. Hence it is easy to imagine what a multitude of people can be reformed if an opportunity for repentance is afforded. (*Letters* 10.96–97)

For a smaller movement, the government would hardly expend resources. In the first century, Luke documents several instances of Christianity's influence as he argued for its innocence to Theophilus (see table 8).

| City | Estimated Population | Reference in Acts | Significance |
|------|---------------------|-------------------|--------------|
| Philippi | 10,000 | Acts 16:11-40 | Jews create an uproar in the city and rulers imprison Paul and Silas after beating them to calm the crowd. Jailer is converted. Magistrates apologize to Paul because they beat Roman citizens. |
| Thessalonica | 35,000 | Acts 17:1-9 | Jews form a mob and claim that the disciples turned the world upside down. City authorities are involved. |
| Berea | 15,000 | Acts 17:10-15 | Jews stir up people. |
| Athens | 28,000 | Acts 17:16-34 | Paul reasons in marketplace and draws the attention of the Areopagus philosophers. |
| Corinth | 50,000 | Acts 18:1-17 | Paul draws the attention of Gallio, the proconsul of Achaia. |
| Ephesus | 51,000 | Acts 19:1-41 | Paul teaches in a noted school. He is friends with some of the Asiarchs. Riot nearly occurs over the loss of sales for an idol business. Town clerk makes a defense for Paul's disciples. |
| Caesarea | No data | Acts 26:26 | King Agrippa is well aware of the Christian movement. |

TABLE 8: LUKE'S ACCOUNT OF CHRISTIANITY'S INFLUENCE ON THE ROMAN EMPIRE

It is not difficult to imagine Christianity's growth in the major population centers of the empire. For example, Ephesus had an estimated population of 51,000 in the first century (see table 7). Luke is very clear that all of Asia had heard the gospel (Acts 19:10). The influence of the believers caused a decline in the worship of Artemis, undoubtedly the greatest figure of worship in the city as well as in all of Asia. Incredible miracles were being performed, in addition to Paul's daily teaching at the school of Tyrannus and from house to house for three years. So to suggest that 541 people in Ephesus became disciples and that those disciples faithfully shared the gospel with others in the city is not an unreasonable expectation. We will discuss this in more detail in chapter 8.

Even more so, if disciples grow in their knowledge of God, fellowship with other believers, worship in a community, and pray like those assembled in a house in Acts 4, then they—empowered by the Holy Spirit—would boldly declare the word of God and more and more people would become followers of Jesus. For a movement of 541 disciples to grow to 10 percent of a city's population should be expected. For indeed, if the 541 disciples in Ephesus each led one person to Christ every year for fifteen years, there would be more than 8,000 disciples by AD 67, well over the 10 percent tipping point to influence a society. This same scenario was repeated in every major city where the gospel was proclaimed, and it is a plausible explanation for the rapid, multiplicative growth of a church planting movement in the book of Acts (see table 9).

| City | Approximate Year Gospel is Proclaimed | Estimated Population in First Century (Russell 1958) | Population Responding to the Gospel (1.06 percent disciple rate) | Estimated Growth by AD 67 |
|---|---|---|---|---|
| Rome | 30 | 350,000 | 3,710 | 35,000 |
| Alexandria | 30 | 216,000 | 2,290 | 21,600 |
| Damascus | 30 | 31,000 | 329 | 3,100 |
| Tyre | 30 | 20,000 | 212 | 2,000 |
| Sidon | 30 | 12,000 | 127 | 1,200 |
| Cyrene | 30 | 8,000 | 85 | 800 |
| Antioch (Syria) | 32 | 90,000 | 954 | 9,000 |
| Antioch Pisidia | 48 | 17,000 | 180 | 1,700 |
| Perga | 48 | 3,600 | 38 | 360 |
| Corinth | 50 | 50,000 | 530 | 5,000 |
| Thessalonica | 50 | 35,000 | 371 | 3,500 |
| Athens | 50 | 28,000 | 297 | 2,800 |
| Ephesus | 51 | 51,000 | 541 | 5,100 |
| Mitylene | 55 | 23,000 | 244 | 2,300 |
| Miletus | 55 | 15,000 | 159 | 1,500 |
| Rhodes | 55 | 7,500 | 80 | 750 |
| Total | | 957,100 | 10,145 | 95,710 |

TABLE 9: GROWTH OF CHRISTIANITY BETWEEN AD 30 AND 67

Not only do we see the incredible influence that early Christianity had while reading Luke's first historical account, but we see it throughout the documented history of the Roman Empire. For example, in AD 197 Tertullian notes,

Tiberius accordingly, in whose days the Christian name made its entry into the world, having himself received intelligence from Palestine of events which had clearly shown the truth of Christ's divinity, brought the matter before the senate, with his own decision in favour of Christ. (*Apology* V)

The Christian movement was well recorded in the early centuries of the church: Emperor Trajan makes a reference to Christ in AD 107, Pliny the Younger refers to Christian worship in AD 112; Tacitus knew of Christ's execution under Pilate in AD 116; Suetonius records the expelling of Christians from Rome in AD 120; Lucian refers to a person crucified in Palestine in AD 165. Attributions to the Christian faith permeated the social and political conscience of the empire. It was certainly a movement, and the impact is still felt around the world today.

Such a movement deserves proper recognition of its incredible and successful launch to its sustainment over the course of centuries. It was a movement that began with 120 disciples, quickly grew to 14,000, spread to the outer reaches of the empire, and became a driving force of influence in major cities. This was a movement of disciples faithfully committed to seeing more people worship God every day (see table 10).

| Year | Estimated Number of Christians | Estimated Empire Population | Percent of Population |
|------|-------------------------------|----------------------------|-----------------------|
| 30 | 14,000 | 45,000,000 | 0.03% |
| 67 | 95,710 | 51,160,500 | 0.19% |
| 100 | 861,124 | 54,945,000 | 1.57% |
| 150 | 1,925,132 | 65,000,000 | 2.96% |
| 170[13] | 2,389,019 | 40,000,000 | 5.97% |
| 300 | 5,500,000 | 55,000,000 | 10.00% |

TABLE 10: REVISION OF STARK'S ESTIMATES

There was a legitimate church planting movement among unreached people groups in the first century. It was instigated by the Holy Spirit, as demonstrated in the numbers of people converting to Christianity during the first 34 years of the missionary enterprise. Their numbers rose very quickly to nearly 10 percent of the population of major cities in the empire. This can only be explained by

13. A plague between AD 165 and 180 resulted in a dramatic population decline (Littman and Littman 1973, 243-55). Eusebius testifies to the impact Christians had during a similar period (AD 263): "The most of our brethren were unsparing in their exceeding love and brotherly kindness. They held fast to each other and visited the sick fearlessly, and ministered to them continually, serving them in Christ. And they died with them most joyfully, taking the affliction of others, and drawing the sickness from their neighbors to themselves and willingly receiving their pains. And many who cared for the sick and gave strength to others died themselves, having transferred to themselves their death.... . Truly the best of our brethren departed in this manner ..." (*Brotherly Kindness of Christians* XXII).

the responsible actions of new converts who identified with Christ and excitedly took his gospel to their families, friends, and colleagues. The rapid growth was certainly not without its problems, but that is for a different chapter. For now, this rapid, multiplicative, and indigenous movement took the Roman Empire by storm; and in a brief, relatively speaking, 250 years—through hardship, persecution, and plagues—we see the gospel transform multiple people groups spanning from India to Iberia.

The movement that began in Ephesus and spread throughout the province of Asia fits right in the beginning of all this activity. It would become an incredible movement of God, complete with miracles, persecution, imprisonment, and riots. The work of the Holy Spirit in the approximately three years that Paul was in Asia resulted in social upheaval as well as cultural transformation. Most importantly, it resulted in more people worshipping God. Yes, it was a CPM, but this was the result rather than the strategy of the early Christian movement. Paul and his missionary band had a single motivation: the missiologically theocentric focus on God's glory by joining with him to unite all things in Christ.

When you have been involved in missions for a while, you will inevitably hear fantastic stories of phenomenal growth. I would not believe most of them if I had not seen them myself. God is at work in stunning ways still today. Here is just one of those stories:

> As I began my ministry years ago, I was equipped to spread the gospel and plant churches among the unreached in my country. As I met people who had never even heard the name of Jesus, I knew God's church must be established in Northeast India for the rapid spread of the gospel. God had instilled a burning love within me for the lost of this area of India—I desperately wanted to teach them of the same love and forgiveness that had so radically changed my own life. Today, God is multiplying churches across India as we seek him through prayer. God has chosen us, a simple people, to accomplish his mission of reaching the lost. As more leaders are trained, new churches are being planted—resulting in the spread of the gospel and new numbers of believers being added daily. (Schuler n.d., 59)

God is at work in our brother's country. In the last five years, he and other leaders have planted 53,686 house churches, but there is so much more to be done. There are more people groups in his country that have never heard the name of Jesus than in any other country in the world. It is going to take multiple church planting movements to finish the task. This was what happened in Asia in the first century, and this is what inspired Paul to declare, "I no longer have any room for work in these regions" (Rom 15:23).

So far we have introduced *Ephesiology* (chapter 1) and provided evidence for a church planting movement in Acts (chapter 2). As we move forward in understanding the stages of a movement, we will examine the launch of the church in Ephesus (chapters 3–5), along with that church's perseverance in glorifying God by reaching more people with the gospel (chapter 9). In between, the book weaves through the church's grounding in God's plan (chapter 6) and appointment of leaders (chapter 7) who multiplied disciples (chapter 8). This is the story of Paul's missiological theology situated in the grand narrative of God's mission. It rocked the world of his time, and it can rock our world as well.

# CHAPTER 3

# Launching a Movement I: Missiological Exegesis

Vihaan came from the Mishing people, an animistic tribe in Northeast India. There had been no Christian contact with the Mishing until an Indian missionary met Vihaan. As Reyansh, Vihaan's son, tells the story, Vihaan was not overly impressive as a person; but when Christ captured his heart, something significant changed. Reyansh knew a supernatural phenomenon had taken place, and he wanted to become like his dad.

Reyansh was likely in his early twenties when he came to Christ and witnessed his dad's passion for sharing his faith. On a rather inconspicuous day, Vihaan returned from his missionary activities of preaching the gospel in nearby villages when a group of leaders from his village met him at the entrance. "Vihaan," they said, "our village has been experiencing misfortune, and we believe it is because of your Christian god." Without hesitation, the village leaders seized Vihaan, crucified him on the ground, chopped his body into pieces, and threw the pieces into the river. Reyansh understandably wanted revenge, but the Indian missionary who discipled Vihaan told him that he needed to share his faith with the men who murdered his dad.

What a heartbreaking story. I sat stunned when I first heard Reyansh share it. Reyansh is one of many leaders whose stories are astounding. Even more amazing is what God has done through their faithful witness of the good news. The story did not end with Vihaan's death. As Reyansh studied Scripture, the Lord directed him to Jesus' crucifixion. In that story, Jesus was led away with two criminals and innocently crucified among thieves. When Reyansh read what Jesus said next, it was as if God himself were speaking to him. "And Jesus said, 'Father, forgive them, for they know not what they do'" (Luke 23:34). He knew that he had to return to his village and forgive those who crucified his father and mutilated his body.

As was no surprise, the leaders did not want to have anything to do with Reyansh's or his father's Jesus. However, as other villagers observed how Reyansh had forgiven his father's murderers, a change began to occur. Soon people began to come to Christ, and a church started in his village. Within five years, more than a thousand other house churches began among the Mishing and other tribes in the area.

Today Reyansh leads a movement that has spread because of suffering and persecution. Jesus said, "Truly, truly, I say to you, unless a grain of wheat falls into the earth and dies, it remains alone; but if it dies, it bears much fruit" (John 12:24). While the pain of his father's death lingers, the joy Reyansh experiences in the fruit of his martyrdom is as indescribable as the smile on his face when he shares the testimony of how the gospel changes lives and how that results in remarkable movements of the Holy Spirit.

Launching a movement begins with a clear understanding of the gospel we proclaim and how it is good news to the people who hear it. Like Reyansh, it is imperative to find the story of Jesus that will connect with the story of the people we engage. The message of Jesus and the thieves connected with his village. What is the message that will connect with your community?

The next three chapters will focus on developing missiological principles for effectively engaging a community with the message of Jesus Christ. That message is the connecting point between a community's story and God's story. It is the bridge that joins the two together so that they become the same story of God's deliberate act through time to bring people to worship him. First we will begin with an understanding of the gospel Paul preached, then we will move to the principle of missiological exegesis as a first-order issue in developing a missiological theology that tells the compelling story of God who is at work among a people.

## The Gospel of a Movement

God's will is not complicated, but it can be complex. Simply stated, God's will is to reconcile all things to himself through Christ (Col 1:20). The complexity of his will involves the manner in which it is communicated in different cultural contexts. The launch of a movement must involve movement leaders who have the capacity and skills to connect God's story to the story of a culture. However, it starts with a firm understanding of the gospel itself and its impact on our personal lives.

John Stott sums up Paul's gospel well:

The good news of the unsearchable riches of Christ which Paul preached is that he died and rose again not only to save sinners like me (though he did), but also to create a single new humanity; not only to redeem us from sin but also to adopt us into God's family; not only to reconcile us to God but also to reconcile us to one another. (1979, 75)

There was a depth to Paul's gospel that came from a profound yet dark realization of his own disobedience. Not disobedience in the sense of sinful acts, although Paul certainly acted in a sinful manner. He admits as much in his ongoing fight against doing the things he did not want to do and rejoices in his deliverance through Christ (Rom 7:19–20, 24–25). This disobedience, however, was far more profound. It rocked Paul at his very core. So it might be worth a moment to recall Paul's story.

Paul's identity as a Hebrew of Hebrews, a Pharisee whose zeal had no comparison, set him on a path to serve YHWH[14] in the most dedicated manner (Phil 3:5–6). For him, there would be nothing more important than to ensure the integrity of the Jewish people and their relationship with YHWH. Yet, as we know, Paul's identity was rattled by the realization of his unbelief in the very God he believed he served. His absolute ignorance resulted in blasphemy of YHWH, as he persecuted Jesus' followers. His insolent opposition to the God of his fathers amounted to the very rejection of his heritage. It is from this fundamental understanding that Paul's identity, his very existence, denied God's existence. When Jesus met him on the road to Damascus, the depth of his denial overwhelmed his senses: a bright light, thunderous voice, falling to the ground (Acts 9:3–7). He was helplessly confronted by a personal encounter with his living Savior and Lord, the very God he opposed. This resulted in an utter and complete conversion, a repentance from unbelief to belief so intense that everything else would amount to excrement (Greek σκύβαλα, Phil 3:8). Paul reflects this change in his letter to Timothy:

I thank him who has given me strength, Christ Jesus our Lord, because he judged me faithful, appointing me to his service, though formerly I was a blasphemer, persecutor, and insolent opponent. But I received mercy because I had acted ignorantly in unbelief, and the grace of our Lord overflowed for me with the faith and love that are in Christ Jesus. The saying is trustworthy and deserving of full acceptance, that Christ Jesus came into the world to save

---

14. YHWH is the tetragrammaton (literally a four-letter word) spelling of Yahweh. Out of profound respect for God, Jews did not pronounce his name and often substituted other names, such as Adonai, in the Hebrew text. For the weight of the significance of Paul's Jewishness, I use YHWH instead of Yahweh. He went from a deeply religious Pharisee who worshiped YHWH to an intensely personal encounter with the Lord Jesus Christ.

sinners, of whom I am the foremost. But I received mercy for this reason, that in me, as the foremost, Jesus Christ might display his perfect patience as an example to those who were to believe in him for eternal life. To the King of the ages, immortal, invisible, the only God, be honor and glory forever and ever. Amen. (1 Tim 1:12–17)

If we miss the depth of Paul's conversion, then we will not understand the theocentric nature of his writings nor his missiological theology that compelled him to do all for the glory of God (1 Cor 10:31). Our understanding of Paul must lie firmly on the foundation of his experience with God, as he proclaimed "the gospel of the glory of the blessed God" to both Jews and Gentiles (1 Tim 1:11). This was entrusted to him, and he considered everything else unworthy. For Paul, the gospel betrays the depth of humanity's need as well as the height of God's love (Rom 1:16–2:1). Even more, it reveals a glorious God relentlessly pursuing a relationship with his image-bearers (2 Cor 6:16). Paul knew the privilege of delivering this message to others in ways that they would understand so that God would be glorified by more people worshipping him.

## An Indigenous Gospel

There is a definite distinction between the message Paul delivered to the Jews and the message he shared with the Gentiles. Granted, it is the same gospel. Paul proclaimed that the good news of the gospel for the Jews was that the Messiah has come (Acts 13:23) and for the Gentiles that God has overlooked the times of ignorance and called all people to repent (Acts 17:30). Paul knew that the gospel remained one, but it could be expressed in many ways to ensure that God's story connects with others.

As I have listened to the testimonies of many who have come to Christ from Hinduism, Buddhism, and Islam, the breadth of the gospel message is amazing. Some share that God performs incredible healings from diseases, and others share about deliverance from demonic oppression. Still others share that they encountered God because of a vision or a simple conversation with a pastor or Christian neighbor. People are drawn to Christ in many ways. For example, a former Hindu priest and member of the Rashtriya Swayamsevak Sangh (RSS), a Hindu nationalist organization, shared this testimony:

> Things went wrong in my life. My wife got sick. I began to take her to many places for better treatment, but nothing could help her recover from the sickness. I did many pujas [acts of Hindu worship] for my wife's treatment but all the pujas and my hard work were in vain. I spent a lot of money, but my wife could not return to good health. I asked help from people, but no one came to ask about my family situation.

So one day my Christian neighbor came to ask about my family. He shared about God's love and his mercy. After speaking about Jesus, he wanted to pray for my wife. At that time I had no words to refuse, so I said yes because I was so broken and needed immediate help. After his prayer, it was a surprise to me, my wife felt better. Then [my Christian friend] began to come frequently to my house and pray for my wife. Within one month, my wife was healed. I was so surprised to see the power of God; without any medication or treatment she was healed. When I saw the power of God, I believed in him and took the decision to accept Jesus as my Savior and the Lord.

Before baptism, my RSS leader called me and asked me why I will be baptized and accept [the Christian] religion. So I told him everything that happened in our life. He told me to turn back from believing in God, and told me to ask whatever help I needed from [the RSS]. He also offered me a job. After hearing from him, I was so confused. I did not know what to do. But the Holy Spirit reminded me about the great miracle that had been done in my family. Finally, I decided to follow Jesus. Next day I changed my mobile phone number and surrendered my life to Jesus.

Now we are so happy with our spiritual life. And my wife is fine, by the grace of the Lord, and my two sons are also fine. Please pray for my family and me so that we can continue in our spiritual journey.

Christ connects with people at different places, but those places all lead to a final destination: we must believe in him (John 16:9; cf. Rom 10:9–10). At times, however, we complicate the gospel message and make it more about people than about God.

For years I taught a course entitled Theological and Sociological Foundations of Evangelism. At its core, the course focused on understanding the message of the gospel and the sin that would prevent someone from coming to Christ. As seems common in our American evangelical gospel presentations, we often demand a list of sins that must be confessed before salvation can be secured. Even my students, as do many evangelicals, frequently enumerated a fine list of vices that had to be identified and addressed before someone could come to Christ.

This is not only a Western issue but also a global one, as we have exported our theology to other countries. As we drove to the Indira Gandhi International Airport with one of our leaders, he explained the message of the gospel preached by many Christian pastors in India. Their gospel attempted to convince people that drinking or smoking prevented them from going to heaven. Those "sins" had to first be confessed before one could become a Christian.

For example, consider the conversation I had with Rajneesh, a Christian leader from a South Asian country:

**Rajneesh:** In India, culture plays a huge role in every faith. For an instance, we can't ask a new believer to throw out all the idols from his/her home as this will leave a bad impression on him/her. So at first, he/she attends a house church with having a syncretic mind-set.

**Michael:** And then what is the process for a new believer to throw out idols?

**Rajneesh:** It depends on how people do the follow-up. We usually ask them to attend one of our house churches, and then as he/she learns the Word of God, he/she understands that the idols are nothing.

**Michael:** So then what is the first step for one to become a new believer?

**Rajneesh:** Repent and accept Jesus.

**Michael:** Repent from what exactly?

**Rajneesh:** From sin.

**Michael:** Can you elaborate?

**Rajneesh:** Past sin means from everything he/she has done in the past that are sin.

**Michael:** What are examples of this sin?

**Rajneesh:** Disobedience, hatred, unforgiveness, etc.

Rajneesh focused on a gospel message that was anthropocentric in nature. His message communicated the need to change sinful behavior rather than to believe in the one true God. Interestingly enough, idols were not a part of the sinful behavior; rather, they were viewed as a part of culture which presumably would fade away as the "new" believer gathered with others in a house church. This is very different from the manner in which Paul communicated the gospel: the theocentric message of Christ's work and our allegiance to God for his glory. If we misunderstand the depth of conversion and reduce it to simple behavioral changes, we risk proclaiming an anthropocentric gospel leading to syncretism.

Paul knew that forgiveness of sins was based on an individual's faith in Jesus as Lord and Savior, as the one true God—just as he experienced on the road to Damascus. Such faith, rather than an enumeration of a list of wrongdoings, results in salvation that leads to behavior, even identity, change (Mark 2:5–12, Luke 7:47–49). Repentance for the forgiveness of sins (Luke 24:47) means to renounce unbelief in Jesus, who is God and who alone is able to forgive sins. It is not repentance from sins for the forgiveness of sins, as repentance must be from one thing to the corresponding opposite thing—the essence of μετανοέω (*metanoeo*). If it is from our sins, then repentance would mean to sin no more.

This, however, is not possible without Christ, and it promotes a works salvation in a vain attempt to stop sinning. As we see with Rajneesh, such a position takes an anthropocentric view of the gospel. The gospel is reduced to my needs rather than to the glory of Christ.

In contrast, if repentance is from disbelieving that Christ is God, then the corresponding opposite is to believe that Christ is God (Acts 16:31). This is what Jesus taught as the role of the Holy Spirit's conviction (John 16:9). This was Paul's conversion experience as well as his gospel message. Such a theocentric view of the gospel places Christ at the focal point. It is his gospel. It is not about us, but about Jesus and the rightful recognition that he is God.

Interestingly enough, Paul never speaks of enumerating a list of sins as a condition for salvation. He certainly reminds the faithful of their past, but it is by God's grace that we are saved, through faith in Jesus Christ (Eph 2:8–9). Repentance is absolutely required. However, in Paul's gospel repentance is turning from the empty worship of other gods, which was done in ignorance, to the living God (Acts 14:15; 17:30). This was in fact what Paul taught in Ephesus. It is repentance toward God—that is, away from the belief in other deities, like Artemis and the sundry gods and goddesses worshipped in Asia—and trusting in the Lord Jesus Christ (Acts 20:21).

The significance of this gospel message delivered to people in one of the most religiously diverse regions of the Roman Empire cannot be overestimated. There were more than fifty distinct ethnic groups in Asia during Paul's tenure in the area (Charanis 1975, 9). While the worship of Artemis is no doubt central to the beliefs of many, Asia is best described as henotheistic (recognition of multiple deities) and the people as monolatristic (worship of or service to a single deity). A pantheon of gods and goddesses were worshipped in temples and in homes, as each family focused on one particular cultic practice while recognizing many other deities. Paul calling people to repentance toward God represented a monumental shift in their religious lives and belief systems. While the situations were different, that shift was very similar to the one Paul experienced himself: a dramatic calling to follow the one true God who is Lord and Savior for everyone.

The gospel is about believing Jesus is God and giving him glory. When we make it about our sins, then the gospel becomes about us: "Jesus did this for me." In reality, Jesus did what he did to bring glory to God (John 14:31). In other words, Jesus knows that God is most glorified by others worshipping him. It is, after all, the root cause of angelic rejoicing (Luke 17:3–10).

For this purpose, Paul writes, "In him you also, when you heard the word of truth, the gospel of your salvation, and believed in him, were sealed with the promised Holy Spirit, who is the guarantee of our inheritance until we acquire possession of it, *to the praise of his glory*" (Eph 1:13–14; emphasis added). To reinforce the nature of salvation, Paul emphasizes that it is through God's work of love and mercy rather than anything we have done, not even cataloguing and confessing our wrongdoings (Eph 2:4–5).

In Christian discipleship, there will be confession of sins (1 John 1:9), because there is no separation between believing and behaving. That is, if we believe Christ is God, then we behave correspondingly (Eph 5:1). As is clear in Paul's gospel to the Jews, it was about believing in the Messiah who was foretold by the prophets (Acts 17:2–3); and to the Gentiles it was about repentance (Greek μετάνοιά; *metavoia*) from worshipping false gods to worshipping the one true God, in whom "we live and move and have our being" (Acts 17:28). The natural result of believing and worshipping was walking "in a manner worthy of the calling to which you have been called" (Eph 4:1)—a new identity as followers of Christ. As we understand that the gospel is about God's glory, we begin a journey to a movement approach that sees its goal as the nations, tribes, peoples, and languages worshipping before the throne (Rev 5:9). This journey drives us to a distinctly missiological approach to engaging our community and results in a missiological theology that fits the story of the people.

## Missiological Theology of a Movement

Missiology is simply the study of missions. Missiologists, unquestionably more than theologians, like to opine that theology is born from missions—Martin Kähler's idea that "missions is the mother of theology." In many ways, this is true. Theology cannot be created in a vacuum. It is always situated in a context in which people are attempting to explain God as he is understood through a particular cultural lens. Theology is a human endeavor whereby we try to know God. Not only is it a human endeavor, it is also an interpretative task that begins in Genesis, with an explanation of what was happening at the start of human history, and ends in Revelation, with the completion of God's mission. So theologians naturally debate whether we should start with the Bible in developing a theology, or with God himself.

Missiological theology, like any attempt to explain the events of the Bible, is also a human endeavor to interpret and understand God's grand narrative and what he is doing to draw people to himself. The starting point of a missiological theology is God's self-revelation to the nations. It is, by nature, a theology situated in the context of seeking the connecting points between Christ and culture. It is also an active theology, as it recognizes God's redeeming work in history and his call for our participation in his mission. It is a theocentric awareness that all things are summed up in him for the praise of his glory.

In a missiological theology, how we communicate God's story as good news for a people is of utmost importance. As we will see in chapter 5, a missiological theology is formulated when we, as missiological theologians, understand God ourselves, the context in which we are attempting to communicate him to others, and where he is already at work in that context to make himself known. Clark Pinnock communicates the importance of this task of making explicit what God is doing implicitly: "I believe that unless the portrait of God is compelling, the credibility of belief in God is bound to decline" (1994, 101).

So that is where we will start as we delve into Paul's missiological theology—with God. We will amplify this further in chapter 5. Next to a clear understanding of the gospel, this is the beginning point in the launch of a movement.

## The Starting Point of Missiological Theology

From Genesis to Revelation, the Bible tells the story of God's mission in the world. In it we learn of the actions of God the Father, God the Son, and God the Holy Spirit to bring reconciliation between the world and the one true God. These actions, motivated by the Father's love and heart for the entire world, are grounded in the work of Jesus Christ and carried out by the Holy Spirit. Paul effectively explains the unity of God's work in Ephesians. God's mission is to unite all things in Christ (1:10), through the proclamation of the great mystery that the nations are fellow heirs of the promise of Christ through the gospel (3:6). The community of saints has been especially elected and predestined by the Father (1:3–5; 5:1) to be on his mission as his heirs. The Holy Spirit guarantees that special inheritance (1:14) and uniquely empowers (5:19) and emboldens the witness of the church with words that convict the world of its unbelief in Christ (6:17).

To Paul, this is God's mission, in which we are privileged to partner as fellow workers (1 Cor 3:9). The German Reformed theologian Jürgen Moltmann sums it up well: "It is not the church that has a mission of salvation to fulfill in the world; it is the mission of the Son and the Spirit through the Father that includes the church" (1977, 64).

This story of God's work in the world is foundational to our understanding of the purpose of the Bible. It is the story of how God seeks to have a relationship with us and chooses us to share his love with others. The great redemptive work of bringing us into his family as adopted children by Jesus' atoning acts gives us a new identity as his children who take up the work of the family until every people group has had the opportunity to hear of the mystery of God's desire to be in relationship with his creation. For Paul, the first missionary was God (Phil 2:6–7), who relentlessly pursues people and calls us to that same purpose (2 Cor 5:19).

Taking responsibility for the task of proclaiming the gospel to all people as God's co-laborer, Paul distinctly communicated both the continuity of God with Jewish YHWH in Galatia (Acts 13:17–39) and God with Greek Zeus in Athens (Acts 17:24–31), for he saw God at work as much in the Jews as in the nations. Paul's portrait of God—what theologians call "theology proper"—was compelling to both Jews and Gentiles. However, they were not communicated in the same way. In the synagogue, Paul spoke of the God of the Jewish fathers (see table 11). In the public square, Paul spoke of the God of creation (see table 12).

| Pisidian Antioch (Acts 13) | Thessalonica (Acts 17) |
|---|---|
| God of the people Israel (13:17) | Christ suffered and rose from the dead (17:3) |
| • Chose their fathers (13:17) | Jesus is the Christ (17:3) |
| • Made them great in Egypt (13:17) | Jesus is King (17:7) |
| • Gave them land in Canaan (13:19) | |
| • Gave them judges and kings (13:20-22) | |
| God brought a Savior through David (13:23) | |
| John the Baptist announced Jesus' coming (13:25) | |
| Jews in Jerusalem responsible for Jesus' execution (13:27-28) | |
| God raised him from the dead (13:30) | |
| Jesus appeared to his disciples (13:31) | |
| Jesus is the good news that God promised the fathers (13:32-33) | |
| Forgiveness of sins is proclaimed through Jesus (13:38) | |
| Those who believe are freed (13:39) | |

TABLE 11: PAUL'S COMPELLING ARGUMENT FOR GOD TO JEWS
IN PISIDIAN ANTIOCH AND THESSALONICA

Paul's compelling portrait of God for the Jews was firmly situated in the Jewish story. It was a unique story of God's heart to use his people to declare his blessings to all nations. Paul masterfully told the story, and many Jews and devout followers of YHWH believed (Acts 13:43; 17:4). Yet it is the Jewish story and not the story of the nations. Their stories were told differently, as we see in Lystra (Acts 14:15–17), Philippi (Acts 16:31–34), and Athens

(Acts 17:22–31). In his epistles, Paul's portrait of the God of the Jews and the God of all creation beautifully coalesce in a personal, trinitarian God who desires all to be saved and come to the knowledge of Jesus Christ (1 Tim 2:4). The Trinity, of course, is the foundation from which Paul is able to communicate his compelling view of God. C. S. Lewis aptly articulates the idea of a God who makes himself known to Jews as much as to pagans:

> Theology, while saying that a special illumination has been vouchsafed to Christians and (earlier) to Jews, also says that there is some divine illumination vouchsafed to all men. The Divine light, we are told, "lighteneth every man." We should, therefore, expect to find in the imagination of great Pagan teachers and myth makers some glimpse of that theme which we believe to be the very plot of the whole cosmic story—the theme of incarnation, death, and rebirth. (1944, 8–9)

Lewis captures the essence of Paul's missiological theology. In order for Paul to communicate a compelling argument for God to the pagans, he had to know the pagan myths and situate the story of God in their context. Connecting a culture's story in the grand narrative of God's story is an important factor regarding whether Christianity will be viewed as an outsider's religion or as indigenous.

| Lystra (Acts 14) | Athens (Acts 17) |
|---|---|
| Turn from vain worship to a living God (14:15) | God is creator of the universe (17:24) |
| God made heaven, earth, sea, and all that is in them (14:15) | God is Lord of heaven and earth (17:24) |
| God allowed the nations freedom (14:16) | God is creator of humanity (17:25, 29) |
| God's witness was demonstrated through his goodness to the nations (14:17) | God wants to be sought (17:27) |
|  | God is near people (17:27) |
|  | God wants all people to believe in Christ (17:30) |
|  | God will judge the world by Christ (17:31) |
|  | God raised Christ from the dead (17:31) |

TABLE 12: PAUL'S COMPELLING ARGUMENT FOR GOD TO THE NATIONS
IN LYSTRA AND ATHENS

## Connecting Stories and Cultures

Paul's missionary journeys in Acts clearly show his ability to connect the story of God to both the Jewish story and the story of the nations. As a Pharisee who learned at the feet of Gamaliel (Acts 22:3), we would expect him to know the Jewish story, but he also learned the history of the nations he engaged with the gospel. For example, his appeal to the philosophers in Athens to repent from ignorance was largely made on the basis of Paul's ability to connect the Athenian experience with the Christian one. The same is true in Ephesus. When Paul writes to the mostly Gentile believers in Asia, his references to the works of darkness (Eph 5:11) and cosmic powers (Eph 6:12) connects to the magical practices in the city (Acts 19:18–19). The spiritual blessings from the heavenlies (Eph 1:3) is juxtaposed to the stone that fell from the heavens (Acts 19:35). His use of the word *mystery* (Eph 1:9; 3:3–4, 6, 9; 5:32; 6:19; 1 Tim 3:9; 3:16) is in contradistinction to the various mystery religions practiced in Asia.

That connection of history to the present situation gave the nations a sense of what I have called "ancientization" (Cooper 2009a). Ancientization is the ability to relate the past to the present in such a way that the present shares an identity with the past as it sees a coalescing of their stories. It is no longer two histories but one unifying story that legitimizes the present, as a people group attempts to relate their history with the grand story of God's mission in the world. For Paul, there was no historical discontinuity between the Christian faith and other faiths. There was only a continuity with God's work in the world.

Early Christian philosophers picked up on this continuity. Justin, a second-century philosopher who was strolling the coast of Ephesus when he began to understand God's story from an Ephesian believer, held that whatever was taught well by philosophers belongs rightly to the Christians. With that idea, Justin believed that Heraclitus, Plato, and Aristotle were pre-Christ Christians. This λόγος σπερματικός (*logos spermatikos*), as it became known, was divinely and sovereignly instilled in the noble thoughts of the ancients and could rightly be considered Christian.

The North African theologian Origen (AD 185–254) affirmed this understanding as well:

> I am therefore very desirous that you should accept such parts even of Greek philosophy as may serve for the ordinary elementary instruction of our schools, and be kind of preparation for Christianity; also those portions of geometry and astronomy likely to be of use in the interpretation of the sacred Scriptures, so that, what the pupils of the philosophers say about geometry and music, grammar, rhetoric, and astronomy, that they are the handmaidens of philosophy, we may say of philosophy itself in relation to Christianity. (*Letter to Gregory* 1.1)

The idea of *logos spermatikos* stood in stark contrast to the approach of Tertullian (AD 150–225) and Cyprian (ca. AD 200–259), who saw a distinct discontinuity between culture and Christ. As Christianity grew, it seemed to distance itself from an active faith that took risks in the proclamation of Christ and settled into an institutional position that separated itself from its environment. Tertullian, for example, would famously quip, "What indeed has Athens to do with Jerusalem, the Academy with Christ?" (*On the Prescriptions of Heretics* 7).

The separation between Christianity and culture set the institution of the church as the focal point of salvation. Cyprian, as an example of nascent institutionalization, promoted the idea of *extra ecclesium nullus salas* (outside the church, there is no salvation). He wrote, "He can no longer have God for his father who has not the Church for his mother" (*On the Unity of the Church*, 1.6). This institutional mentality continued especially after the Christianization of the Roman Empire. Paul, however, was quite different as he observed God at work in culture. He did not separate the God of his fathers from the God of all creation. Instead, he helped people see this continuity by first understanding their religious beliefs, cultural practices, and history—what I am calling "missiological exegesis."

## Missiological Exegesis

Missiological exegesis is the task of the missionary that is focused on understanding the peculiarities of a people group with a view to seeing how God is at work in those peculiarities. Paul used three primary techniques as he learned about the people he engaged with the gospel: dialogue, observation, and historical study.

The English word *dialogue* comes from the Greek διάλογος (*dialogos*) and means "conversation." We see a few cognates in the New Testament, such as διαλέγομαι (*dialegomai*), διαλογιζομαι (*dialogizomi*), and διαλογισμο (*dialogismo*). Of the thirteen times *dialegomai* is used in the New Testament, ten of those are in Acts. All of the uses in Acts deal with the Apostle Paul. When Luke uses it to describe Paul's missionary work, it is often translated in the New American Standard Bible as "reasoning" (six times in Acts 17:2, 17; 18:4, 19; 19:8, 9), "talking" (two times in Acts 20:7, 8), or "discussion" (two times in Acts 24:12, 25). Dieter Kemmler comments that the New Testament use of *dialegomai*, consistent with Attic Greek, is best reflected as "reasoned, or discoursed argumentatively, either in the way of dialogue … or in that of formal and continuous discourse" (1975, 35–36)—a practice common in philosophical schools.

When Luke writes of Paul's dialogue with others, it seems apparent that he was conversing with various people and his conversation occurred most likely in a Socratic manner (Marshall 1980, 283). This is consistent with the understanding that Paul's missionary journeys resembled that of traveling sophists or peripatetics and his instruction with that of the Hellenistic schools (Alexander 1995, 61). Paul took on familiar forms in order to communicate effectively.

Luke tells us that while Paul was in Athens on his second missionary journey, "he reasoned [*dialegomai*] in the synagogue with the Jews and the devout persons, and in the marketplace every day with those who happened to be there" (Acts 17:17). This style of public discourse was as much about sharing information as it was about gathering information. While Paul dialogued, he was learning about the Athenians. Paul's desire for those he engaged was to believe the truth about the God he was sharing. We see this clearly in Ephesus. Luke writes,

> And he entered the synagogue and for three months spoke boldly, reasoning [*dialegomai*] and persuading them about the kingdom of God. But when some became stubborn and continued in unbelief, speaking evil of the Way before the congregation, he withdrew from them and took the disciples with him, reasoning [*dialegomai*] daily in the hall of Tyrannus. (Acts 19:8–9)

Characteristic of Paul's dialogue was respect. For example, at the Areopagus he seems to identify the searching for spirituality of the Athenians as a positive desire to know truth (Acts 17:22). The Lukan scholar William Larkin states, "Here we have a respectful recognition of religious endeavors but not an acknowledgement that they lead to true, saving faith" (1995, 255). Respect for religious beliefs does not mean consent. Paul regarded all people as created in the image of God, and because of the image-bearer nature of those he encountered, he respected their attempt to seek God, albeit they sought him in vain.

The very fact that his encounters were dialogical in nature demonstrates his respect for others. Paul's "respectful recognition of religious endeavors" was not out of ignorance. Luke recounts, "Now while Paul was waiting for them at Athens, his spirit was being provoked within him as he was observing the city full of idols" (Acts 17:16 NASB). Paul's "observing" (Greek θεωρεω, *theoreo)* has the idea that in his observation he was also trying to understand what he encountered.

Paul's respectful dialogue and observation eventually resulted in an invitation by the philosophers at the Areopagus. Luke only records a summary of the exchange that ensued, but the detail he provides helps us see that respectful dialogue, observation of culture, and knowledge of history were instrumental in Paul's formulation of a missiologically theocentric gospel message. Luke records, "Men of Athens, I observe [*theoreo*] that you are very religious in all respects.

For while I was passing through and examining the objects of your worship, I also found an altar with this inscription, 'TO AN UNKNOWN GOD'" (Acts 17:22–23 NASB).

As Hans-Josef Klauck notes, the opening address at the Areopagus has the same structural elements as classical travel accounts in which dialogue and observation were important ways to convey information (2003, 75). Out of regard for the beliefs of others and what he had learned, Paul respectfully acknowledged the spiritual journey of his hosts.

Paul's understanding of the religious beliefs of Athenians came not only from his observation but also from knowledge of their history. Twice Paul quotes from their own philosophers (Acts 17:28): "In him we live and move and have our being" and "For we are indeed his offspring." We are unsure of the provenance of the first quote. Nevertheless, according to Klauck, "There is not in fact a literal verbal parallel to this passage, but its components are found in early Greek philosophy, in the reflections about the being and the significance of Zeus, the highest god" (2003, 87).

The second quote is most certainly a reference from Aratus' Φαινόμενα (*Phenomena*). The third-century BC Greek philosopher was commissioned to write a treatise on the stellar constellations. In his opening stanzas, he paints a different picture of the Zeus of Homer and Hesiod, who wrote of him four centuries prior. Instead, Aratus describes Zeus as follows:

> From Zeus let us begin; him do we mortals never leave unnamed; full of Zeus are all the streets and all the market-places of men; full is the sea and the havens thereof; always we all have need of Zeus. *For we are also his offspring;* and he in his kindness unto men giveth favourable signs and wakeneth the people to work, reminding them of livelihood. He tells what time the soil is best for the labour of the ox and for the mattock, and what time the seasons are favourable both for planting of trees and for casting all manner of seeds. For himself it was who set the signs in heaven, and marked out the constellations, and for the year devised what stars chiefly should give to men right signs of the seasons, to the end that all things might grow unfailingly. Wherefore him do men ever worship first and last. Hail, O Father, mighty marvel, mighty blessing unto men. Hail to thee and to the Elder Race! Hail, ye Muses, right kindly, every one! But for me, too, in answer to my prayer direct all my lay, even as is meet to tell the stars. (Φαινόμενα, 1; emphasis added.)

What is striking is Paul's recognition that Zeus of the Athenians is the God he proclaimed, albeit not the jovial Zeus who enjoyed making folly of humans. Aratus' Zeus was benevolent, a god who cared and looked out for humans.

Paul recognized a direct correlation and presented it to the philosophers. Nearly four centuries prior to Paul's arrival in Athens, God was at work making himself known so that one day the Athenians would worship the one true God. This was not a redemptive analogy. It was not contextualization. It was the proper identification of God's work and explicitly connecting his story with the story of a people.

The manner in which Paul dialogued with religious others, observed their culture, and studied their history continues to be the first step in a model for effective engagement of a culture. It was characteristic of Paul's disciples and should also be characteristic of us. It was a pattern seen repeatedly at Ephesus. As we read in Acts 19, the gospel had spread all around Asia and upset the religious practices of those who worshipped Artemis, particularly those in Ephesus. Instigated by a silversmith named Demetrius, an uprising ensued that was primarily motivated by economic loss as Christianity displaced the worship of the Ephesian goddess and the manufacturing of pagan shrines. Luke describes the situation:

> A man named Demetrius, a silversmith, who made silver shrines of Artemis, brought no little business to the craftsmen. These he gathered together, with the workmen in similar trades, and said, "Men, you know that from this business we have our wealth. And you see and hear that not only in Ephesus but in almost all of Asia this Paul has persuaded and turned away a great many people, saying that gods made with hands are not gods. And there is danger not only that this trade of ours may come into disrepute but also that the temple of the great goddess Artemis may be counted as nothing, and that she may even be deposed from her magnificence, she whom all Asia and the world worship." (Acts 19:24–27)

Soon after Demetrius rallied people to his cause, the crowd grabbed two Christians, Gaius and Aristarchus of Macedonia. As we read the text, the environment is growing increasingly hostile, and we begin to get a sense that things aren't going to end well for Paul's two disciples. We don't know how long the two were held hostage, but it was long enough for Paul to have contact with friends who were Asiarchs (Acts 19:31)—officials who presided over religious rites and public games in Asia. The fact that Paul developed friendships with them tells us something about the level of mutual respect they had for each other. The increasing threat potential of the crowd caused Paul's friends to advise him against intervening.

What happens next would have never been expected unless the Christians of Asia had a good reputation. Indeed, Paul expected such a reputation from Christian leaders. When Paul instructed Timothy in regard to the appointment of an overseer, he wrote, "Moreover, he must be well thought of by outsiders, so that he may not fall into disgrace, into a snare of the devil" (1 Tim 3:7). At the height of the riot, the crowd chanted in unison for two hours, "Great is Artemis of the Ephesians!"—only to be quieted by a single brave soul who would intervene on behalf of Gaius and Aristarchus.

> And when the town clerk had quieted the crowd, he said, "Men of Ephesus, who is there who does not know that the city of the Ephesians is temple keeper of the great Artemis, and of the sacred stone that fell from the sky? Seeing then that these things cannot be denied, you ought to be quiet and do nothing rash. *For you have brought these men here who are neither sacrilegious nor blasphemers of our goddess.* If therefore Demetrius and the craftsmen with him have a complaint against anyone, the courts are open, and there are proconsuls. Let them bring charges against one another. But if you seek anything further, it shall be settled in the regular assembly. For we really are in danger of being charged with rioting today, since there is no cause that we can give to justify this commotion." (Acts 19:35–40; emphasis added)

In my estimation, this is the most remarkable testimony about Christians ever given: "For you have brought these men here who are neither sacrilegious nor blasphemers of our goddess" (Acts 19:37). The Ephesian goddess cult was an interesting conflation of the goddess worship of Asia and Greece, even the goddess worship of the ancient Near East. We are most familiar with the Greek Artemis, the goddess of the hunt and moon. She was the twin sister of Apollo, who fell in love with Orion. Jealous of the attention Artemis gave to Orion, Apollo tricked her into killing him. Distraught by the betrayal, Artemis appealed to Zeus, and Zeus placed Orion in the sky chasing the seven sisters (Pleiades), just as he was doing when he first met Artemis. The Greek Artemis was the protector of women and young girls. She was often associated with women's rites of passage, such as marriage rituals and childbirth customs (Brinks 2009).

The Asian Artemis, or Artemis Ephesia, as she was more accurately called, was most known for her "multi-breasted" figure. Artemis Ephesia was believed to be a symbol of fertility and was the focal point of worship in Asia. Perhaps adopted from ancient Near Eastern mother-goddess worship, Artemis Ephesia was considered the patron of childbearing and was responsible for the salvation of women and children during birth. Alongside of this role, she was viewed as the legitimate wife of the Ephesians, as she was known as the founder of Ephesus and protector of the Amazons (LiDonnici 1992, 21).

The temple of Artemis Ephesia, which gained the distinction of being one of the seven ancient wonders of the world, was originally constructed in the eighth century BC and would eventually be destroyed in AD 263. Over the centuries, the temple was razed on multiple occasions. The numerous reconstructions of the temple were often funded by private donations of adherents, as was the custom for funding temple-building campaigns. The Greek historian Strabo (64 BC to AD 24) recounts, "But when it was set on fire by a certain Herostratus, the citizens erected another and better one, having collected the ornaments of the women and their own individual belongings, and having sold also the pillars of the former temple" (*Geography* 14.1.22).

Both the Greek Artemis and Artemis Ephesia had some association with wild beasts. Statues of Artemis Ephesia depict griffins, lions, leopards, and other creatures, testifying to the title given her by Homer as queen of the wild beasts (*Iliad* II.21.470). These representations add color to Paul's comment in 1 Corinthians: "What do I gain if, humanly speaking, I fought with beasts at Ephesus? If the dead are not raised, 'Let us eat and drink, for tomorrow we die'" (1 Cor 15:32; see Frayer-Griggs 2013).

Acts 19 and Paul's letters to the Ephesians and Timothy accurately portray aspects of the worship of Artemis. Shrines of Artemis were crafted and sold as much for the artisans as for the upkeep of the temple. Artemis' name was invoked in inscriptions for magical practices, which is evidenced in the destruction of magical texts in Acts 19:18–19. *The Papyri Graecae Magicae*, an ancient source of magical spells dating between 100 BC and AD 400, is laced with references to Artemis (see Betz 1986). Her association with marriage also might have been the motivation for Paul to write the beautiful marriage illustration that differentiated Christianity from the worship of Artemis (Eph 5:22–33; LiDonnici 1992).[15] Even the difficult passage on Paul's view of women in 1 Timothy 2 becomes clear in the context of the belief in the goddess as the legitimate wife. He also directly addresses Artemis' association with the salvation of children and women in 1 Timothy 2:13–14.[16] These were culturally conditioned correctives, not necessarily normative standards for all churches.

The accuracy with which Luke and Paul write of the cultural and religious context of Ephesus emphasizes the importance of missiological exegesis that is respectful but also uncompromisingly theocentric. There is little doubt that such a deep level of understanding of the people Paul engaged was a primary reason for Christianity developing profound roots in Asia. Christianity would ultimately become the indigenous religion of the region for more than thirteen centuries.

---

15. In the second century AD, Xenophon of Ephesus described the festival of Artemisia as a celebration of marriage when Ephesian families paraded their eligible children in a procession through the streets (see *Ephesian Tales of Anthia and Habrokomas*).

16. In chapter 9, we will discuss 1 Timothy 2:8-15 in the context of morality as one key to sustaining a movement.

For years, my academic research focused on contemporary Paganism. This research placed me in very unique situations with some of the most spiritually sensitive people I have ever met. While I did not agree with their beliefs, I did respect their search for truth. In an attempt to emulate Paul's work, I read ancient and modern sources, observed religious rituals in backyards, on geological outcroppings, and around stone monuments, as well as interviewed hundreds of practicing Pagans in order to understand who they were and what they believed. My goal was to earn their respect, as well as the right to share about the one true God who relentlessly pursues us. The principle that guided my research was the same as described by the town clerk of Ephesus.

During those years in the academy, I would occasionally be invited by a church to teach about Paganism. On one occasion an invitation came to speak to an apologetics class in a suburban Chicago megachurch. They were interested, so I thought, in Wicca and Druidry and the reasons why they were two of the fastest growing religions in the West. When I entered the classroom, it appeared to be more like a night club than a lecture hall, so I thought that this would be a sensitive group of Christians who genuinely searched for effective ways to engage culture. As I approached one of the round tables where a group of people were conversing, they stopped talking and introduced themselves, and then one of them made the following comment that about knocked me to the ground: "So you must be here to give us ammunition to shoot down Paganism?"

Such disrespect for others, whether they are pagans, Hindus, Muslims, or Buddhists, had no place in Paul's missiological theology. It should have no place in ours either.

Missiological exegesis is a first-order exercise whereby we understand the people whom God has been relentlessly pursuing. It begins with a respectful dialogue with people and observation of their practices and customs. It dives deeply into their history in order to understand how God has engaged them. Ultimately, missiological exegesis leads to the development of a missiological theology that connects the story of a people with the story of God. That connection will determine whether Christianity is viewed as a foreign religion or as an indigenous one.

༉

After a training session in Northeast India, Reyansh said, "Michael, let's go share our faith," to which I replied, "Let's do it."

As is common when I am with our national partners, Reyansh wanted me to share and he would translate. "People like to hear the white person more than me," he said.

I agreed to share, but having been in many of these situations, I knew that Reyansh could communicate more effectively than me. So off we went to a Muslim area of the city.

As we walked along a dirt path next to the railroad tracks, we came to a family sitting outside. The women were talking, the children were playing, and an older man was preparing a canister of milk he was taking to sell at the local market. I introduced Reyansh and myself, and then began to ask about their culture and beliefs. Before we were too far along in the conversation, I noticed that the women and the man were fascinated with whatever Reyansh was saying in his obviously embellished translation. Finally, I said to Reyansh, "Now tell them about Jesus."

Reyansh went on and shared about his story. Slowly a crowd of around twenty people gathered as the message about Jesus captivated them. You could see it in their eyes and on their faces. Reyansh's testimony about what the Lord had done in his life was far more interesting than the white guy who came to visit. He connected his story as he learned their story to show them God's story.

Launching a movement is an act of God the Holy Spirit empowering believers to be witnesses. That empowerment sees with God's eyes and seizes the opportunity to join with him. The place where this happens is where you are currently. It does not require you to go on a short-term mission trip or to become a missionary. God wants the people in your proximity to know him, and he has given you what is necessary to make that message clear. It is his gospel, and with a bit of hard work in dialoguing with others, observing their culture, and studying their history, you can share his message with those who have not heard. Our only response is to follow Paul's example of missiological theology and to join God in connecting his story with the story of your community (1 Cor 11:1).

However, there is another step in the process of launching a movement before we can effectively communicate his story: missiological reflection, the subject of the next chapter.

# CHAPTER 4

# Launching a Movement II: Missiological Reflection

We flew into Kathmandu on a summer afternoon after several days with our leaders in Northeast India. Tapan, Nagesh, and Aadesh met us at the airport. There might not be a better feeling than seeing the smiling faces of brothers who live with the constant threat of incarceration because of their work. The stress of government restrictions, the pressures on their families, and the needs of the saints wore heavily on the hearts of our brothers; and those first hours together were telling. We could see in their faces and hear in their voices their need to take a step back and for us to encourage them from God's Word.

The daily threat they felt was palpable. Even as I write, three Nepali leaders were recently detained and an American was deported for training pastors in the capital city. Just as the government and religious authorities in Ephesus took notice of that new Christian movement, the challenges in Nepal are a sure sign that Christianity is a movement in the little country at the top of the world.

As is so often the case, times of simple reflection on a book of the Bible not only bring refreshment to our souls but also enlighten our minds in regard to our ministries. Sometimes they reveal blind spots; at other times they affirm what we are doing. This occasion, set within sight of the Himalayas, was one of those times when God showed us both our strengths and where we needed strengthened. So the five of us took an entire day to focus on 2 Timothy.

In my opinion, there is no better letter to encourage those who are in the midst of challenging situations than this very personal epistle written near the end of Paul's life to his very dearest friend and son in the faith. We will look at Timothy more when we begin our discussions on leading and multiplying a movement. At this moment, however, as we opened God's Word together to humbly read and allow the Holy Spirit to teach and encourage us, the collective wisdom of our small hermeneutical community began to reveal and affirm God's direction. We were doing theology in community—the work of missiological reflection—as missiological theologians.

In the previous chapter, we discussed three salient features of missiological exegesis: dialogue with others, observation of culture, and study of history. In this chapter, our focus will be on missiological reflection, with specific attention given to what we believe about God. This core doctrine is fundamental to our ability to connect God's story to the story of a people. However, in this chapter I will not prescribe belief. Instead, I will encourage discovering God as we build a framework based on a reading of Scripture that is more than an intellectual exercise of the head. The framework is a missiological exercise of the heart, in recognition that God's ultimate purpose is for more people to worship him.

In this framework, the reader or hearer of God's Word will act as a missiological theologian who interprets Scripture with an eye to the completion of God's mission in the world. This manner of reading God's Word is often overshadowed by the proliferation of theological texts and a sundry list of theological formulations. Shawn Redman shares the sentiment succinctly: "Many missionaries do not realize that the Bible can (and should) guide their mission practice because they lack the ability to see anything other than theology in the Bible" (2012, 292).

Our goal, then, is to recover a missiologically theocentric reading of the Bible that is applicable to contemporary cultural engagement and moves us to the completion of God's mission. The first aspect of this goal is understanding ourselves as missiological theologians—theologians, like my friends in Nepal, who come to the Scriptures in a community, trusting the Holy Spirit to guide and teach.

## Missiological Theologians

If missiological exegesis, as we discussed in the previous chapter, is dialogue with others, observation of culture, and study of history, then missiological reflection is the intermediate step toward the intersection of this exegesis with a theology that will connect with culture. It is the hard work of understanding where we ourselves land on the theological spectrum, and it leads to the challenge of making the gospel make sense in a culture. In Athens, we see how Paul integrated his missiological exegesis into a message that was particularly focused on the philosophers at the Areopagus (Acts 17:22–34). Similarly, the letters to the churches of Asia give us an idea of how Paul communicated a theocentric message in the Asian context (Ephesians, Colossians, Philemon, 1 and 2 Timothy). Through our observation of Paul's work, it is apparent that he is not simply a theologian espousing doctrine. Rather, Paul is a missiological theologian connecting the story of God with the story of a people.

God does not use just anyone to launch a movement. Certainly it will be someone who understands God's vision for the harvest and his heart for gospel work. More importantly, God uses a worker passionate for his glory and willing to risk everything to make Jesus' name famous. That undoubtedly describes the Apostle Paul. Upon his conversion in Acts 9, Paul received a mission to take the gospel to the Jews, Gentiles, and rulers, which he faithfully carried out to the end of his life. While we have tagged him with the moniker "the apostle to the Gentiles," he never wavered from Jesus' calling on his life. Ananias' shock must have been astounding when Jesus appeared to him and said, "Go, for [Paul] is a chosen instrument of mine to carry my name before the Gentiles and kings and the children of Israel" (Acts 9:15). The one-time persecutor of Christians was now an adopted son.

Paul's own account of his conversion underscores his mission:

> And when we had all fallen to the ground, I heard a voice saying to me in the Hebrew language, "Saul, Saul, why are you persecuting me? It is hard for you to kick against the goads." And I said, "Who are you, Lord?" And the Lord said, "I am [εγώ εἰμι] Jesus whom you are persecuting. But rise and stand upon your feet, for I have appeared to you for this purpose, to appoint you as a servant and witness to the things in which you have seen me and to those in which I will appear to you, delivering you from your people and from the Gentiles—to whom [ὧν] I am sending you to open their eyes, so that they may turn from darkness to light and from the power of Satan to God, that they may receive forgiveness of sins and a place among those who are sanctified by faith in me." (Acts 26:14–18)

The fact that God himself was calling Paul did not escape him. When Paul cries out, "Who are you, Lord?" Jesus answers with a title that Paul would recognize as YHWH: "I am (Greek εγώ εἰμι) Jesus" (see Ex 3:14; John 8:58). God was calling Paul to be a bondslave and witness. In Greek, "to whom" (Greek ὧν) Jesus is sending Paul is in the plural, and as Luke records in the early history of the church, Paul obeyed his calling to carry the gospel to everyone—Jews and Gentiles.[17]

---

17. It is unfortunate that we read "Gentiles" as its own distinct ethnic group, different from the Jews and Samaritans. The reality is, "Gentiles" is a catch-all word that describes distinct ethnic people groups who are not Jews or Samaritans. Just in Asia, as you might recall, there were more than fifty distinct ethnic groups with their own culture, religious beliefs, and practices.

Being 2,000 years removed from Paul's Damascus Road experience, we are tempted to look at him as a theologian—and that he was, but it was a secondary role next to him being on God's mission. Paul was not one to sit in an ivory tower waxing eloquently to a group of listeners, even though he and his colleagues, guided by the Holy Spirit, were responsible for the development of much of early Christian doctrine. Neither was he simply a missionary, one who was sent with God's mandate to proclaim good news to the nations, although his vision was to go where the gospel had never been (Rom 15:4). For Paul, being on God's mission made him a missiological theologian—anachronistic for sure, but it rightly captures Paul at his core: one chosen by God to see what God was doing in the world and to connect the good news of Jesus Christ to people of different cultures, all for the praise of God's glory.

| Scripture | Description |
| --- | --- |
| Acts 22:3-21 | Jew, born in Tarsus, educated by Gamaliel, persecutor of the Way, appointed to know God's will, witness to everyone, sent to the Gentiles |
| Acts 22:25 | A Roman citizen by birth |
| Acts 26:5 | Lived as a Pharisee |
| Romans 1:1 | A servant of Christ Jesus, an apostle |
| 1 Corinthians 1:1 | Called by the will of God as an apostle of Christ Jesus |
| 2 Corinthians 1:1 | An apostle of Christ Jesus by the will of God |
| Galatians 1:1 | An apostle through Jesus Christ and God the Father |
| Ephesians 1:1 | An apostle of Christ Jesus by the will of God |
| Philippians 1:1 | Servant of Christ Jesus |
| Philippians 3:5-6 | Circumcised on the eighth day, tribe of Benjamin, Hebrew, Pharisee, persecutor of the church, blameless according to the law |
| Colossians 1:1 | An apostle of Christ Jesus by God's will |
| 1 Thessalonians 2:7 | Gentle |
| 1 Timothy 1:1 | An apostle of Christ Jesus by command of God |
| 1 Timothy 1:12 | Judged faithful, appointed to service |
| 2 Timothy 1:1 | An apostle of Christ Jesus by God's will |
| 2 Timothy 1:11 | Appointed a preacher, apostle, and teacher |
| Titus 1:1 | Servant of God, an apostle of Jesus Christ |
| Titus 1:3 | Entrusted with preaching the word |
| Philemon 1 | A prisoner for Christ Jesus |

TABLE 13: PAUL'S SELF-IDENTITY

Herein lies a dilemma. When we view Paul strictly as a theologian, then his writings might be reduced to a moral theology that governs the lives of adherents. When we view Paul simply as a missionary, then his writings become a narrative of what he accomplished. However, if we view Paul as a missiological theologian, then the majority of the New Testament focuses on a theocentric—that is, God-centered—mission for God's glory through the announcement of his Son and the making of disciples of every people group on the planet. Paul becomes a model to emulate rather than a figure to be admired (1 Cor 11:1). It is for this purpose that Paul encounters the risen Savior on the road to Damascus.

> Now as he went on his way, he approached Damascus, and suddenly a light from heaven shone around him. And falling to the ground, he heard a voice saying to him, "Saul, Saul, why are you persecuting me?" And he said, "Who are you, Lord?" And he said, "I am (εγώ εἰμι) Jesus, whom you are persecuting. But rise and enter the city, and you will be told what you are to do." (Acts 9:3–6)

At that miraculous moment, Paul was forever captured by the great I am (εγώ εἰμι)—Jesus Christ—and he never looked back. The individual God uses to launch and ground a movement first surrenders himself to God's will (Eph 1:1). Paul did not wait for God to give him a new vocation. He did not need a geographical "calling." He simply took on a new identity as God's fellow worker and followed God's will—that all should hear the good news of the glorious Lord.

## Bracketing Our Theology

Paul came from a distinct Jewish Christianity, yet he undoubtedly understood the boundaries of his Jewishness as well as the impact it could have on Christianity. Nevertheless, when he was with Jews, he did as the Jews (Acts 21:23–26; 1 Cor 9:20; Phil 3:5–6); but when he engaged other cultures, he bracketed those beliefs as a missiological theologian so that he could communicate effectively. Bracketing belief does not disregard our background, nor does it pretend that our background cannot somehow impact our theologizing. Bracketing belief is the act whereby we seek the Holy Spirit to help us see what God is doing in a culture and begin to make connections between his work and the work of making him known, while suspending our theological bias (Acts 17:16). In Athens, Paul observed a city full of idols. While this naturally repulsed Paul's Jewishness, it did not prevent him from engaging in dialogue to understand what he observed. Ultimately, he made a connection between the altar to an unknown god and the God who created the universe (Acts 17:23–25).

Holding tightly to our own culturally conditioned theological constructions is potentially harmful for cross-cultural work and might even be harmful in an ever-changing spiritual climate such as in the West. While we should be well-versed in various theological systems, we want to encourage the emergence of indigenous theologies that exhibit the healthy, historic boundaries of the Christian faith while maintaining adherence to the faithful testimony of Scripture as understood in its socioeconomic and geopolitical context. At the same time, we also recognize the responsibility to guard against theological innovation. This might at times result in an uncomfortable tension between our views and those of others. However, consider Paul once again in Athens: a Jewish Christian who observed a city full of idols yet recognized that Zeus as described by a stoic philosopher (Acts 17:28) is equivalent to YHWH of his ancestors (Acts 17:29). This was an amazing step toward an indigenous Christianity.

## Defining a Missiological Theologian

It is easy to imagine how ineffectual Paul would have been in Athens and Ephesus if he were to have communicated a Jewish Christian theology. The consequence of imposing a personal, culturally conditioned theology on a culture often results in a transplanted gospel disconnected from a people. The truth is that our theological constructions may or may not be applicable to other cultures, and we need to be willing to allow the Holy Spirit to work as much in us as in our brothers and sisters in different contexts so that we see an indigenous theology emerge without our cultural trappings. The implication of such a submitted posture is that the missiological theologian's task of missiological reflection falls among the most important and challenging work he must accomplish as he does theology in a community of cultural others. It is not an easy task.

The early church had many examples of leaders reflecting on theology in community. One such leader was part of a trio known as the Cappadocian Fathers. Gregory of Nazianzus (AD 329–390), writing at a time of considerable theological debate over the nature of God,[18] describes the theologian in this manner:

> In the former discourse we laid down clearly with respect to the theologian both what sort of character he ought to bear, and on what kind of subject he may philosophize, and when, and to what extent. We saw that he ought to be,

---

18. Along with Emperor Theodosius, Gregory would call the second ecumenical council in Constantinople in AD 381 to affirm the creed developed at Nicaea and to strengthen the position for the third person of the Trinity.

as far as may be, pure, in order that light may be apprehended by light; and that he ought to consort with serious men, in order that his word be not fruitless through falling on an unfruitful soil; and that the suitable season is when we have a calm within from the whirl of outward things, so as not like madmen to lose our breath; and that the extent to which we may go is that to which we have ourselves advanced, or to which we are advancing. (*Oration* 28.)

*Pure, collaborative, peaceful,* and *learned* are adjectives that aptly reflect what Gregory defined as the character of a theologian. We, of course, see similar characteristics in Paul's description of the leaders in 1 Timothy 3 who were charged with maintaining and teaching correct doctrine. Gregory, who eventually became known as "the Theologian," writing amid the context of increasing debate on whether or not someone could truly describe the incomprehensible God, invited theologians to join him in ascending the "holy mountain" to understand the ineffability of God, who can only be known through his own self-revelation rather than through philosophical formulations (Oration 42).[19]

As Gregory encouraged *pure, collaborative, peaceful, and learned* theologians, a young Berber theologian from Numidia (roughly modern-day Algeria and Tunisia) emerged on the scene following a dramatic conversion. Augustine's (AD 354–430) early life as a theologian marked him as a formidable force for orthodoxy in the Western church. Just as any theologian, he was also susceptible to his past and personal biases contributing to his theological formulations.[20] It seems, however, that later in life his dogmatism diminished in recognition that perhaps he did not hold all the answers. In one of his final treatises, which he never completed, Augustine took a notable approach to the task of theologizing:

> In matters that are obscure and far beyond our vision, even in such as we may find treated in Holy Scripture, different interpretations are sometimes possible without prejudice to the faith we have received. In such a case, we should not rush in headlong and so firmly take our stand on one side that, if further progress in search of truth justly undermines this position, we too fall with it. (*The Literal Meaning of Genesis*, 1.18)

With Gregory's description of a theologian and Augustine's realization that differing views of Scripture might lead to different theological conclusions, we see that the work of a theologian takes humility and teachability.

---

19. Gregory's description of the theologian did not simply remain a description, but a model that he exemplified as he practiced the work of a theologian. Always desirous to work in community and to seek consensus, Gregory was one of the early and great theologians of the church (see Mason 1899; Von Campenhausen 1998, 101-15).

20. Some modern scholars see Manichaeism's influence on Augustine's theology. See Von Campenhausen, (1969, 260); Runciman (1982, 16); Frend (1984, 662); Phipps, (1980).

We would not think of Gregory or Augustine as missiological theologians by any stretch of the imagination. Nevertheless, their discipline in the manner they theologized is applicable as much for the systematic or biblical theologian as it is for the missiological theologian.

A missiological theologian, then, is an individual who takes seriously the work of God in a culture and the work of God in the interpretative activity of theologizing. He is a consummate learner who is never satisfied in the application of theology to culture, but always testing it in a community of learners so that the theology which emerges in a context will genuinely connect to the people as if it were always meant to be. Indeed, since God is at work in culture, this is one of the most exciting tasks a missiological theologian will accomplish.

First, however, the missiological theologian needs to be completely satisfied with his own theology and how God's story connected to his own. This process of reflecting on theology is beautifully modeled in the lives of Gregory and Augustine and should also be demonstrated in the life of the missiological theologian. If the missiological theologian does not know the breadth of good doctrine, then the risk of heresy becomes greater, as does the risk of moral failure—topics for the next three chapters.

## A Framework for Missiological Reflection

A missiological theologian will naturally have a broad understanding of doctrine. Whether this is achieved through formal education or personal study, it is evident that the good doctrine of a missiological theologian focuses on a profound but simple doctrine of God. In his classic big green volume, *Christian Theology*, Millard Erickson writes, "One's view of God might even be thought of as supplying the whole framework within which one's theology is constructed and life is lived. It lends a particular coloration to one's style of ministry and philosophy of life" (1984, 263). Naturally, then, we must start with the doctrine of God. A key component to a doctrine of God is seeing the Bible through the lens of his mission.

### The Starting Point of Missiological Reflection: The Grand Narrative

It is not uncommon to see a statement such as the following on an evangelical church's website or in its bylaws: "The Scriptures, both Old and New Testaments, are the inspired Word of God, without error in the original writing, the complete revelation of his will for the salvation of men and women, and the divine and final authority for all of Christian faith and life." Undoubtedly, the Scriptures are unique. Sixty-six books spanning 1600 years were written by forty authors from every walk of life: kings, prophets, philosophers, poets, a physician, businesspeople, and religious leaders. The Old Testament is the preparation, the Gospels are the manifestation, Acts is the propagation, the Epistles give the explanation, and Revelation is the completion.

As an overarching theme, God's mission in the world conveys the story of the incomparable God who actively engages his creation to unite all things in Christ (Col 1:20). From its foundation, God's mission in the world is about his relationship with his creation (Col 1:16). As the story unfolds, we learn of Adam and Eve, created in God's image and made completely satisfied in their relationship with their creator. After their desire for self-glorification is manifested at the tree, the unsearchable God continues to pursue them and provide for them, even promising them that one day the woman would bear a child who would destroy Satan (Gen 3). Then, through a covenant relationship with Abram, God reveals the mystery of his intention to bless every nation (Gen 12). Ultimately, the incomprehensible God sends his Son to demonstrate his commitment to unite all things in Christ and then sends the Holy Spirit to Jesus' followers so that they would be witnesses who shared in this ongoing historic activity. Ultimately, the work will be completed, as John foretold to the churches in Asia when he wrote Revelation. This is a message often repeated by Paul to the churches in the Roman Empire, and it is a message they took to the world as they identified as Paul's fellow laborers in God's work.

| Topic | Bible Passages | Romans | Ephesians |
|---|---|---|---|
| Beginning of God's mission | Genesis 1–3 | Romans 1:19–32; 5–7; 8:19–23 | Ephesians 1:4–10 |
| God's mission to bless the nations | Genesis 12 | Romans 9 | Ephesians 3:1–13 |
| Jesus sent to show God's mission | Gospels | Romans 10; 15:1–13 | Ephesians 2:11–22 |
| Holy Spirit empowering Jesus' followers on God's mission | Acts 1–28 | Romans 2–3; 6–8; 12–14 | Ephesians 1:11–14; 4:3–4; 5:17–21 |
| Completion of God's mission | Revelation 1–22 | Romans 11 | Ephesians 6:10–20 |

TABLE 14: GOD'S MISSION IN THE WORLD (SEE COOPER 2019)

The story of reconciliation is foundational to our understanding of the purpose of the Bible. It is the story of how God seeks to have a relationship with us and desires for us to share his love with others, because he ultimately knows that we will be most satisfied when we direct our worship to him (John 15:8–11; 1 Cor 5:15; 10:31). The great redemptive work of adopting us into his family by Jesus' atoning act gives us a new identity as his children who take up the mission of the family until every people group has had the opportunity to hear of the mystery of God's desire to be in relationship with his creation (Eph 1:5; 3:6; 5:1).

While there is little doubt that the unifying theme of the Bible is God's engagement of the world so that more people will worship him, it is not an exclusively Jewish story. The Gospel of John nicely captures this juxtapositioning of the Jewish story with the world's story. Written from Ephesus sometime between AD 67 and 95, John connected Jesus' story with the rest of the world in a simply and profoundly written example of missiological theology. We will address the topic of the Fourth Gospel as missiological theology in more detail in the next chapter. For now, God's story of connecting with all people is seen in John's use of κόσμος (cosmos)—world. More than all the other Gospels combined, John uses the word fifty-eight times to communicate that God's work was not merely a Jewish work but a global work of cosmic proportion. Consider table 15 which illustrates John's emphasis on Jesus' ministry to all people.

| Verses in John's Gospel | Jesus' World Connection |
| --- | --- |
| 1:9 | The true light came into the world. |
| 1:10 | He made the world. |
| 1:29 | He takes away the sin of the world. |
| 3:16 | God loves the world. |
| 4:42 | He is the Savior of the world. |
| 6:14 | He is the prophet who is to come into the world. |
| 6:33 | He gives life to the world. |
| 8:12 | He is the light of the world. |
| 8:26 | He declares to the world what he has heard from the Father. |
| 12:19 | He is the Son of God who came to the world. |
| 12:47 | He came to save the world. |
| 14:31 | His work demonstrated to the world his love for the Father. |

TABLE 15: THE WORLD AND THE FOURTH GOSPEL

Over the centuries of theological work attempting to formulate systems to describe a unifying theme, theologians have unwittingly marginalized God's missionary activity to a subset of theology called missiology. Missiology became one of many divisions to be studied rather than the primary motivation of theological pursuit. Redman noted, "The genuine mission activity in Scripture is drowned out by a hurricane of contemporary 'theological' force …, leaving Christians and non-Christians with the perception that Scripture has little to say in terms of mission" (2012, 292).

The unfortunate consequence is a weakened missionary activity in the church and a preference for the academic study of theology. While an academic study of theology certainly has merit, if theology stays in the classroom, or even in the church, its value is diminished, resulting in the church becoming insular and institutional. Instead, a theology that will have as much value in the classroom and church is one that will be actively sharing God in the community. John's Gospel beautifully communicates such a story, as John makes deliberate attempts to connect the story of Asia with Jesus' story.[21] However, to get to this place in our own theologizing we need a pathway, and one stepping stone is doing theology in community.

## Doing Theology Collaboratively

Theology is never intended to be done in isolation. As we will see in the chapter on leading a movement, Paul did theology in community. We do not often recognize this notion, but it is clear to be seen. The simple fact that the majority of Paul's epistles were coauthored testifies to the value he placed on working out theology with others. Doing theology in community was a natural act of the early church, as they gathered together guided by the Holy Spirit to learn more about God and their new identity as his children (1 Thess 5:27; Col 4:16).

Paul, of course, was not the only apostolic influence on Ephesus. As mentioned, the Apostle John arrives in the great city after Paul's martyrdom as one of the last remaining apostolic eyewitnesses to Jesus. In his first epistle, he clearly communicates the notion of doing theology in community: "But the anointing that you (Greek plural ὑμεῖς) received from him abides in you (Greek plural ὑμῖν), and you have no need that anyone should teach you (Greek plural ὑμᾶς). But as his anointing teaches you (Greek plural ὑμᾶς) about everything, and is true, and is no lie—just as it has taught you (Greek plural ὑμᾶς), abide in him" (1 John 2:27). An obvious reference to Jesus' teaching on the Holy Spirit, John rearticulates the idea later to the churches in Asia: "But the Helper, the Holy Spirit, whom the Father will send in my name, he will teach you (Greek

---

21. I disagree with Keener and others who suggest that the Ephesian context had little, if any, impact on the development of the Fourth Gospel. See Craig S. Keener, *The Gospel of John: Two Volumes* (Grand Rapids: Baker Academic, 2010).

plural ὑμᾶς) all things and bring to your remembrance all that I have said to you (Greek plural ὑμῖν)" (John 14:26). In both verses, John writes in the second person plural, emphasizing that these are community tasks rather than those of individuals and that they involved the Holy Spirit working in each individual as they learned together rather than in isolation.

In 1912, Rolland Allen summed up this idea of the Holy Spirit's work as he wrestled with what is still one of the perennial challenges of missions today: "If we have no faith in the power of the Holy Spirit in them [our disciples], they will not learn to have faith in the power of the Holy Spirit in themselves. We cannot trust them, and they cannot be worthy of trust" (Allen 1912 [1959], 196). What the Apostle John captured in the ministry of Jesus is critical for us to grasp. No doubt it is dangerous to trust the Holy Spirit's working in someone's life. However, there is no misgiving that the Holy Spirit is working. He is far more concerned for the doctrinal integrity of the church than us, and when brothers and sisters gather together, like our time in Kathmandu, God's Spirit works in our lives in ways that we cannot imagine.

## Hermeneutical Community

During my doctoral studies, Paul Hiebert introduced me to the idea of a hermeneutical community. Hiebert suggested that such a community serves as a safeguard against personal theological biases (1994, 101). In his day and still in ours, the prominent theology on the mission field is that which emerged during the Reformation. Hiebert argued that the medieval church was culturally ethnocentric and naturally held biases that were not relevant in contemporary missions in different cultures (ibid., 95–96). The theologies emerging out of the twelfth to seventeenth centuries addressed issues relevant to that time and for that place. To do theology, then, becomes a missiological exercise that involves the voices of Christians from other cultures who can adequately address issues occurring in their contexts. In the spirit of the three-self model of Henry Venn and Rufus Anderson (nineteenth century), this fourth self—"self-theologizing" (ibid., 96–97)—holds the idea of developing indigenous theologies in a community of believers that are culturally relevant for a particular community.

I am not certain that I was ever successful in convincing Dr. Hiebert, however strongly I argued, that the hermeneutical community needed to expand to include more than just the contemporary cultural actors but also other actors throughout the history of the church who modeled a community hermeneutic. As W. H. C. Frend points out, the theology of the early church was formulated in an environment influenced not only by Plato and the

Gnostics but by Buddha and Zoroaster (1984, 316). Such a pluralistic context closely connects to the sundry pluralistic contexts around the world today—increasingly in the Western world, as well—and those early voices should play a role in a missiological theology. However, even the early theologizing of the church needed boundaries in determining correct doctrine, and a little-known monk provided such a framework.

## Vincentian Canon

Vincent of Lérins (died c. 450) lived at a monastery off the coast of France. Advancing in years and seeing the development of various theological positions, such as Celestius' teaching on works salvation and Augustine's theology of original sin, Vincent desired to develop a standard upon which he might trust in the event that he was unable to judge proper theological orthodoxy. He became known for his consensual method of determining correct doctrine: the Vincentian Canon. It is summarized in Latin as *teneamus quod ubique, quod semper, quod ab omnibus creditum est* (let us hold to what is believed everywhere, all the time, by everyone).

> In the Catholic Church itself, every care should be taken to hold fast to what has been believed everywhere, always, and by all. This is truly and properly "Catholic," as indicated by the force and etymology of the name itself, which comprises everything truly universal. This general rule will be truly applied if we follow the principles of universality, antiquity, and consent. We do so in regard to universality if we confess that faith alone to be true which the entire Church confesses all over the world. [We do so] in regard to antiquity if we in no way deviate from those interpretations which our ancestors and fathers have manifestly proclaimed as inviolable. [We do so] in regard to consent if, in this very antiquity, we adopt the definitions and propositions of all, or almost all, the bishops and doctors. (Vincent of Lérins, *Commonitorium*, chapter 2)

Motivated by Arianism and other influences that threatened orthodoxy, Vincent set forth the idea that correct theology is that which has been believed always, everywhere, and by all. As Rudolf Morris, Vincent's English translator, suggests, "This principle, however, does not exclude progress or doctrinal development. But it must be progress in the proper sense of the word, and not a change" (1949, 260). Vincent himself understood this progress as a maturing of doctrine rather than a creation of something different.

Commenting on the Vincentian Canon, the Russian Orthodox theologian George Florovsky states:

> These two aspects of faith [church and apostles], or rather—the two dimensions, could never be separated from each other. Universitas and antiquitas, as well as consensio, belonged together. Neither was an adequate criterion by itself. "Antiquity" as such was not yet a sufficient warrant of truth, unless a comprehensive consensus of the "ancients" could be satisfactorily demonstrated. And consensio as such was not conclusive, unless it could be traced back continuously to Apostolic origins. (1995, 74)

The Vincentian Canon enjoyed centuries as a guiding principle in theological reflection (Oden 1993, 11). I first learned about Vincent in a doctoral class with Thomas Oden, an avid proponent of the canon and a self-professed paleo-orthodox, who proposed that theology should not be looked at narrowly, but rather with boundaries. In fact, he believed that the rediscovery of boundaries would be the primary occupation of twenty-first century theology (ibid., 13). It is in the context of boundaries that missiological reflection is best conducted. Those boundaries were initially set in the first five centuries of our faith. It is in this spirit that a consensual understanding of correct doctrine can be developed.

## Boundaries of Theology

Defining the boundaries of consensual theology is challenging. In the early church, heresy played a significant role in determining these orthodox theological boundaries. In the first five centuries of the church, theological issues, when taken to extreme, molded an understanding of what was or was not correct apostolic tradition that was believed everywhere by all. These various issues generally revolved around an aspect of the doctrine of God—most often an aberrant Christology, as noted in table 16.

| Period | Heresy | Description |
|--------|--------|-------------|
| 2nd cent. | Docetism | Christ appeared to have flesh, but was actually a ghost. |
| 2nd cent. | Adoptionism | Impersonal power comes on Jesus, who has lived a holy life, and God adopts him as a son. |
| 2nd cent. | Modalism | One God expressed in three different types. |
| 2nd cent. | Monarchianism | God the Father enters Mary's womb, suffers, dies, and rises from the dead. |
| 320s | Arianism | Christ is subordinate to the Father and is a created being. |

| 380s | Apollonarianism | Christ is human and his soul is replaced with the Logos. |
|------|-----------------|---------------------------------------------------------|
| 430s | Nestorianism | Two separate natures of Christ. Logos passes through Mary. |
| 450s | Monophysitism | The single nature of Christ is divine and clad in flesh. |

TABLE 16: HERESIES DURING THE FIRST FIVE CENTURIES

In addition to the various Christological heresies, other theological opinions were often asserted. Known as *theologoumenon*, the opinions of early theologians were permitted, but where clear connection with apostolic tradition could not be asserted, they were not held as authoritative doctrine. This did not suggest that such *theologoumenon* were heresy; rather they were simply theological ideas being explored as theologians attempted to connect with philosophy and contemporary culture. During those early centuries, philosophy played an important role in theological development as the church looked for ways to connect to the culture. Quoting the second-century Neopythagorean philosopher Numenius, Origen agreed that "Who is Plato but Moses in Attic Greek?" (*Against Celsus* 8.13).[22] Not all that dissimilar from Paul in Athens, these early Christians actively looked for God's work in culture.

As theology developed over the centuries, many theological opinions were put forward as theologians wrestled with various doctrines. Their attempts to describe God, the process of salvation, the church, or the end times, among many other theological constructions, resulted in diverse views of what Scripture taught on any given doctrine. Where deviation from the nature of God occurred, such as in Arian Christology now found in Mormonism, Jehovah's Witnesses, Oneness Pentecostalism, and to a lesser degree in contemporary hierarchical complementarianism, heresy often resulted. In other cases, deep theological convictions of opinions—the nature of the Eucharist, for example, or the practice of pedobaptism—separated believers from fellowship with one another, resulting in a proliferation of denominations from the sixteenth century until today. In a very real sense, Christianity might rightly be called the first "postmodern" movement, as everyone had their own truths in relation to their doctrinal and denominational preferences.[23]

---

22. This is the same Origen who connected Plato's understanding of the stars representing souls to the Christian idea of the preexistent soul (see *De Principiis*, book 1).

23. "Postmodern" really is not the correct nomenclature for this phenomenon, although the word has stuck in our current milieu. "Hypermodernism" is a better term, as it describes the logical trajectory of modernism. For an excellent discussion on this subject, see Harold A. Netland, *Encountering Religious Pluralism* (Downers Grove, IL: InterVarsity Press, 2003).

If there is a solution to our contemporary theologizing, it might be found in rediscovering a missiological understanding of God's nature and will. Few evangelicals, if any, would disagree with the primacy of God's mission of gospel proclamation. As a dear friend used to say, "You cannot be evangelical if you are not evangelistic." However, God's mission cannot simply be viewed as an added part of Scripture or of one's theology. It should rightly be viewed as the unifying theme which governs all of the church's activity as adopted children in God's family. Redman poignantly asserts, "Correct interpretations of Scripture are most often surrounded by correct understandings and practices of God's mission (Gen 41–50; Dan 3–7; Acts 10:44–48; 11:15–18), while obscured interpretation occurs precisely when mission is obscured (Jonah 1–4; Matt 8–12)" (2012, 8).

To ensure proper interpretation, theology is best reflected upon collaboratively in a community of those committed to God's mission rather than to maintaining a doctrinal or denominational agenda. This missiological reflection is an interpretive act whereby God's will—that is, his desire to unite all things in Christ—becomes the hermeneutical key for communicating about him and his mission.

⁂

Up to this point, I have laid out a framework whereby the missionary, pastor, or church leader is a missiological theologian who reflects on theology in a hermeneutical community that includes the theological developments in the early church and the boundaries of orthodoxy. A missiological theologian certainly has personal theological convictions that he is willing to bracket as he and the community consider how to communicate the story of God to a culture so that God's story is seen as their story. It is important, then, to have a clear and simple understanding of who God is as we reflect missiologically on how to communicate him to others. To that subject we will turn in the next chapter.

I was standing in the front of the worship center of a church in Houston, about to deliver the story of Jesus and his friends six days before Passover (John 12:1–8), when someone asked, "Are you ready?" Our son Zachary was with me on that weekend, as we conducted an Ephesiology Lab workshop[24] with a number of the key leaders of the church. He responded, "Well, you know what Einstein said: 'If you can't explain it to a six-year-old, you don't understand it yourself.'" If we cannot explain God simply, then we might not understand him ourselves.

---

24. You can learn more about the Ephesiology Lab at https://ephesiology.com/ephesiology-laboratory.

As a guide in constructing our view of God, we might consider an explanation that explicitly focuses on his nature as a missionary. Such a missiologically theocentric perspective is by necessity simple, as it seeks to tell the story of God in a way that can be understood and connected to the story of the people he is engaging. Paul told that story in Athens and John tells that story in Ephesus. It is a story that emanates from their profound understanding of God and their ability to connect their understanding of him with the stories of cultures.

Ultimately, this is the goal of our missiological exegesis and reflection—what I am calling a missiological theology. It is not a complex process, but it is one that will ensure the emergence of a theology that is culturally relevant and sustainable in the life of a movement. When a theology is rooted in indigenous soil with proper boundaries, then it ceases to be an imported theology and opens opportunities to connect a culture with God's redeeming work in history. This will become apparent as we examine the missiological theology of John. He connected God's story to the culture's story as he proclaimed the λόγος (*logos*) to the Ephesians who had read about him for nearly five centuries before he arrived in the flesh.

# CHAPTER 5

# Launching a Movement III: Missiological Theology

Bishop Chito Ramos of The Alliance of Bible Christian Communities of the Philippines (ABCCOP) leads a movement of 850 churches in his country. The Philippines is a diverse nation, with more than two hundred ethnic groups spread across approximately two thousand inhabited islands. Currently, most ethnic populations have been engaged with the gospel, leaving twenty-four remaining ethnic groups that have less than 2 percent population of Christians and six ethnic groups that have no Christian witness at all.

The alliance formed in the 1970s when three mission organizations—Send (FEGC), Overseas Mission Fellowship, and World Team (RBMU)—came together with a church planting vision for the archipelago nation. With the arbitrary decision made in the 1995 by missiologists to consider a country reached with the gospel when the evangelical population reached 2 percent (Cooper 2018), the mission organizations recognized their work with ABCCOP was complete as the church planting alliance became indigenously led.

Today ABCCOP is made up of tribal (45 percent), rural (40 percent), and urban (15 percent) churches all around the archipelago. In 2016 and 2017, the alliance started 185 churches. By the end of 2019, they reported 403 new churches started. With more than one hundred home missionaries, the alliance has a vision to start an additional 500 churches in 2020. Bishop Chito rightly captures the significance of a theocentric missiology which is at the heart of a missiological theology and essential to a movement:

Can we really be excessively theocentric? I believe that the more theocentric we become, the more balanced our perspective would be in terms of doing ministry as a whole. Our theocentricity would bring us to be all the more sensitive to the needs of people, and yet not lose our eternal perspective.

We cannot be too theocentric! To ensure our focus remains on God, we work toward a missiological theology imbued with God's heart for his creation. In the last chapter, we discussed missiological reflection—that important task of gathering in a community to do theology together. As we have had conversations with the people we hope to engage, observed their religious and cultural practices, and learned their history, we are looking for the intersection of God's story with theirs. This is a theocentric missiology, in which the intersection of these stories, when effectively communicated, is the essence of missiological theology.

Years ago, some talked about this as a redemptive analogy (Richardson 1976). However, missiological theology is much more than an analogy. It is the effort of a missiological theologian who directly observes God at work in a culture and makes his work known to that culture in such a way that the culture is transformed. Missiological theology is grounded in God's will and multiplies his worshippers as people see that their story and God's story are the same story. This is the point where a culture grasps that our God is their God.

## The Doctrine of God: Formulating a Missiological Theism

At the core of a missiological theology is a compelling view of God. If we do not have a compelling view of God ourselves, it will be difficult to connect his story with the story of a culture. So we must wrestle with this most profound question. In other words, reflecting missiologically on who God is will help us think through the best way to communicate him in other cultures. Clark Pinnock summarizes this idea nicely:

> No doctrine can be more important than the doctrine of God. It is the principal doctrine in any theology, because apart from it the vision of faith cannot be stated. The whole creation is grounded in God, and the flow of history is the sphere of the outworking of his purposes. The doctrine is of more than academic interest; it is also of great missiological and practical importance. How can we commend belief unless we have formed a convincing conception of God for ourselves? (1994, 102)[25]

---

25. I realize the "danger" in quoting someone who espoused Open Theism. However, the gravity of Pinnock's statement cannot be ignored no matter our view of God. Besides, Pinnock's theological ideas fall within the boundaries of orthodoxy while not being authoritative doctrine, an example of *theologoumenon*.

Not only can our doctrine of God be a determining factor of belief, it is a determining factor in our own philosophy of life and missions. We will naturally engage culture based upon what we believe about God. For example, if we believe God is just, then our engagement will likely be confrontational. Similarly, if we believe God is righteous, then our engagement will likely focus on moral behavior. Granted, God is just and righteous, and he is many other things as well, not the least of which is relational. As we have seen throughout history, God is in pursuit of relationships with his creation. Missiological theology, then, is our human attempt to formulate a doctrine of God in such a way that it makes sense to us so that we can make it make sense to others. As I noted in the previous chapter, this is an exercise best accomplished in a community of people committed to God's mission of more people worshipping him.

**Evangelical Views of God**

Many evangelical theologians wrestle with the question of God, their reflections generally falling into one of three categories: classical theism, free will theism, or open theism. As the "openness of God" debate ignited in the mid 1990s in the United States, several classical theists accused open theists of a deviation from the doctrine of God. At the core of the debate was the philosophical question of whether God knows the future if it had not happened. To the classical theist, since God is omniscient, he absolutely knows the future. However, to the open theist, if the future has not occurred, then God could not know something that has not happened.

A sort of heresy trial took place in the Evangelical Theological Society to determine whether those who identified as open theist could remain a part of the academic society and still be considered evangelical. One of the outcomes of the debate was the publication of volume 45.2 of the *Journal of Evangelical Theological Society* in 2002 and a text that outlined four views of God: *Perspectives on the Doctrine of God: Four Views* in 2008. In the text, Bruce Ware (modified Calvinist perspective), Paul Helm (classical Calvinist perspective), Roger Olson (classical Arminian perspective), and John Sanders (open theist perspective) defended their respective positions as they laid out their viewpoints on which interpretation most faithfully holds to Scripture. As the four contributors laid out the views of the others, there was general agreement that the definitions of each view accurately reflected that particular position.

For example, Ware, Helm, and other classical theists would agree that, according to the open theist John Sanders, classical theism is understood as follows: "According to classical theism God is simple, impassable, immutable, absolutely unconditioned by any external reality, controls all that happens, never takes any risks, has no emotions, and never responds to creatures" (Sanders 2008, 222). Classical theism is best represented by Augustine (354–430), Calvin (1509–64), and Reformed theology in general.

Similarly, open theism is represented by the Cappadocian Fathers, Clark Pinnock, and John Sanders. Bruce Ware, in the 2002 journal and with some agreement from Sanders, defined open theism as follows:

> Open theism affirms God's exhaustive knowledge of the past and present, but it denies exhaustive divine foreknowledge, in that it denies that God knows— or can know—the future free decisions and actions of his moral creatures, even while it affirms that God knows all future possibilities and all divinely determined and logically necessary future actualities. (Ware 2002, 193)

Free will theism, perhaps the third wheel in the openness debate, is represented in the works of Justin Martyr (100–165), Jacob Arminius (1560– 1609), and John Wesley (1703–91). Here is how Roger Olson described it:

> According to Christian free will theists, God cares so much about personal, loving relationships that he does not control or dominate everything creatures do. Instead, God limits his power and control in order to allow humans (and perhaps some other creatures) limited, situated freedom of decision and action. In free will theism, God is in charge (because he is God and therefore the omnipotent Creator of all) but not fully in control (because he chooses to relinquish some control to others). (2008, 148–49)

In spite of the obvious differences in their understanding of God, in regard to the attributes of God, evangelicals broadly agree that he is immaterial, necessary, personal, wholly good, self-sufficient, omnipresent, omnipotent, and omniscient—although there are nuanced views of these attributes, depending on the theological system. Where evangelicals disagree is formulated in table 17.

| Attribute | Classical Theism | Free Will Theism | Open Theism |
|---|---|---|---|
| Pure Actuality | God cannot be acted upon. | God can be acted upon. | |
| Sovereignty | God is all-determining. | God is not all-determining. | |
| Eternality | God is timeless. | God is timeless. | God is everlasting. |
| Self-Existence | God is absolutely unconditioned. | God chooses, but is not forced, to be conditioned by creatures. | |
| Immutability | God never changes. | God's being does not change, but his will, thoughts, and emotions can change. | |

| Impassibility | God is not affected by his creation. | God sovereignly chooses to be affected by creatures. | |
|---|---|---|---|
| Foreknowledge | God's knowning is eternally definite and determined | God has exhaustive definite fore-knowledge, timeless knowledge of future contingent events. | God has knowledge of all past and present things and all future determined things. |

TABLE 17: EVANGELICAL VIEWS OF GOD'S ATTRIBUTES

While each representative can muster arguments—both theological and philosophical—for their position and against the other positions, no position can ever adequately describe God. These human attempts at constructing a theology are just that: human attempts. If we are honest, there is much we can learn from each view that has merit for our personal understanding of God. Yet, as often seems to be the case in theological debates such as those surrounding the doctrine of God, the issues addressed were not on the minds of the authors of Scripture. In essence, we create an argument from silence based on interpretive choice rather than on clear scriptural indication.

That does not suggest the invalidity of the arguments. No doubt that evangelical theologians aspire to interpret Scripture faithfully in their attempts to construct theology. This has been the case for theologians from early on in the history of the church. The Berber theologian Tertullian (AD 160–220), for example, argued for the Trinity when Scripture does not explicitly make a statement about the Trinity. The Egyptian deacon Athanasius (AD 296–373) argued for the unity and equality of the Godhead, even though competing views used Scripture to argue a different position. Both the Trinity and the equality of the Godhead are pillars of sound, authoritative doctrine and provide boundaries in determining whether or not a belief system is heretical. However, to arrive at those conclusions required debate, as the early church did theology in community. The consensus view of the church on both theological issues has been held universally around the world for nearly two millennia. In much the same way, even though there is not consensus, the various opinions of God are helpful to the church as we do theology in community. They certainly enrich our understanding of who God is.

**Arriving at a Consensus View**

At this point in the history of theology, there is not clear agreement on our understanding of God, as demonstrated by the incongruencies of the classical, free will, and open views. Nevertheless, the various views of God currently held by evangelicals fall within the boundaries of the historic faith and can be held with charity as the conversations continue. These various views are best understood as *theologoumenon*, or theological opinions, rather than as an authoritative doctrine of God. In the fourth century, Gregory of Nazianzus recognized the challenge we face when we attempt to define God in our words:

> Therefore, we must begin again thus. It is difficult to conceive God, but to define Him in words is an impossibility, as one of the Greek teachers of Divinity taught, not unskillfully, as it appears to me; with the intention that he might be thought to have apprehended Him; in that he says it is a hard thing to do; and yet may escape being convicted of ignorance because of the impossibility of giving expression to the apprehension. But in my opinion, it is impossible to express Him, and yet more impossible to conceive Him. For that which may be conceived may perhaps be made clear by language, if not fairly well, at any rate imperfectly, to anyone who is not quite deprived of his hearing, or slothful of understanding. But to comprehend the whole of so great a Subject as this is quite impossible and impracticable, not merely to the utterly careless and ignorant, but even to those who are highly exalted, and who love God, and in like manner to every created nature; seeing that the darkness of this world and the thick covering of the flesh is an obstacle to the full understanding of the truth. (*Oration* 28.4)

We should take heed of Gregory's gentle recognition that it is not possible to formulate an exhaustive and infallible doctrine of God. As Gregory, undoubtedly one of the great theological thinkers of his day, wrestled with understanding God, he realized the impossibility of the task. In essence, as others were describing God in precise terms, Gregory stood above the fray to say that if you think you know him, then you really do not. He concluded, "For how is he [God] an object of worship if he be circumscribed?" (*Oration* 28.7).

What we take from Gregory is the fact that our attempts to circumscribe or delineate a doctrine of God will always remain incomplete. The conversations are important, but the formulations only point to the fact that we do not really comprehend what we might think we comprehend. Well over a century ago, Arthur Mason, the English translator of *Orations*, summed up Gregory's thinking on God:

> We may assuredly know by the study of the world around us that God is, but we cannot find out what he is. We can arrive at negative truths concerning him, that he is incorporeal and the like, but not at any adequate positive conception. We are compelled to use figurative and anthropomorphic language concerning him, and it is hard to recognize constantly that such language is only figurative. Idolatry is the result of failure to recognize it. (1899, xiii)

Additionally, the current debates on the various views of God are largely Western and articulated by Western evangelical theologians in contexts where the pursuit of academic knowledge is celebrated and awarded, even though they might be acts of hubris if we take Gregory seriously. In the context of missions, I wonder about the relevance of these debates for the rest of the world. The complexity of the sundry terms used to describe God requires a level of philosophical sophistication that seems outside of the manner in which God is described in the Bible. It is not that these discussions no longer have merit, but their value remains academic for most, devotional for a few, and inaccessible for many. Their missiological value, nevertheless, should not go without a challenge. If we in the Christian community cannot arrive at a consensus view of God in relationship to his missiological agenda to unite all things in Christ, then it will be difficult to commend belief in him.

## Theological Consistency and the Doctrine of God

An important aspect of commending belief in God is consistency in our theological propositions. Consistency of theological statements is always a challenge. The logical outcome of a statement can be a determining factor in whether or not belief in God is congruent with a culture's story. It is not that we are allowing culture to define God. However, if God is at work in culture, like Paul observed in Athens and Ephesus, then something of God can be discovered there. What we discover about God in a culture must correspond with our doctrine of God.

We must also be aware that we might have conceived of God in ways that could work contrary to what we observe in culture. For example, when a classical theist argues that God is all-determining, then the natural consequence is double predestination: God has determined some to salvation and others to damnation. To many religious people around the world, this sounds characteristically like the fatalism we see in Vodou, Hinduism, and to some extent in Islam. Similarly, when an open or free will theist argues that God's will can change, then the natural consequence is uncertainty in God's actions. To the traditional religionist or animist, appeasement of this God is the only way to ensure well-being and guard against misfortune. The missiological theologian needs to weigh these doctrinal issues seriously, as their articulation in cross-cultural contexts might have unintended consequences in an emerging Christianity.

## Toward a Missiological Theism

Arriving at a theological consensus is not a panacea for the mission of the church or the proclamation of the gospel. Nevertheless, it does recognize that there are some aspects about God that we can understand and others that are beyond our ability to understand. This was not an issue for Paul, John, or the first-century church. Instead, their preoccupation was communicating the God they knew to a people who did not know their God or knew him in some incomplete form. This missiological theism relates our understanding of God in such a way that can be clearly seen in his character as described in the biblical texts and observed in culture rather than in the construction of philosophical arguments.

As we reflect on the question of God with the eyes of a missiological theologian, we must be able to explain who he is to ourselves before we attempt to explain him to others. Albert Einstein's often quoted aphorism, "Everything should be made as simple as possible, but no simpler," holds true as much in theology as in physics. To that end, a missiological theism is an endeavor to focus our theological attention on the missionary nature of God as our first-order understanding based upon a simple reading of the biblical texts and not a philosophical formulation.

Missiological theism does not assume the biblical authors are addressing issues that are not explicit in the texts themselves. Instead, missiological theism understands that God—first and foremost—wants to be known, is making himself known, and desires to be worshipped. These characteristics of the eternal God cannot change. God's interaction in human history must be described by his mission. His active pursuit of people through self-revelation in his creation and creatures, as well as in his Word—both propositionally and personally—demands that we view him as the preeminent missionary relentlessly chasing after a personal relationship with those who bear his image. As a result, missiological theism might describe God's attributes in the following manner.

| Attribute | Missiological Theism |
|---|---|
| Pure Actuality | God is completely glorious without addition or subtraction. His will is singular. What he was is what he is and what he will always be. (Eph 1:5, 9, 11; 3:9, 20-21; 1 Tim 3:16) |
| Sovereignty | Inasmuch as God's sovereignty relates to his plan, it will not change. (Eph 1:4; 2:1; 3:11; 4:6; 1 Tim 6:15-16) |
| Eternality | God is, has always been, and will always be. (Eph 3:11; 1 Tim 1:17). |

| Self-Existence | God is absolutely unconditioned in his will. He necessarily exists and will bring more people to worship him. (1 Tim 1:17; 2:5-6) |
|---|---|
| Immutability | God cannot change in his character, essence, or will. (Eph 1:18-23; 2 Tim 2:13) |
| Impassibility | God chooses to be affected by creatures only in relationship to his will; that is, his will does not change, will not be thwarted, but can be delayed due to creatures. (Eph 4:30; 1 Tim 2:1-4) |
| Foreknowledge | God's foreknowledge is not causative; he foreknows inasmuch as he is sovereign. (Eph 1:5; 2:10) |

TABLE 18: ATTRIBUTES OF GOD IN MISSIOLOGICAL THEISM

There is no other doctrine so profound as the doctrine of God. As we reflect on who he is and what he has done, we cannot help but see a God so distinct from others and so worthy of worship. He is the God who compelled Gregory to exclaim rhetorically, "For what will you conceive the Deity to be, if you rely upon all the approximations of reason? Or to what will reason carry you, O most philosophic of men and best of Theologians, who boast of your familiarity with the Unlimited?" (*Oration* 28.7). How utterly silly it is of us to think that we might be capable of formulating a comprehensive doctrine of God or that our philosophical construction of him best explains who he is.

Yet, as incomprehensible as he is, he did not leave himself without a witness. Moving from our missiological exegesis and reflection, the missiological theologian begins to connect the activity of God in the culture with the one true creator God we can only know from his own revelation. As we have seen, Paul was a master at connecting these stories. However, he was not alone. The Apostle John also made that connection when he was asked by church leaders in Asia to write about the Savior.[26] A missiological theism sees God for who he says he is, sees what God is doing in culture, and is constrained by God's own self-revelation. No more and no less, as it exclaims with Gregory the utter mystery of he who desires to restore all things to himself and is at work doing just that. What a privilege for the missiological theologian to be considered God's co-laborer.

## Formulating a Missiological Theology

Paul's missiological theology—his theocentric message to the churches in Asia—connected people to God's story. Their story was not an appendage to God's story. It was intricately intertwined from the beginning, just as God had

---

26. Irenaeus writes, "John, the disciple of the Lord ... published the gospel while living in Ephesus in Asia" (*Against Heresies* 3.1.2).

promised to bless every nation (Gen 12). Paul's ability to relate God's story with the story of the nations was due in large measure to his dialogue with others, observation of their culture, and study of their history. His method of missiological exegesis helped form the foundation of an awareness of an ethnic group that ensured Christianity would take root in the culture.

This type of missiological theology was not uncommon. The Gospel of John, the Fourth Gospel, provides a wonderful model of a text that offers a deliberate focus on addressing specific cultural issues and connecting them to Jesus' story. John's unique contribution to the Ephesian corpus testifies to the importance of connecting stories. Matthew's Gospel did that with the Hebrews. Mark's did the same with the Romans, and Luke's with Theophilus. Now, less than forty years after the arrival of the light of the world, John is connecting Jesus' story with the Ephesians.

## The Gospel of John as Missiological Theology

There are at least two things that first-year Greek students observe in the Gospel of John. First, and perhaps foremost, is how relatively easy it is to translate the Gospel from Greek to English. The simplicity of words and grammatical structure helps build the confidence of budding new Greek scholars. Second is how difficult it is to interpret John's Gospel. Even with the simplicity of the language, the thoughts and ideas conveying John's unique expression of Jesus' story are some of the most profound in all of Scripture.

The profound nature of John's Gospel is due in part to the diversity of opinion related to the reason why he wrote such a different perspective than the Synoptics—Matthew, Mark, and Luke. D. A. Carson summarizes the mood of Johannine studies:

> There is much more of the same, all of it worthy of lengthy discussion. But the dominant impression of the field of Johannine studies today is of considerable disagreement as to what the text says or implies, and disarray as to the best methods for studying the book. (1990, 40)

Even so, Carson writes,

> Whether the Fourth Gospel was interpreted so as to ground some form of Christian mysticism, or so as to make clear the truth of justification by faith, there was at least no doubt that it was the product of the apostle John, that in some ways it is the most focused of the four canonical Gospels, and that fundamental reconciliation between John and the Synoptics can be achieved. (ibid., 29)

Perhaps even more interesting, most scholars have agreed that the provenance or origin of John has little impact on our understanding of the Fourth Gospel. In fact, Craig Keener argues,

> Although the evidence for a Syro-Palestinian provenance is not absolutely compelling, it is not weak and would be the most likely proposal if the evidence for Roman Asia is judged as better. At the same time, it should also be noted that establishing a provenance in Ephesus is not essential for interpreting the Gospel. Ephesus was mostly representative of other Greco-Roman cities of the eastern Mediterranean, so the same general milieu would inform the Gospel there as in many other places. (2010, 146)

Keener's insistence that the culture of Ephesus is not necessary for interpreting the Gospel is remarkable and flies in the face of every first-year Bible student who learns that context is king. The *Sitz im Leben* (roughly "setting in life"), a German term that biblical scholars use to communicate the context of a text, is critical to understanding and interpreting the purpose of a text. Along with the *Sitz im Leben*, authorial intent—the reason why the author wrote—also influences our understanding of the text. To dismiss the *Sitz im Leben* of the Fourth Gospel will result in a complete misunderstanding of John's message. As we consider the unique contribution of John's Gospel to Jesus' story, the background of Ephesus is absolutely necessary.

So we begin there; and the story of how this Gospel came to be is worth repeating. We do not know exactly when John arrived in Ephesus, but we have no doubt that he lived there, most likely sometime between Paul's death in AD 67 and the conclusion of the persecution of Emperor Domitian in AD 96. Eusebius, the fourth-century bishop and renowned "Father of Church History," adds clarity to John's presence in Ephesus (although not necessarily to the writing of the Gospel) after the death of Domitian, when John returned from exile in Patmos:

> Listen to a tale, which is not a mere tale, but a narrative concerning John the apostle, which has been handed down and treasured up in memory. For when, after the tyrant's [Domitian's] death, he returned from the isle of Patmos to Ephesus, he went away upon their invitation to the neighboring territories of the Gentiles, to appoint bishops in some places, in other places to set in order whole churches, elsewhere to choose to the ministry some one of those that were pointed out by the Spirit. (*HE* 3.23.6)

Irenaeus (AD 130–202) relates a story he heard from Polycarp (AD 69–155) that places John in Ephesus at the time of Cerinthus:

John, the disciple of the Lord, going to bathe at Ephesus, and perceiving Cerinthus within, rushed out of the bath-house without bathing, exclaiming, "Let us fly, lest even the bath-house fall down, because Cerinthus, the enemy of the truth, is within." (*Against Heresies* 3.4.4)

Cerinthus (died ca. AD 100), a Jewish Christian from Egypt, contended that Jesus received the Christ at his baptism. Some believe this to have been an early form of Gnosticism, but to connect Cerinthus to the late second-century heresy is anachronistic. He was most likely a Judaizer, as he continued to hold a strict Jewish position on the Sabbath and circumcision. His teaching presumably flourished during the late first century in Asia and was perhaps influenced by Egyptian mystery religions, as he denied the divinity of Jesus.

Some have suggested that Cerinthus impacted Paul's ministry, even to the point of being the focus of his epistle to the Galatians as well as the Jerusalem council (Acts 15) in AD 50, but there is no good reason to make such an assertion. Jerome certainly indicates the possibility when he writes, "I refer to Cerinthus, Ebion, and the rest who say that Christ has not come in the flesh, whom [John] in his own epistle calls Antichrists, and whom the Apostle Paul frequently assails" (*Commentary on Matthew*, Preface, 2). However, such a vague reference cannot be assumed to have been the occasion for Paul, who had no aversion to calling out false teachers by name (2 Tim 1:15; 2:17), to write Galatians.[27]

Recounting Polycarp's ministry as bishop of Smyrna, a city north of Ephesus on the Aegean coast, Irenaeus remembers hearing him teach what he had learned from the apostles, especially sitting at the feet of John, as he came to faith in Christ as a young man (*Against Heresies* 3.3.4). John later appoints him as bishop of the church in Smyrna (Tertullian, *Prescriptions* 32.2). Polycarp died a martyr's death in AD 155 for being an "atheist," since he did not believe in the Roman gods. Repeatedly asked to repent from his unbelief and to renounce Christ, Polycarp testified, "Eighty-six years have I served him and he has done me no wrong. How can I blaspheme my King and my Savior?" (*Martyrdom of Polycarp*, 9). The date of Polycarp's death, and his age helps place John in Ephesus around AD 69, if not before.

Relating what he knew from Clement, Eusebius indicated that John only wrote his Gospel out of necessity (*HE* 3.24.5), something that seems apparent in Jerome's preface to his commentary on Matthew's Gospel:

---

27. Cerinthus and the Ebionites have both been mistakenly identified as proto-Gnostic. Their beliefs certainly found a home in later Christian Gnosticism, but Cerinthus and the Ebionites were clearly situated in the milieu of their day. Both Cerinthus and the Ebionites emerged out of the Judaizing Christians and their doctrines developed in concert with Christianity and Plato.

When [John] was in Asia, at the time when the seeds of heresy were springing up … he was urged by almost all the bishops of Asia then living, and by deputations from many Churches, to write more profoundly concerning the divinity of the Saviour, and to break through all obstacles so as to attain to the very Word of God (if I may so speak) with a boldness as successful as it appears audacious. Ecclesiastical history relates that, when he was urged by the brethren to write, he replied that he would do so if a general fast were proclaimed and all would offer up prayer to God; and when the fast was over, the narrative goes on to say, being filled with revelation, he burst into the heaven-sent Preface: "In the beginning was the Word, and the Word was with God, and the Word was God: this was in the beginning with God." (*Commentary on Matthew*, Preface, 2)

Charles Hill suggests that Eusebius' reference is actually a fragment from Papias' book (written ca. 110), *Expositions of the Sayings of the Lord* (1998, 582–629). Papias, a hearer of John and friend of Polycarp, became the second bishop of Hierapolis (*Irenaeus, Against Heresies* 5.33.4).[28] If Hill is correct, then John's Gospel was well known throughout Asia in the late first century. Additionally, Polycarp and Papias could have been among the bishops who requested that John write about the Savior, although it seems more probable that they became involved in the ministry in Asia later, as both seem to know the entire Johannine corpus. This could suggest a date for the Fourth Gospel in the range of AD 68 to 90.

Granted, many scholars have given attention to the nascent Gnosticism and Docetism that might have emerged in John's day. However, this seems unreasonable if we date the Gospel early. Few scholars give attention to the city of Ephesus and the worship of Artemis and Dionysus as a contributing influence on the content of this unique Gospel. Even more, the striking prologue emphasis on λόγος (*logos*) and the connection to the philosophy of Heraclitus of Ephesus (535–475 BC) is largely ignored. Granted, there are nearly six hundred years between Heraclitus and John. Nevertheless, Heraclitus' *logos* philosophy was renowned in Ephesus and Asia, much more so than the teaching of Cerinthus, which only survives in the writings of his antagonists.[29]

---

28. Papias' own testimony on being a disciple of John is conflicted. Whatever the case, he certainly learned the Johannine traditions.

29. The main source for Cerinthus' teaching includes Irenaeus, *Against Heresies* (1.26.1; 3.2.1, 2; 3.3.4; 3.11; 16); and Ephiphanius, *Panarion*. Eusebius writes about Cerinthus in *HE* 3.28.

Diogenes Laërtius writes in the fifth century BC that Heraclitus' book, *On Nature*, was housed in the temple of Artemis[30] and, "... acquired such fame that it produced partisans of his philosophy who were called Heracliteans" (*Lives of Eminent Philosophers*, IX, 6). As Kahn points out, Heraclitus' philosophy attracted the attention of many during John's day and later into the third century, "Down to the time of Plutarch [AD 46–120] and Clement [of Alexandria, ca. AD 150–215], if not later, the little book of Heraclitus was available in its original form to any reader who chose to seek it out" (1981, 5).

Paul and Luke must have also known about Heraclitus. For two years, Paul reasoned (Greek διαλέγομαι; *dialegomai*) the word (Greek λόγος; *logos*) of the Lord to Jews and especially Greeks in the philosophical school of Tyrannus, where Heraclitus would have no doubt been taught (Acts 19:9–10). While we do not know much about this school, the language Luke uses to describe it indicates its connection to Greek philosophy. The Greek, σχολαί (*scholai*), is a term used to describe the location where philosophers taught (Lidell and Scott's *Greek-English Lexicon*), and διαλέγομαι, as we saw in chapter 3, is the manner in which philosophers engaged students. As we have seen, Paul was a student of culture, so it is only natural that he would have studied the major philosophy that emerged out of Ephesus just like he did with that which emerged out of Athens.

Heraclitus, writing during the period when the Jews were returning from the Babylonian exile and constructing the Second Temple, was regarded as highly as Plato and the later Stoics. Even Christian philosophers held him in high regard. Justin Martyr (AD 100–165), who heard the gospel while in Ephesus, thought of Heraclitus, along with Socrates, as a pre-Christ Christian. He writes,

> We have been taught that Christ is the first-born of God, and we have declared above that He is the Word of whom every race of men were partakers; and those who lived reasonably are Christians, even though they have been thought atheists; as, among the Greeks, Socrates and Heraclitus, and men like them; and among the barbarians, Abraham, and Ananias, and Azarias, and Misael, and Elias, and many others whose actions and names we now decline to recount, because we know it would be tedious. (*First Apology*, 46)

---

30. Diogenes writes, "As to the work which passes as his, it is a continuous treatise *On Nature*, but is divided into three discourses, one on the universe, another on politics, and a third on theology. This book he deposited in the temple of Artemis and, according to some, he deliberately made it the more obscure in order that none but adepts should approach it, and lest familiarity should breed contempt." Only fragments of *On Nature* exist today.

So was John dealing with a proto-Gnosticism or Docetism in his prologue, or with an existing *logos* belief in Ephesus? Gnosticism and Docetism do eventually become formidable competitors of Christianity, but not until later in the second century. Could John have foreknown these systems of belief? Absolutely, but why would we need to force a tenuous prophetic declaration by the apostle when he clearly wanted to connect Jesus' story to those in Asia?

The Fourth Gospel is an evangelistic presentation focused on addressing the religious and philosophical systems in Asia, and specifically those associated with the goddess Artemis and the god Dionysus, as well as with the philosopher Heraclitus. John was not concerned with embellishing the Synoptics with his personal eyewitness of Jesus, nor was he concerned with the chronology of Jesus' ministry. It also seems unreasonable to suggest that the destruction of the Jewish temple or the Jewish War would have influenced his writing. If the Gospel is dated to the beginning of the Jewish War, when John arrived in Ephesus, the temple's destruction has no bearing on the Gospel. In fact, the significance of John's references to the temple (John 2:14–21; 7:14–28; 8:2–59) must be juxtaposed to the importance of the temple of Artemis to the Ephesians. If, in fact, John's audience comprised non-Christian Ephesians, they would have had no regard for the Jewish temple, if they had even known about it at all. It makes more sense that John's references to the temple in his Gospel positioned Jesus as the most high God who was greater than any god or goddess worshipped in temples made by human hands. Jesus superseded the worship and rituals occurring in a temple, no matter where the temple was located—Jerusalem or Ephesus.[31]

John's Gospel was a message that would have connected with a people who were proud to live in the city of a wonder of the ancient world, where "all Asia and the world worship" Artemis (Acts 19:27).[32] His primary concern was connecting Jesus' story with the story of those in Asia in such a way that they would clearly see that the one true God, εγώ είμι, is the creator and sustainer of the κόσμος (John 6:35–51; 8:12; 9:5; 10:9, 11–14; 11:25; 14:6). It is he alone who gives the right to become children of God, rather than Artemis, who acted as the protector of childbearing (John 1:12). Jesus performed genuine signs, like the wedding feast miracle, that would clearly demonstrate his primacy above Artemis, the goddess of matrimony (John 2:1–12). It is Jesus who can respond to religious leaders and call them to be born again, in distinction from Dionysius who was twice born of Zeus

---

31. See Andreas Kostenberger, "The Destruction of the Second Temple and the Composition of the Fourth Gospel," *Trinity Journal 26 (2005), 205-42*, for a discussion of the impact of the temple's destruction. I obviously disagree with Kostenberger's assessment.

32. Luke typically uses οἰκουμένη (inhabited earth) rather than κόσμος (world).

(John 3:1–15). Jesus had special knowledge of people, like the woman at the well (John 4:1–45)—who, like some women in Asia, consorted with men in the antics of the symposium. Jesus' reference to being the living bread signifies his preeminence above other gods and goddesses, whose theophaginic rituals connected the practitioner with the deity. Only Jesus can take away the hunger of humanity (John 6:22–59).

John's superb missiological theology made Jesus real to those who had never heard of him. The fact that he was an eyewitness further testified to the authenticity of Jesus as "the true light, which gives light to everyone" (John 1:9), who came into the world to give abundant life (John 10:10). Jesus was rejected and despised by his own people (John 1:11), but those other nations—and John was writing in a context where there were as many as fifty distinct ethnic groups—would find solace in a personal God who sacrificed himself and was resurrected to new life so that they might also receive eternal life (John 4:39–42, 46–53; 10:16; 12:20–26; 16:8–9; 17:20–21). This was a message for the entire world, a word that John repeats in order to make clear that Jesus is the one true God and Lord, supreme over all others.

In spite of Keener's conclusion—"An Ephesian provenance does not affect interpretation as much as we might hope" (2010, 146)—it seems clear that the uniqueness of the Fourth Gospel provides compelling evidence for John as a missiological theologian. The heart of the gospel is to tell the story of Jesus, and John brilliantly portrays Jesus in a way that made sense to those in Ephesus and Asia. John is connecting with the Ephesians on philosophical, religious, cultural, and ethnic levels to communicate Jesus' story in a way that it did become their story. It was no longer just the Jewish story of a Messiah. It was the story of the one true God who would restore the world, including the world of those in Asia.

## Steps to Launching a Movement

John clearly understood the culture and history of Asia. He must have read Heraclitus to make the connection with the *logos*. He understood the significance of the temple of Artemis for the lives of the Ephesians and juxtaposed Jesus, who has supremacy over any temple. John knew about the religious rituals of theophagy (eating the gods) and matrimony. He demonstrates a profound awareness of the importance of women in Ephesian culture as he relates the story of Jesus' relationships with women (Samaritan woman, Mary Magdalene, Syrophoenician woman). His deep understanding of his context and his thoughtful engagement when relating Jesus to his audience demonstrates a missiological theology that connected Jesus' story with the people's story.

This manner of connecting stories ensured that Christianity would be an indigenous system of beliefs and contributed to the ongoing expansion of the movement that was as much a Jewish movement as it was a Greek movement. In fact, it was God's movement, as he continued to go before the early disciples to make himself known. The task they enjoyed was showing those they engaged how God was at work among them. To do that meant they had to be where the gospel was needed and they had to allow the Holy Spirit to show them what God was doing to grab the attention of those he was pursuing.

The effectiveness of these early efforts demonstrated a thoughtful understanding of the context, as they dialogued with people, observed their culture, and studied their history. They knew the story of those they were engaging and they connected that story with God's story so that it became a unified story of God's relentless pursuit of more people worshipping him. This model of developing a missiological theology is one contemporary missions must emulate if the gospel has any hope of connecting to culture.

※

Ultimately, the outcome of missiological exegesis and reflection is a missiological theology. It is not a complex process, but it is one that will ensure the emergence of a theology that is culturally relevant and sustainable in the life of a movement. When a theology is rooted in indigenous soil with proper boundaries, then it ceases to be an imported theology and opens opportunities to connect a culture with God's redeeming work in history.

Theology attempts to answer the questions of what and why we believe as we do. In answering those questions, theology forms the basis of who we are as Christians—in other words, it provides a sense of identity. That identity, while being worked out for the Christian theologically, is expressed within a cultural context. Thus, the expression of Christianity in a particular context is to some degree a result of the search for a meaningful identity that relates theology and culture. This is missiological theology, and it is as much evangelistic as it is focused on making disciples of all nations.

Missiological theology stands above other systems of theology (Reformed, Covenant, Dispensational), as its focus is on the proclamation of the activity of God in the world to draw people to worship him. What emerges out of a context where missiological theology is developed, like in Ephesus and Asia, is a Christianity firmly rooted in the apostolic tradition with a color of the contemporary culture. There is no place better to see this than in Paul's circular letter to the churches in Asia.

Paul's missiological theology—his theocentric message to the churches—compelled the believers to stay on their mission to proclaim the gospel so that more people would worship God (John 1:14). It was now their story, and they held the responsibility to propagate it as adopted children into God's family charged with joining him to unite all things in Christ. It was this theological grounding that empowered the church to press forward with the advancement the gospel. To that we now turn.

# CHAPTER 6

## Grounding a Movement: Missiological Theology II

After a long flight from South Asia and a restless night's sleep, I awoke to attend our church the next morning. Our youngest son, Christopher, was home so he drove as jet lag was taking its toll on this weary traveler. Our mission organization's regional director and I had been in South Asia meeting with church leaders in five cities to learn more about their movements and how we might encourage them as they were beginning to reach new levels of growth—phenomenal growth. It was not uncommon to meet with leaders who were responsible for between five hundred and one thousand house churches, and even more. The rapid growth of Christianity in that part of the world is out of control—at least out of our control. Ensuring the theological fidelity of this movement has brought new challenges to what it means to keep the words of the faith and of good doctrine (1 Tim 4:6).

During the trip, I began to think more concretely about what was needed to ground a movement biblically and theologically so that people would continue to press forward in making disciples and not devolve into an institution. This grounding had to be more than simply teaching the latest church planting strategies. Then it struck me as it did back in Romania thirty years ago. The answer might be found in the church of Ephesus. The fantastic events at the church's birth, along with her rich history of spreading the gospel all over Asia (Acts 19:10), is reminiscent of what we see happening today in the Global South and the Global East. This is the story of Chito in the Philippines. It is Juan's story in Colombia and Reyansh's in India. It is Beni's testimony in Nepal, as well as Jean's in Burkina Faso. It is like this story from a tribal leader in a South Asian country:

During the summer of 2017, I suffered from a severe sickness for about three months. I was bedridden, and my whole body was swollen and had become very weak. My appetite was gone, and I was not able to walk properly. It was on 14th August, a film about Jesus Christ was shown just next to my house. Since I was too weak to stand and walk, I requested my wife and another to take me to the venue where the film was shown. They carried me to my neighbor's courtyard.

I watched the film until the end. As soon as I finished watching, tears rolled down from my eyes. I was bitterly crying. The works and the promise of everlasting life and the sacrifice of Jesus Christ on the cross for humanity had deeply touched my heart. I then realized how sinful I was. I repented and believed in my heart that Christ is truly the Savior of this world and it is through him alone one can have everlasting life.

The next morning, I invited *The Jesus Film* operator to share more about Jesus Christ and asked him to pray for my sickness. He shared about Jesus' miracles of healing the sick and raising the dead. He then prayed for my sickness. And to my surprise, after a couple of days my health started improving. My three-month-old sickness was gone. I started eating food. It was a miracle in my life. I never ever thought that I would receive a new life through a film about Jesus Christ and that I would receive a miraculous healing through the prayer of his servant. Both me and my wife have repented and accepted Jesus Christ as our personal Lord and Savior. We took water baptism on 20th August, 2017. We share our testimony to people wherever we go.

No doubt God is at work around the world today just as he was two thousand years ago. An unwavering passion grounded God's movement across the known world in the first century. That passion was nothing less than God's glory manifested in more people worshiping him. In the Roman province of Asia, that passion was wonderfully addressed in Paul's letter to the Ephesians. The letter, as does John's Gospel that we considered in the previous chapter, lays out the convictions of Paul's missiological theology.

You will recall that missiological theology is the result of missiological exegesis—dialogue with people, observation of culture, study of history— and missiological reflection—the first step in connecting God and culture. Its focus is to develop an effective way to communicate God's story with the story of the people so that they are, in reality, the same story. Just as God determined the boundaries of the nations, so he also placed a longing in our souls to be connected to him. Missiological theology makes the implicit searching and grabbing for God explicit, when people realize that he is not far from them (Acts 17:27).

As we have discussed in chapter one, a movement has stages. After its emergence, a movement's convictions will solidify. Those convictions will define its future. It is largely based upon these defined convictions and how they are enacted in the lives of believers that a movement will either experience exponential growth or decline into an institution.[33] Admittedly, applying contemporary theories to an ancient movement is anachronistic. However, we can make observations of the movement in Asia that will help us determine fundamental characteristics that led to the growth of the church. From those characteristics, we can evaluate our current situation and make proper application.

Here is our challenge, though. While there are particular sociological factors that contribute to the growth of a movement, we must also recognize that Christianity is a movement like no other. Paul's epistle to the Ephesians will reveal to us both the sociological factors and the salient characteristics that contribute to the long-term success of a missiologically theocentric movement empowered by the Holy Spirit. The end result is not a strategy for how to produce a movement, but a model for what a movement looks like. Such a model recognizes that we play a particular role—planting and watering like Paul and Apollos—but God causes the growth (1 Cor 3:6).

Penned as a circular letter most likely intended for believers all over the region, Ephesians answers the questions regarding God's purpose and where the church fits into his divine plan. John Stott summarized Ephesians in this way: "The whole letter is thus a magnificent combination of Christian doctrine and Christian duty, Christian faith and Christian life, what God has done through Christ and what we must be and do in consequence" (1979, 16).

It has long been assumed that Paul wrote Ephesians while he was in prison in Rome or Caesarea, although he could have been writing from a prison somewhere in Achaia or Asia, even in Ephesus.[34] At any rate, he is focused on helping the believers understand that God is most glorified when his purpose is fulfilled. Four times in the first chapter Paul refers to God's will:

---

33. Remember, decline is not necessarily negative. It could signify that the movement has become mainstream in society. It could equally signify a loss of momentum due to persecution, a lack of mobilized members, or a compromised leadership.

34. Robinson (1910) outlines a plausible case for Paul being in prison in Ephesus. Here are the salient points: 1) There is an early church tradition of imprisonment based on *Acts of Paul and Thecla; 2)* The ruins of St. Paul's Prison in Ephesus; 3) An undocumented imprisonment with Andronicus and Junia (Rom 16:7) had to take place prior to Acts 20:1-4) Prisca and Aquila risking their lives for Paul (Rom 16:3-4) fits with events in Ephesus; 5) Tension at the synagogue, and the upheaval due to Demetrius, suggests a scenario that might include prison; 6) Paul fought wild beasts at Ephesus (1 Cor 15:32), perhaps a euphemism for persecution (more likely a reference to the struggle with Artemis worship); 7) Paul suffered afflictions in Asia (2 Cor 1:8ff); 8) Paul indicates that he was often in prison even prior to Caesarea and Rome (2 Cor 11:23). If Robinson is correct, then an early imprisonment in Ephesus seems most likely. In addition, Paul indicates he was in Ephesus for three years (Acts 20:31). However, Luke seems to leave a gap between Paul's three months of teaching in the synagogue and his move for two years to the school of Tyrannus (Acts 19:8-10). Paul could have been imprisoned during this nine-month gap (Acts 20:19). Whatever the case, an Ephesian imprisonment is just as plausible as a Roman imprisonment and adds more color to the movement in Asia.

by his will (1:1); the purpose of his will (1:5); the mystery of his will (1:9); the counsel of his will (1:11). He is not indicating four different desires of God. God's will is a singular focus, the very essence of what brings God the most glory, and the primary reason why Paul was appointed an apostle (1:1) and why we are adopted children—chosen and predestined.

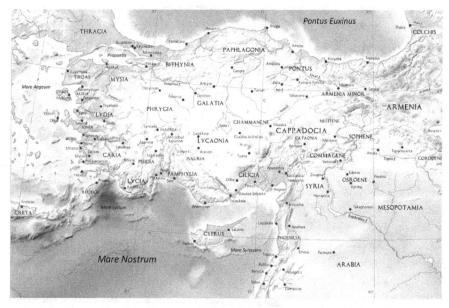

FIGURE 3: MAP OF ASIA MINOR

In our Western Christian individualism, we tend to think Ephesians 1 is focused on us. After all, we are the ones who have received every spiritual blessing (1:3). We are the ones whom God chose (1:4) and predestined (1:5, 11). Therefore, we have the privilege of figuring out what God's purpose is for us. So, then, much of our time revolves around the question "What is my purpose in life?" It is a great question. However, the theocentric emphasis of Ephesians 1 demands that the question of God's will be placed on God, not on us. Paul is not concerned about our purpose in life. He is concerned that we understand God's purpose; once we understand it, other ancillary questions will become clear.

As Christopher and I were driving to church that Sunday morning, I asked him, "What is God's will?" As a first-year university student, this was no doubt of critical importance for his future. I'm not sure what I expected him to say, but what he did say would have never crossed my mind. "Well, that's easy. We are Coopers, and God's will is to evangelize the lost."

If I had been the one driving, I'm certain that in my foggy jet lag we would have swerved off the road and into the ditch. Christopher answered the question that emerges from Ephesians 1:3–14. God's perfect plan is that all things will be united in Christ, and our identity—whether a Cooper, Ramos, Kone, or Hsieh—revolves around our participation in his mission for his glory.

Recognizing our identity as believers is an essential part of being a follower of Christ. That identity gives us a sense of belonging to a community of believers who are on God's mission, who are behaving in a way that is consistent with that community, and who are grounded in our belief that it is all about God's glory. Belonging, behaving, and believing are at the core of what I have called religious satisfaction (Cooper 2009a). Complete satisfaction comes only when we have a clear understanding of those three aspects of our identity. If we are muddled on any one of them, then we are susceptible to distractions and open to exploring other ways to find fulfillment in our lives, whether through substance abuse or similar addictions, other religions, false doctrines that tickle our ears—or even through good ministry programs like those that distracted the church in Ephesus (Rev 2:1–7).

True satisfaction for the Christian is founded in a theocentric understanding of God's will. This foundation, when properly a part of our identity, forms the basis on which a movement will cascade into an unstoppable Spirit-led force in fulfilling the Great Commission. If this is not understood, a movement will institutionalize, with a focus on discovering our will as individuals or our will as a local expression of Christ, even our will as a mission agency. The movement then becomes about us rather than about God.

## The Foundation of a Movement

Ephesians 1:3–14 is a beautiful, doxological passage written from Paul's passion for the preeminence of God. In fact, the entirety of Ephesians is focused on his supremacy. In six chapters, Paul makes explicit reference to the Father, Son, or Holy Spirit no less than 133 times in 155 verses. Put a different way, there are 2,422 Greek words in the letter. This means that Paul refers to God once in every 18 words! To miss the theocentric nature of the epistle is to misunderstand Paul's focus on God's glory reflected as much in us as individuals empowered by the Holy Spirit as in the church, the body of Christ, charged with declaring a mystery. It is a letter written so that we would understand that everything is about him and his glory. As Theodoret taught in the fourth century, we should never shun the name whereby we have been saved. "Let us rather learn from this blessed language how we are bound to glorify our benefactor, by connecting the name of Christ with our God and Father" (*Letter to John the Economus*, 146).

In the original, verses 3–14 comprise one massive sentence that, as Foulkes recognizes, is "impossible to analyse" (1989, 53). In spite of this challenge, we will attempt to unpack the passage a bit further, because unless we understand God's will, it is nearly impossible to ground a movement in its divine responsibility as co-laborers who are identified with the family of God. Paul writes:

> Blessed be the God and Father of our Lord Jesus Christ, who has blessed us in Christ with every spiritual blessing in the heavenly places, even as he chose us in him before the foundation of the world, that we should be holy and blameless before him. In love he predestined us for adoption to himself as sons through Jesus Christ, according to the purpose of his will, to the praise of his glorious grace, with which he has blessed us in the Beloved. In him we have redemption through his blood, the forgiveness of our trespasses, according to the riches of his grace, which he lavished upon us, in all wisdom and insight making known to us the mystery of his will, according to his purpose, which he set forth in Christ as a plan for the fullness of time, to unite all things in him, things in heaven and things on earth.

> In him we have obtained an inheritance, having been predestined according to the purpose of him who works all things according to the counsel of his will, so that we who were the first to hope in Christ might be to the praise of his glory. In him you also, when you heard the word of truth, the gospel of your salvation, and believed in him, were sealed with the promised Holy Spirit, who is the guarantee of our inheritance until we acquire possession of it, to the praise of his glory. (Eph 1:3–14)[35]

As mentioned, Paul refers to God's will three times (vv. 5, 9, 11) in a paragraph of 204 Greek words without any punctuation. This singular purpose (Greek τοῦ θελήματος αὐτοῦ—lit. "the will of his") points to what he determined from the beginning, that at the appropriate time God will "unite all things in [Christ], things in heaven and things on earth" (v. 10).[36]

---

35. Some suggest that Ephesians 1:3-14 is in the form of a *berakhah*, a genre of Hebrew blessing, identifying the passage as an early Christian hymn. Scholars of Ephesians attempt to find a symmetry to the passage, such as a Trinitarian symmetry (Cambier, 1963), Christological symmetry (Kramer, 1967), or Greek rhetorical symmetry (Robbins, 1980). For a complete discussion on early scholarship of the passage, see Barkhuizen (1990). Ultimately, Barkhuizen concludes that any attempt to reconstruct the passage is speculative (1990, 407). I am not so certain that genre or style of writing were on Paul's mind as he sat in chains in a dark, damp prison cell. It seems much more reasonable that Paul was thinking about God and the blessing he had received and then related it to the context of Asia with the myriads of gods and goddesses "promising" blessings, and presented an argument for true spiritual blessings coming from God through Christ. Ultimately, Paul is laying out the fact that these blessings were according to the purpose of God's will to unite everything in Christ.

36. The notion of "God's will," I suggest, is in distinction to the "will" of gods and goddesses worshipped by those in Asia. For instance, Pausanias, the second century AD Greek geographer, writes what is certainly a broadly held understanding of the "will." He states, "The Megalopolis was founded by the Arcadians with the utmost enthusiasm amidst the highest hopes of the Greeks, but it has lost all its beauty and its old prosperity, being today for the most part in ruins. I am not in the least surprised, *as I know that heaven is always willing something new, and likewise that all things, strong or weak, increasing or decreasing, are being changed by Fortune, who drives them with imperious necessity according to her whim*" (*Description of Greece*, 8.33.1; emphasis added).

It is a mystery that Paul later explains as a work only accomplished through Christ. Namely, he broke down the barrier between the Jews and the nations so that now we are together being built "into a dwelling place for God by the Spirit" (2:22). Just so there is no confusion, he once again clarifies, "This mystery is that the [nations][37] are fellow heirs, members of the same body, and partakers of the promise in Christ Jesus through the gospel" (3:6).[38] Although once hidden, God now revealed the mystery which is to be proclaimed by the body of Christ (3:10). It is a spiritual activity that rolls back the darkness of this present world to reveal the glory of God shown in "the immeasurable riches of his grace in kindness toward us in Christ Jesus" (2:7).

A fourth-century theologian known by the name Ambrosiaster, said this:

> The pleasure of God, whose counsel cannot be changed, was to show in Christ the mystery of his will. This happened at the time when he chose that he should be revealed. Now his will was this, that he should then draw close to all who were in sin, either in heaven or in earth. God gave Christ to bring believers the gift of forgiveness of their sins through faith in Christ. (*Epistle to the Ephesians*, 1.9.1)

Chapter 1 of Ephesians, then, is all about God and the accomplishment of his will in uniting everything in Christ. As the foundation of his glory, the question of being chosen and predestined comes into perspective and points to their—i.e. choseness and predestineness—connection to God's perfect plan. Foulkes honestly acknowledges, "This doctrine of election, or predestination, is not raised as a subject of controversy or speculation. It is not set in opposition to the self-evident fact of human free will. It involves a paradox that the New Testament does not seek to resolve, and that our finite minds cannot fathom" (1989, 55). Whatever being chosen and predestined mean, they somehow must be tied to the mystery of God's work in Christ that is to be proclaimed by the church.

Ephesians, it is important to remember, was written to groups of saints all around Asia rather than to individuals. By the time of Paul's writing, there could have been as many as 150 house churches in the city of 51,000 inhabitants (see table 7 in chapter 2). Thus, when Paul says, "even as [God] chose us in [Christ]" (1:4), he is not referring to an individual, but to a collective body of believers—the church—which has been chosen before the foundation of the world.

---

37. Greek ἔθνη (*ethne*; plural, "nations"). As previously mentioned, an unintended consequence of translating *ethne* as Gentiles is the impression that the Gentiles are a homogenous people group just as the Jews.

38. Like the issue of "will," I suggest that Paul's use of "mystery" is in distinction to the "mysteries" often associated with Pagan cultic practices at the temple of Artemis. For example, Pausanias observed while traveling in Alea, "The Caphyatans have a sanctuary of the god Poseidon, and one of the goddess Artemis, surnamed Cnacalesia. They have also a mountain called Cnacalus, where every year they celebrate mysteries in honor of their Artemis" (*Descriptions of Greece*, 8.23.4).

Having a theocentric perspective takes the choosing, as well as the time of the choosing, away from any individual and focuses on God's ultimate plan of revealing the mystery through what he has chosen before the foundation of the world—namely, the church (Eph 3:10). A missiologically theocentric reading of Ephesians 1 demands that the attention is placed on God's will accomplished in Christ and what he has done to ensure its fulfillment. I think Foulkes is correct when he writes that "from eternity to eternity God works all things according to his perfect plan" (1989, 54)—including the church's election and predestination.

### Our Identity in Adoption

So Paul writes, "In love [God] predestined us for adoption to himself as sons through Jesus Christ, according to the purpose of his will" (1:4–5). Key to an understanding of Paul's concept of predestination is an understanding of adoption. When Romania opened up to the West in 1990, images of children in orphanages flooded American television. We lived in Romania at the time and saw firsthand the deplorable conditions many of those children were subjected to: sleeping in their waste; tethered to their cribs; deprived of human touch and emotion. Their plight propelled many to act. Some, out of a deep concern for the well-being of the children, saw themselves on a rescue mission to save them from tragic situations. Others, out of a deep desire to bring these precious children into a new family, saw themselves providing a forever family. Most, no doubt, wished both for those children.

Paul's understanding of adoption was similar to many contemporary adoptions. In a very real sense, our adoption as sons and daughters was God's rescue mission because we were "children of wrath" (2:3). However, our adoption through Jesus Christ is so much more. In Paul's time, Greek adoption was common for boys, while rare for girls. It was much more than a rescue. Greek adoption gave a new identity to the child, including an expectation that the one adopted would now fulfill the will of the family. Often these adoptions were due to no male heir to an estate, so the identity of an adopted son was taken very seriously. It was a genuine inheritance and privilege that gave the adopted child every right and responsibility of the family. As Hugh Lindsay remarks,

> A son adopted during the lifetime of the adopter on his decease had immediate and uncontested rights to his inheritance, and was effectively in as strong a position as a natural son of the adoptive parent. ... The adoptive son was required to relate to his adoptive father as though he were his biological son. (2011, n.p.)

Our adoption into God's family is the same. We are given a new identity in Christ and a new purpose to fulfill the family's business as if we were biological children—namely, proclaiming the mystery of our Father's will. Paul further emphasizes our adoption when he writes, "Therefore be imitators of God, as beloved children" (5:1). In other words, we are to be about our heavenly Father's mission, fulfilling our identity in the family of God by declaring the gospel to every nation.

Much of Western evangelicalism has relied on the Reformers for an understanding of election and predestination. The complex theologies that emerged—double predestination, the sovereign will of God, the permissive will of God, free will theism, classical theism—raise questions that were never on the mind of Paul and have drawn our attention away from God's mission in the world, much like Jesus' disciples were distracted by end-times theology (Acts 1:6–7; cf. Matt 24:36; Mark 13:32). I like how C. S. Lewis puts these issues: "There is no more tiresome error in the history of thought than to try to sort our ancestors on to this or that side of a distinction which was not in their minds at all. You are asking a question to which no answer exists" (1944, 10–11).

Granted, the Reformers rightly brought our attention back to God's Word, salvation by grace through faith, and the priesthood of believers. In addition, the French reformed theologian John Calvin, for example, helped to define our predestining to adoption in three points. First, Calvin asserted that our adoption meant that we are to be pure and holy as is reflected in the Father. Second, we are to behave toward our Christian brothers and sisters as we do toward God. Finally, we have a responsibility to be gracious and forgiving toward those who are outside the Christian family (Westhead 1995, 113). All three are important aspects of adoption. Strikingly absent from Calvin's understanding of adoption, however, is the Christian responsibility to join with God in the work of declaring the mystery of salvation to the nations.

Regarding the sixteenth-century Reformers, Robert Glover, a missionary statesman who served in China, noted, "Despite their clear conceptions and statements of fundamental doctrines of evangelical faith, they showed a remarkable ignorance of the scope of the divine plan and of Christian duty in relation to the gospel" (1931, 40). Though perhaps overstated, Glover did make a common accusation against the Reformers.

Taking a more conservative posture, Thorsten Prill concedes that Matthew 28:18–20 did not factor into the Reformers' understanding of missions. Instead, Luther believed that his writings would be the purveyor of the gospel (Prill, 2017). The face of European Christianity was no doubt impacted. Nevertheless, one of the primary challenges we face in Western evangelical theology is rediscovering the proper meaning of "evangelical" in relationship to our responsibility as adopted children of God to take the good news to all people groups.

With a theocentric reading that places the focal point of Ephesians on God's will, there is no need to think about our purpose. Our identity has put us in a new position as "created in Christ Jesus for good works, which God prepared beforehand" (2:10). These works, purely due to the theocentric context of the letter, must be tied to God's will. They are not things we search for, as they are already prepared. Now, just as Christ expects of his adopted brothers and sisters, we are to be witnesses in Jerusalem, Judea and Samaria, and to the ends of the earth (Acts 1:8). This is not a progressive witness, but rather a simultaneous one. There is no question of where we are to be witnesses. Jesus is not leaving room for us to wait on making disciples until some future prompting of where to go. It is now, and it is to all nations without discrimination.

## The Battle for a Movement

A missiologically theocentric movement determined to fulfill God's mission is a target for spiritual warfare. There is nothing that Satan would like more than to see the efforts of the spread of the gospel reduced to an institution. He is very aware of how his story ends. He knows that Christ will be and is already victorious. His only course of action is to slow the progress of the gospel as long as possible so that his kingdom will continue to dominate the earth. His purpose has not changed. He attempts to steal God's glory for himself, and he leads people, even Christians, to think they can do the same.

Satan has been opposing the work of God from the beginning of creation. That is precisely why Paul reminded the churches of Asia to "stand against the schemes of the devil" (Eph 6:11). Paul warns about these schemes in multiple contexts. In 2 Corinthians 4:4, the devil blinds the minds of the unbeliever. In 2 Corinthians 11:14–15, he appears as an angel of light. In 2 Corinthians 12:17, he uses physical ailments to frustrate the plans of God. In 1 Thessalonians 2:18, he opposes and hinders the Christian. All these tactics have one objective: to slow the movement of God by any means. Satan knows he cannot stop it, but he can certainly hamper its effectiveness and prolong his demise.

Perhaps one of the most descriptive understandings of the forces of darkness is found in Ephesians 6. Paul's teaching on the spiritual battle that lies before Christians is situated in the letter after he lays out his understanding on a number of important relationships for believers: to God (chapter 1), to others (chapter 2), to God's mission (chapter 3), to leaders (chapter 4), and to other brothers and sisters (chapters 4, 5, and 6). Notice, it is at the end of the letter that he addresses "the spiritual forces of evil in the heavenly places" (6:12). He juxtaposes these forces with the emphasis that our battle is not "against flesh and blood." The battle is not against God, his mission to reach the nations, our leaders, or our brothers and sisters. Instead, it is against the evil forces trying to delay the inevitable.

It is interesting that the majority of Ephesians pertains to proper Christian relationships in connection to God's mission. Paul seems to be alerting us to a scheme of the devil to distract, thwart, and break us from these relationships, as it will result in losing God's perspective on his mission. When Satan is successful, our focus becomes anthropocentric. If he can make us believe that the world revolves around our mission and our vision for ministry, then God's plan to unite all things in Christ will become a secondary or even tertiary act, consequently prolonging Satan's doomed reign on earth. We might do good things, but not the main thing.

## The Armor of God

How then should the Christian respond? Writing from a prison, Paul would have had a detail of soldiers around him. Of course, he was familiar with the armor of a soldier, so he used it as an analogy for preparing the body of Christ for spiritual battle. His focus was not on an individual Christian fighting the spiritual battle alone. Rather, the body of Christ was to engage in this battle together in unity as one force. So Paul begins, "Therefore take up the whole armor of God, that you may be able to withstand in the evil day, and having done all, to stand firm. Stand therefore ..." (Eph 6:13–14a).

Perhaps more striking, Paul's emphasis on standing firm in his letter to the Philippians was a reference to the battle tactics of Philip II of Macedon (382–336 BC), who gave his name to the great city that received the gospel in Acts 16.[39] The believers at Philippi would no doubt understand the military imagery. "Only let your manner of life be worthy of the gospel of Christ, so that whether I come and see you or am absent, I may hear of you that you are *standing firm in one spirit, with one mind striving side by side for the faith of the gospel*" (1:27; emphasis added).

Philip was held prisoner in Thebes at a young age and learned battle tactics from a Theban general. During his internment he developed a strategy that became known as the Macedonian phalanx, which was key to the expansion of Greece under Philip's son, Alexander the Great. That strategy revolved around two important tactics. First, Philip further enhanced the phalanx, enabling a steady offensive approach and offering the most protection from opposing forces. The phalanx placed the offensive

---

39. Paul's use of "standing firm," as well as the battle imagery, could indicate that he was writing from prison somewhere in Macedonia during his travels in that region, as recorded in Acts 20:1-3. This could place the date of writing Ephesians around AD 57. The fact that Paul also writes about our citizenship in both Philippians (3:20) and Ephesians (2:19) might lend further credibility to the notion that he wrote Ephesians from Macedonia. The use of both the battle and citizen images does not necessarily indicate that the letters were written from the same place and during the same period of time. The fact that Timothy was the coauthor of Philippians but not of Ephesians suggests different locations for the two letters.

force in a side-by-side, compact formation that was difficult to penetrate and made it possible to advance on the opposition while more productively standing firm on the ground that had been gained. Second, Philip utilized the spear that gave those at the front line of the phalanx a greater range to hold off the enemy as the phalanx advanced to take more ground (Anson, 2010). Paul must have also had in mind the Roman *testudo*, the famous formation of soldiers advancing their might in a shell-like formation to ensure safety from the flaming arrows of the enemy. These battle strategies did not escape Paul as he outlined the pieces of armor that would prove successful against the schemes of the devil(6:13–17).

Much has been written regarding the relationship between the vital body parts that each piece of armor protected. The belt buckled around our waist reminds us of doing away with everything that might encumber our faith so that we can stand on truth (6:14a). The breastplate protects our vital organs, without which we would have little hope of living righteously (6:14b). The sandals help us stand for the peace that only comes through the gospel (6:15). The shield enables us to extinguish the attacks of Satan as we rely upon the author and perfecter of our faith (6:16). The helmet protects the brain, the storehouse of the knowledge that gives us assurance of the completion of God's will (6:17a).

When I have heard the armor of God taught, it is usually from a defensive posture, with the emphasis on the armor protecting us as individuals against the attacks of Satan. Yet Paul knew the success of Philip and later of Alexander, and he certainly knew the Roman Empire's success in expanding the *Pax Romana*. The effective armed forces of Greece and Rome were not passive in their aggression. They were forceful, violently overpowering the opposition in order to establish the reign of their respective empires. This was, no doubt, in Paul's mind when he wrote about the spiritual battle.

Paul's charge to put on the full armor of God was not a charge to defend against the attacks of evil forces. It was a charge to protect the body of Christ with spiritual armor as it moved in unity, side by side, to advance the spread of God's kingdom around the world by proclaiming the gospel of peace. That is why Paul is sure to remind the church to take up the sword of the Spirit, which is the word of God (6:17) and to pray (6:18) that words may be given in the proclamation of "the mystery of the gospel" (6:19). This prayer was not simply for Paul, but for all who are ambassadors charged with the responsibility to boldly declare the reconciliation of God with the nations through the work of Christ.

The fourth-century North African Neoplatonic philosopher, Marius Victorinus, understood this. "The gospel is to be carried abroad. It is to be preached among the nations. Wherever, then, it is preached, it must be heard. But so that all may hear, one must use one's feet to travel. And so do we travel with haste and urgency" (*Commentary on the Letter to the Ephesians* 2.6.15).

## The People of a Movement

Paul's letter begins with a declaration of God's will and our participation in it, and then ends with the armor that protects us as we advance his will around the world. Sandwiched between the foundation and the battle of a movement are the people of a movement. Paul provides us with the meat of instruction that grounds the understanding of our identity as adopted children on God's mission.

Paul's letters were commonly heard rather than read. There were no efficient means of reproduction to ensure a wide distribution of content. Even if there were a way to get printed content into the hands of the masses, the masses were largely illiterate. Scholars estimate that only 3 to 10 percent of the Roman Empire could actually read (Harris, 1991). That percentage might have been higher within the Jewish population, as well as in an educated city like Ephesus. Nevertheless, the fact that books were for the elite limited their distribution to the masses.

This was not a hindrance to the spread of the gospel. In fact, it very well could have contributed to the rapid multiplication of disciples. The oral transmission of Christian teaching meant that Christianity was accessible to all, not just to the elite, and that everyone could share the message easily. For it to be accessible also meant that it was understood. The apparently complex theology that emerges from Ephesians was not complex to the original audience. It could not be complex since it had to be transmitted orally.

As we approach the missiological theology of Ephesians, we have to read the letter as simply as we can, without the lens of the twenty-first century educated reader. A simple reading does not mean that Ephesians was less profound. It was extraordinarily profound! In fact, we could easily say that it was revolutionary as much for the Gentiles as for the Jews. The clear and unassuming message that God intends to unite all things in Christ and that Christ's work that brought the nations (*ethne*) near by his blood (Eph 2:13) has broken the barrier between people groups was as radical as anything the original audience would have encountered.

These believers understood that the context of this profundity fully aligned with fulfilling God's will. In that context, the stage is set for understanding an important aspect of the missiological theology that takes up the bulk of Paul's attention: the people of a movement. In essence, Paul is saying that if you believe what he has laid out in the first chapter, then the remainder of the letter is what it looks like to live that out (behaving) in a community (belonging). In essence, this is our identity as saints.

As he does in Romans and Colossians, Paul outlines correct doctrine (chapters 1–3), then correct conduct (chapters 4–6). He frames his letter with theology proper (1:3–6), Christology and soteriology (1:7–12), pneumatology (1:13–14), anthropology (chapter 2), missiology (chapter 3), ecclesiology and practical theology (4:1–6:20), all grounded in the context of fulfilling God's plan to unite all things in Christ. It seems that Paul is trying to answer general theological and practical questions that might arise when a community focuses on God's will. His motivation is on everything being accomplished to God's glory.

The people of a movement will always be motivated by the completion of God's mission in the world. They will be missiologically theocentric, as they join with him to see the name of Jesus lifted above all others (1:21). The movement is founded first on a relationship with the Creator. Ephesians wonderfully gives us a missiological theology that begins with God, who gives every spiritual blessing to the saints (1:3), in contrast to the myriads of gods and goddesses thought to bless worshippers in Asia. Paul's missiological theology tells of our uncreated God, who created us in Christ Jesus for good works (2:10), rather than a god who is crafted by human hands (Acts 19:25–27). He tells us of God, who called us to a life of imitation (5:1) through the filling of the Holy Spirit (5:19), rather than the drunken debauchery associated with Dionysus.[40]

The inheritance that is ours from our adoption is guaranteed by the sealing of the Holy Spirit (1:13), rather than by the theophaginic practices associated with the myriad of gods and goddesses in Asia. That inheritance demands a response that compels us on God's mission in the world, advancing the good news together as the body of Christ, ever mindful that our battle is not against flesh and blood (6:12).

The churches in Asia were not living in a theological or missiological vacuum. Ephesians was not written *ex nihilo*. The churches had a theology that Paul was reinforcing (see table 19). That indigenous theology emerged out of his missionary encounter with culture. To the church in Corinth he said, "I have become all things to all people that I might save some" (1 Cor 9:22). So we should expect nothing less while he was in Ephesus, especially since he wrote 1 Corinthians from this city. As he reasoned daily in the philosophical hall of Tyrannus (Acts 19:9) and taught from house to house (Acts 20:20), the theology we see is at the same time faithful to the story of Jesus and relevant for the people of Asia. It is another beautiful example of missiological theology.

---

40. No doubt Paul was contrasting the Christian life of being filled with the Holy Spirit and the Dionysian practice of drunkenness. Dionysus, as significant as Artemis, his half-sister, had a prominent place in Ephesus. "At any rate, when [Mark] Antony made his entry into Ephesus, women arrayed like Bacchanals, and men and boys like Satyrs and Pans, led the way before him, and the city was full of ivy and thyrsus-wands and harps and pipes and flutes, the people hailing him as Dionysus Giver of Joy and Beneficent" (Plutarch, *Life of Antony 24.3*).

| Acts 18:18-19:41 | Acts 20:17-38 | Ephesians |
|---|---|---|
| Learned about Jesus accurately | | 1:7; 2:11-22 |
| | Repentance toward God | |
| Taught about Jesus as Lord | Faith in our Lord Jesus Christ | 1:13 |
| Power of the Holy Spirit to be witnesses | The Holy Spirit leads us | 1:17; 3:16; 4:3; 5:19 |
| | Testifying to the gospel of the grace of God | 2:8-9 |
| Persuading about the kingdom of God | Proclaiming the kingdom | 5:5 |
| God works miracles of healing and exorcism | | |
| | Declaring the whole counsel of God | |
| | The Holy Spirit appoints leaders | 4:1-8 |
| Evil spirits know Jesus and his followers | | 2:1-3; 6:10-12 |
| | Leaders care for the church | 4:10-16 |
| Handmade gods are not gods | | 2:10; 5:5 |
| Missiological theology contra the Artemis cult (Savior, Leader, Blessing, Will, Marriage) | | 1:3-14; 5:22-33 |
| | Church of God was purchased by Christ's blood | 1:7; 2:13 |
| | God's grace builds up and gives an inheritance | 1:6-7, 11, 14, 18; 2:5-8; 4:7 |
| Respect others' beliefs | | |
| | We must help the weak | |
| | It is more blessed to give than to receive | |

TABLE 19: THE THEOLOGY OF ASIA: WHAT PAUL AND THE DISCIPLES TAUGHT IN EPHESUS

Ephesians does not represent new theological material. David Wenham points out that the same themes of wisdom, revelation, knowledge, mystery, good pleasure, and all things in Christ are seen in 1 Corinthians (1995, 132). We see them as well in Colossians, which closely parallels Ephesians. The military theme of standing firm is repeated in Philippians. Ephesians does not represent theological innovation nor is it deutero-Pauline, but rather it represents missiological ingenuity that introduces the nations to the God who has brought peace through the work of Christ and given us an inheritance as adopted children—a matter of utmost importance to both Jews and Gentiles. The unique contribution of Ephesians to the Pauline corpus is its emphasis on God's glorification through the uniting of the faithful saints into his kingdom and our responsibility to be implicated in his mission to the nations.[41]

A simple reading of Ephesians gets us to the place of seeing the missiologically theocentric focus of Paul. While we learn about relationships between people and leaders, relationships with the nations, relationships within the family—in other words, relationships within the body of Christ—Paul does not want the people of a movement to be distracted from God's purpose. It is as those relationships are united in Christ that we together are chosen to be on God's mission as predestined heirs. We are those who have a new identity and who are about God's glory. So, Paul prays:

> I do not cease to give thanks for you, remembering you in my prayers, that the God of our Lord Jesus Christ, the Father of glory, may give you the Spirit of wisdom and of revelation in the knowledge of him, having the eyes of your hearts enlightened, that you may know what is the hope to which he has called you, what are the riches of his glorious inheritance in the saints, and what is the immeasurable greatness of his power toward us who believe, according to the working of his great might that he worked in Christ when he raised him from the dead and seated him at his right hand in the heavenly places, far above all rule and authority and power and dominion, and above every name that is named, not only in this age but also in the one to come. (1:16–21)

Paul's prayer reaffirms what he has just taught. It is not disconnected from his missiological theology. The wisdom and revelation of knowing God is the understanding of his divine plan to unite all things in Christ (1:9–10). The hope of our calling is our election (1:4) and predestination (1:5, 11) to fulfill his will. Our inheritance is sealed with the Spirit (1:13–14) to ensure us that we

---

41. It is worth noting what we do not see emerging in the theology of Asia, which is indicative to Paul's missiological theology. There is no explicit reference to Judaism or to the Law and Prophets in Ephesians, although we can discern Jewish influence on Paul. Paul's emphasis on the Trinity is in contradistinction to the Jewish YWYH. Granted, for Paul there is no difference, but to the Jews, this was blasphemous.

are adopted children (1:5). The power that raised Jesus from the dead is the same power that enables us to declare to others, just as we heard that Jesus is seated at the right hand of God (1:14). John Chrysostom said, "He has made known to us the things that are in his heart" (*Homilies on Ephesians* 1); and at the very heart of God is his glory.

## Relationships with the Nations

After his doxological introduction and prayer for the believers, Paul reminds the church of their past and what Christ has done. While we were dead in our sins, directed by our lusts, and children of wrath, God saved us (2:1–9). It was a salvation as much from ourselves and our own devices as to the fulfillment of God's plan. The new creation, language that parallels the Septuagint account of God creating Adam and Eve in his image, was also a new identity crafted by God, in contrast to what the Ephesians would have been accustomed to seeing from the silversmiths who crafted images of Artemis. We are God's workmanship, not that of some other deity or craftsman, which results in good works (2:10).

The nineteenth-century English pastor, Robert Dale, stated it well:

> As the branch is created in the vine, we are created in Christ; as the fruits of the branch are predetermined by the laws of that life which it receives from the vine, so our "good works" which are the result of our union with Christ, are predetermined by the laws of the life of Christ which is our life and the strength of all our righteousness. (1897, 151)

Paul has already explained those good works, but he amplifies them as he continues to write about the mystery entrusted to him to declare to the nations that they are included in God's divine plan of uniting all things in Christ (Eph 3:1–9).[42] This, now, is the responsibility of the church through the empowering Spirit (Eph 3:10–21). Stott calls it "the circle of divine communication" (1979, 73). The good news came from God to Paul, Paul to the nations, and finally from the church to the spiritual realms. This was for all to know—a declaration of God's divine plan that was established from the foundation of the world. He chose the church to declare it—empowered by the Holy Spirit, knowing her inheritance as a part of God's family, and charged with the responsibility to announce his glory to the nations.

---

42. Remember, there are more than fifty people groups in Asia that are culturally distinct and ethnically diverse.

Chrysostom, teaching in the fourth century, captures the idea:

> In the body it is the living spirit that holds all members together, even when they are far apart. So it is here. The purpose for which the Spirit was given was to bring into unity all who remain separated by different ethnic and cultural divisions: young and old, rich and poor, women and men. (*Homilies on Ephesians* 9.4.1–3)

## Relationships with Believers

As this diverse body of believers has been brought together through the message of peace, we are now to walk in a manner worthy of our calling (4:1). This calling is not to a vocation, but to what Paul has already described. We are to walk by imitating God, as is right since we are his children (5:1) who have received an inheritance in the kingdom (5:5). He does not want us to forget that we are united in Christ, Jews along with the nations, as was his intention from the beginning (2:11–3:13). A few years earlier, Paul had written to the churches in Galatia, "And the Scripture, foreseeing that God would justify the [nations][43] by faith, preached the gospel beforehand to Abraham saying, 'In you shall all the nations be blessed'" (Gal 3:8).

Now we are citizens with the rest of the saints (2:19–22). We are fused together in a work that only Christ could do. We have already heard from John Chrysostom on two occasions, but in a church 1,500 miles south of Ephesus in Antioch of Syria, this man who was renowned for his eloquent sermons spoke to a congregation in the fourth century. Chrysostom was a straightforward exegete concerned with the accurate interpretation of Scripture, as he learned while studying at the School of Antioch. His desire was for his listeners to gain practical applications of Scripture for their daily lives. Concerned for his flock, he would write, "I cannot let a day pass without feeding you from the treasures of Scripture" (*Homilies from Genesis* 1.82.2). In his *Homilies on Ephesians*, which he preached in AD 393, Chrysostom taught on this wonderful union shared by believers:

> Bind yourselves to your brethren. Those thus bound together in love bear everything with ease... . If now you want to make the bond double, your brother must also be bound together with you. Thus he wants us to be bound together with one another, not only to be at peace, not only to be friends, but to be all one, a single soul. Beautiful is this bond. With this bond we bind ourselves together both to one another and to God. This is not a chain that bruises. It does not cramp the hands. It leaves them free, gives them ample room and greater courage. (*Homilies on Ephesians* 9, 4.1–3)

---

43. For footnote 37 on *ethne*.

The work that Christ has accomplished in breaking down the barrier between the Jews and the nations created a bond between believers that is worth preserving at all costs (2:14; 4:3). That bond only intensifies when we realize that we are all on the same mission to bring God glory for his sake, as the gospel advances in a grand cosmic battle.

In 1986, during my college years, I experienced my first summer evangelism project with Cru. Camping at the seaside of Sopot, Poland, just after that project, I was overwhelmed with excitement for finishing the Great Commission in Eastern Europe and the Soviet Union. That fall, on the inside flap of my newly purchased Bible—a replacement for the one stolen from our campsite—I taped a note card with a quote from C. S. Lewis. In his classic book, *Mere Christianity*, Lewis wrote, "Enemy-occupied territory—that is what the world is. Christianity is the story of how the rightful King has landed in disguise, and is calling us all to take part in a great campaign of sabotage" (1952, 46). When we are bound together in God's mission, nothing can stop the people of a movement on the "great campaign of sabotage"—not even the forces of darkness.

## Relationships with Leaders

To accomplish this task, Christ gave gifts to the church (4:8). Some were apostles, others prophets, still others evangelists, and some shepherd-teachers. It would not be correct for us to read the clergy of the church into these gifts, or even the elders—although they were certainly leaders in the church. More than likely, these were deacons, a point I will argue in the next chapter. These gifted men and women were charged with a solemn responsibility to build up and ensure unity in the church. The manner in which they were to do this was by equipping people for ministry (4:12).[44] It was a team effort; each, in his or her own capacity, was to contribute to the maturation of Christ's body with the goal of accomplishing God's will.

We live in a day when much of ministry has focused on the professional. We see the institutionalizing impact on the church when the works of service are delegated to those with formal education or ordination. When teaching in the majority world, I am inevitably approached by a brother or sister who asks something to the effect of whether I would lay hands on them so that they could baptize new believers.

This perception that authority is somehow transmitted from a "professional" has a long history, dating back to the early second century. Under the constant stress of persecution, early leaders were challenged with upholding the faith.

---

44. διακονία (*diakonia*) is the Greek used in 4:12. We will fully discuss the responsibility of movement leadership in the next two chapters.

Such assurance, so they thought, could only come from apostolic succession. It was vital to the early church that the leaders had a direct line of authority from Paul or Peter or one of the other apostles. So, for example, Clement of Rome (ca. AD 90) would reprimand the church in Corinth for expelling leaders who had been appointed by Paul (*1 Clement*). Ignatius of Antioch (ca. AD 110) would encourage the church at Ephesus to obey their bishop, Onesimus, ostensibly the slave Paul had freed in Colossae (*Letter to the Ephesians*).

What is noteworthy in Paul's letter to the Ephesians is the absence of any personal greeting to leaders in the churches of Asia. With Paul's attention on God's mission, we should not be surprised. No doubt Corinth was fresh on his mind, with the divisions over who baptized who (1 Cor 1:10–17). Such distraction did not promote the unity and single-minded focus on God's will that Paul demands in Ephesians, nor did it honor his God who was uniting all things in Christ.[45] These gifted people responsible for maturing the church had a single goal: to equip the saints for works of ministry (4:12). It was not about building up their own ministries. It was about building up the body of Christ to do the work of Christ.

Typically I respond to my friends in the majority world with a question: "Are you obedient to the Great Commission to make disciples of all nations?"

"Oh yes, Dr. Michael," is generally the reply.

"Then the authority to baptize has already been given to you by Jesus himself."

As we are on God's mission, our authority as believers is transmitted to us directly from our risen Lord: "All authority in heaven and on earth has been given to me. Go therefore and make disciples of all nations, baptizing them in the name of the Father and of the Son and of the Holy Spirit, teaching them to observe all that I have commanded you. And behold, I am with you always, to the end of the age" (Matt 28:18–20).

Only Christ is the head of the church. The promoting of individuals into positions of authority must be done with care and must recognize the gifting of the entire church for ministry. When those in authority do the ministry, then we are in jeopardy of becoming an institution—recruiting volunteers rather than equipping disciples to make more disciples—as we will see in chapters 7 and 8.

※

---

45. The fact that Paul does not mention the names of people he knew in Ephesus or Asia could indicate an early date for the writing of the letter, perhaps as early as AD 53 or 54, at the beginning of the work in Ephesus.

Lest we think that Paul's letter was a moral theology or that Paul was a moral philosopher, we would do well to pay attention to the life of the author himself. Paul clearly had a missiologically theocentric agenda: the declaration of God's glory to the nations and the advancement of the kingdom by its heirs. It was as much his calling as it was the calling of all who were predestined to adoption through Christ. All that he does is to the praise and glory of God, "who is the blessed and only Sovereign, the King of kings and Lord of lords, who alone has immortality, who dwells in unapproachable light, whom no one has ever seen or can see. To him be honor and eternal dominion. Amen" (1 Tim 6:15–16).

This conviction grounded the movement in Asia, and it was reinforced by the sound doctrine of its leaders, something we will discuss in the next two chapters. The moment when God's glory is no longer the focus of equipping the saints, the movement might continue to do good things, but it will cease to do the main thing that will sustain its growth—the subject of chapter 9.

The election and predestination topics so common among Western theologians, beginning with Augustine and then to Calvin and now the Reformed theology of many evangelicals today, place the focal point of texts like Ephesians 1 on us. Such an anthropocentric application risks losing the passion of the first-century movement of God that sought his glorification by declaring the mystery of his will so that more people would worship him. Unfortunately, our human nature tends to make Scripture about ourselves. In so doing, we incessantly attempt to discover God's will for our lives in fulfillment of an elusive calling that gives us purpose.

What Ephesians teaches us is that God's will is not about us. Instead, it is about God's glorification through his gracious activity of drawing together a movement of the elect, who are about their Father's work for his praise and glory. Our satisfaction and our identity, then, are wrapped up in three things: our *belonging* to a community solely focused on God's mission; our *behavior*, which is always moving in the direction of fulfilling God's will; and our *beliefs*, when they rightly emphasize God's glory.

A theocentric reading of Ephesians places God's will as the unifying theme of the letter. God's will—period. It also takes any question regarding our purpose and relegates it to obscurity, as the question is already answered. Being in God's family means our identity focuses on doing God's business. His mission. When we miss this point, our movement becomes an anthropocentric institution in search of purpose.

Retaining the God-focused fulfillment of our adoption emboldens a movement intent on God's glorification by proclaiming the gospel to the nations so that more tribes, languages, and people will be worshipping before his throne

(Rev 7:9). That was the work of the first love of the church in Ephesus, and it must also be the first love of a movement whose vision is more people following Jesus every day (Eph 6:24). That first love, however, must be modeled by the leaders of a movement, who will pass it on to faithful people who will teach others—matters we will address in the next two chapters.

# CHAPTER 7

# Leading a Movement

"Are you prepared to be like the other missionaries?" asked Canon Moses, executive director of the Anglican-initiated Here's Life in Uganda. My friend, Rev. Justus Miwanda, and I were meeting Canon Moses at the Namirebe Guest House in Kampala, trying to discern which tribes in the country were still unengaged. Our information indicated that four people groups were yet to hear the gospel. Two of them, the Nubi and a group of South Asians, were near Kampala. The other two—the Lulba, a group of refugees from the Sudan civil war (in the northwest), and the Ik (in the mountains of the northeast)— were close to the border of the war-torn country of South Sudan.

It is interesting to think that Christianity has been in Africa since one of the first so-called "deacons," Philip, explained the gospel to the Ethiopian eunuch in Acts 8:26–40. I am sure that Jesus and his family discussed spiritual things with the people they encountered in Egypt when they were displaced from their homeland as well (Matt 2:13–15). For more than two thousand years there has been a Christian presence on the continent. At the birth of modern missions, Africa was a focus of many efforts that were so effective that nearly every sub-Saharan African country has a majority Christian population. So it might come as a surprise that there are still tribes in some countries who have not heard the news of great joy that is for all people. In addition to the four tribes in Uganda, there are sixteen tribes in Ethiopia, nine tribes in Burkina Faso, and eight tribes in Ghana who do not have a Christian worker among them. The task is still not finished in Africa.

As we were planning our next steps to engage these people groups, we were fully aware that many might be resistant to the gospel. I wondered what Canon Moses really meant by his question, so I asked him to clarify it. He said that the first Western missionaries came to Africa with their belongings packed in a coffin, knowing there was a good chance they would not return home. The history of missions on that continent, even modern history, is dotted with the gravestones of many missionaries who were killed by those they were trying to reach or who died of various diseases. These challenges continue to confront Christian missionaries around the world. We were reminded of this when we heard the story of one Ugandan pastor who was caned for reaching out to the Nubi, a Muslim tribe about a two-hour drive outside of Kampala.

God uses special people to lead and multiply a movement, if for no other reason than these are people ready to count the cost so that more people will worship God. The next two chapters form a critical juncture for a movement. It is no exaggeration to say that a movement will thrive or fail based on its leaders. Their commitment to trusting the Holy Spirit to work in the lives of those they equip and empower is risky in the human sense; but as we learned in the previous chapter, God's desire is to see all his adopted children engaged in his work of bringing more worshippers to him.

Movement leaders should inspire followers of God to join them in the awesome privilege of being on God's mission to unite all things in Christ. These leaders recognize Jesus as the head of the church and that Jesus is building his church (Matt 16:17–18) as they make disciples (Matt 28:18–20). Paul and Timothy absolutely exhibited this movement leadership. However, they were not alone. There were at least twenty-six named disciples who worked in Asia to spread the good news (see table 22). Two other apostles also connected with the movement; John and Peter were movement leaders focused on God's mission. Along with the other movement leaders, they called the disciples to join together to see God's glory proclaimed and inspired other disciples in Asia as well.

In this chapter we will look briefly at Peter and John, and then we will turn our attention to Paul's band of movement leaders who were called "deacons." It is important to understand the development of leadership structures in the early church and the fact that there were hints of institutionalization beginning in the second century. Finally, we will consider the Ephesian model of movement leadership that became instrumental in the ongoing growth of the saints in the movement.

## Movement Leaders

If we learn anything from studying the lives of the first leaders of the Christian movement—those original twelve disciples who walked with Jesus—it is that they were rough around the edges. They came from all walks of life—fishermen, zealots, a tax collector—with diverse interests and understandings of why Jesus came (Mark 8:27–29). When we read their stories in the canonical Gospels, we find ourselves wondering if they really get it. Yet these same disciples were empowered by the Holy Spirit and used by God in fantastic ways as co-laborers in connecting his story with the story of the nations.

Peter, perhaps the boldest of the first disciples, always seemed to have his proverbial foot in his mouth. His relationship with John must have been fun to watch, as God used the two of them together in marvelous ways. Through their witness, the gospel was proclaimed to the Jewish religious authorities (Acts 3:17–26) as well as to Samaritans (Acts 8:14–17), and the lame were healed (Acts 3:1–10). Ultimately, they both connected with the movement in Asia: Around AD 64 or 65, Peter encouraged the churches suffering persecution through a letter; and in AD 68 or 69, John moved to Ephesus, perhaps to escape the Jewish War, and eventually wrote his Gospel.[46]

In chapter five, I discussed the significance of John's Gospel as an example of missiological theology. John uniquely connected with the Ephesian culture to tell Jesus' story and dovetailed it in such a way that the Ephesians also saw their story. While John's Gospel is evangelistic in nature and written to connect with the nations, Peter's focus is the disciples living throughout Asia. Specifically addressed to the "elect exiles of the Dispersion" (1 Peter 1:1), Peter wrote as one who knew Christ. His message to these believers is clear: Christians are to arm themselves with the same attitude as Christ; they are to stop sinning; live according to God's will because the end is near; gently and respectfully preach the gospel to non-Christians; be attentive and serious in prayer; treat others with love; and serve others with the gifts that God has given them.

Peter is fully aware that this will not be an easy assignment, but neither was Jesus' suffering (2:21–23). The social upheaval, both religious and economic, that the Way created across Asia had resulted in slanderous accusations, ostracism, mob riots, and local police action (2:13–17; 3:13). As Peter turns his attention to the movement leaders, they are to bear witness to the true grace of God (5:12), bringing doctrine and practice together so that Christians will know how they should conduct themselves in the face of anti-Christian hostility, never shrinking from making a defense for the faith.

Peter's letter and John's Gospel show us one thing for certain: their lives had been so radically impacted by Jesus that they were not the same people we met when they were called (Mark 2:16–20). John, one of the Sons of Thunder

---

46. I have suggested a date prior to AD 70 for John's Gospel, primarily due to the lack of reference to the destruction of the Second Temple.

(Mark 3:17), who postured himself at the request of his mother to sit with Jesus in his kingdom (Matt 20:20–21), became known as the disciple of love (1 John 2:5, 10, 15; 3:1, 10, 11, 14, 16–18, 23; 4:7–12, 16–21; 5:1–3). Peter, as we learn from John, was impulsive, as when he cut off the ear of Malchus (John 18:10); contemptuous, as when he would not allow Jesus to wash his feet (John 13:8–9); and humiliated, when he denied Christ (John 13:36–38; 18:15–18, 25–27). However, Peter was also loved by Christ and forever changed by God's grace (John 21:15–19).

The love of Christ that changed Peter and John so thoroughly also changes a movement leader from someone who lords authority over others to someone who serves others like Jesus (Matt 20:25–28). Consider how Peter described this kind of leader in his letter to the churches in Asia:

> So I exhort the elders among you, as a fellow elder and a witness of the sufferings of Christ, as well as a partaker in the glory that is going to be revealed: shepherd the flock of God that is among you, exercising oversight, not under compulsion, but willingly, as God would have you; not for shameful gain, but eagerly; not domineering over those in your charge, but being examples to the flock. And when the chief Shepherd appears, you will receive the unfading crown of glory. (1 Peter 5:1–4)

At the core of movement leadership is a love for God and a love for people. It is that love which demonstrates, as John reminds us, that we are disciples of Christ (John 13:35). This love is blind to human hierarchy and only sees Christ as the ultimate movement leader, the head of the church. Love—that all-important characteristic of a movement leader—cannot be downplayed. It is motivated by God's glory and understands that God is most glorified when more people worship him. Equally so, it understands that joy is found in our identity in Christ (John 15:11) rather than in an assumed authority over others. It recognizes that there is one head of the church, Jesus, and its attention is focused on equipping the saints to make him known around the κόσμος (*cosmos*).

## Paul and His Band of Movement Leaders

As we observed in grounding a movement (the previous chapter), the responsibility of leadership fell largely on a group of people who were charged with equipping the saints for works of ministry (Eph 4:11–12). Before we address Paul and his community of movement leaders, the question we have to raise, related to leadership and the growth of the early Christian movement, is: What form or structure might explain such significant growth? One of the keys to answering this question is understanding the people who were in the middle of the growth. What did they do to launch a movement of rapidly multiplying disciples all over the Roman province of Asia, Asia, and the Roman Empire? Addressing these two questions requires us to hold our contemporary forms of leadership loosely in recognition that the modern-day church—the present phenomenon that typically meets in a structure and requires multiple layers of leadership to care for both the spiritual lives of congregants as well as the physical infrastructure that has evolved to serve them—is not the same as the simple house-church movement that exploded across the Roman Empire in the first century.

To begin to take the step to hold our leadership forms loosely will also require us to understand that the manner in which New Testament leadership has been interpreted for the modern-day church organization is vastly different from the leadership that actually emerged in the first-century movement. Our contemporary interpretations of leadership are often founded on English translations that betray a particular bias in regard to ecclesiastic structures. Translators undoubtedly have the best of intentions when bringing the biblical text from the original language to the language of a culture. Nevertheless, it is challenging to bracket one's interpretative act from not being informed by one's experience and cultural context.

When we do theology in community, we mitigate these biases. Yet a community bias might emerge out of local cultural contexts, necessitating a larger hermeneutical community that includes brothers and sisters from different cultures participating in the process of missiological theology. It sounds like a daunting undertaking, and it is. However, taking the time to ensure proper translation, interpretation, and application is a step to developing mature disciples who will be able to effectively take God's story and connect it to the stories of the people. Church polity is one of those areas where a bias appears to have crept into the interpretation of leadership roles early in the church's formation, and the bias continues into the twenty-first century.

One area where a bias clearly appears is in the contemporary church's understanding of the position of a deacon. In the English Standard Version (ESV) of the New Testament, the Greek word διάκονος (*diakonos*) is translated in four ways—"servant," "attendant," "minister," or "deacon." In total, the word is used twenty-eight times, and the translators only chose to render it literally as "deacon(s)" three times—and only in Paul's epistles (Phil 1:1; 1 Tim 3:8, 12). In the ESV, it is most commonly translated "servant" (eighteen times) or "minister" (seven times). Seven of the eighteen references to *diakonos* as "servant" are found outside of the Pauline corpus and exclusively in three Gospels (Matt 20:26; 23:11; Mark 9:35; 10:43; John 2:5, 9; 12:26).

Paul uses the word twenty-one times, and the ESV translates it as "servant," "minister," or "deacon." Two of those references are directed as a description of Jesus (Rom 15:8; Gal 2:17), and two references are to Satan's emissaries (2 Cor 11:15). Twelve times the word *diakonos* refers to Paul or one of his associates. In seven of those cases, the word refers to a male associate or to himself and is translated "minister:" Epaphras (Col 1:7), Paul (Eph 3:7; Col 1:23, 25), Tychicus (Eph 6:21; Col 4:7), and Paul and Timothy (2 Cor 3:6). In five cases, it is translated "servant" and refers to both male and female associates as well as to himself: Phoebe (Rom 16:1), Apollos and Paul (1 Cor 3:5), Paul and Timothy (2 Cor 6:4), Paul (2 Cor 11:23), and Timothy (1 Tim 4:6). While an argument can be made for the lexical range in Paul's use of *diakonos* to include all three iterations (servant, minister, deacon), such an argument is not necessary. In fact, since Paul uses δοῦλος (*doulos*; "bond servant") twenty-eight times, one must ask why he would use two different words to communicate a similar idea, especially since he uses *diakonos* in such a precise way as a "leader" in the church (Phil 1:1; 1 Tim 3:8, 12).

The question that emerges from the translation of the word *diakonos* in the Pauline corpus is why to prefer "minister" or "servant" over "deacon." In reference to Christ and Satan's emissaries, an argument can be made for translating the word "servant." In the remaining verses, however, there doesn't seem to be a clear context in which a preference for "minister" or "servant" is warranted over "deacon." Does this mean that we throw out eighteen centuries of church leadership structures in which the office of deacon meant carrying out "menial tasks and duties," as Thabiti Anyabwile noted (2012, 25)? Are these "menial tasks and duties" sacred responsibilities that we see demonstrated in Scripture? The responses to these two questions will help determine the church's identity as an institution or a movement.

As I look at the type of New Testament leadership that grows a movement, I am inclined to translate the word *diakonos* consistently whenever it is used in relationship to people. In doing so, the group of leaders at the heart of the movement—Paul, Timothy, Apollos, Tychicus, Epaphras, and Phoebe— were all *diakonoi*, who served the church in the following ways: as apostles (Acts 19:22; Eph 3:7), as prophets (2 Cor 3:6, 12–18), as evangelists (1 Cor 3:5–6; 2 Tim 4:5), or as shepherd-teachers (Eph 6:21–22; Col 4:7–8; 1 Tim 4:6). Such an interpretive translation puts Ephesians 4:11–12 in context: "And he gave some as the apostles, as the prophets, as the evangelists, as the shepherds who are teachers (τοὺς δὲ ποιμένας καὶ διδασκάλους, *tous de poimenas kai didaskalous*), to equip the saints for the work of ministry (εἰς ἔργον διακονίας, *eis ergon diakonias*), for building up the body of Christ" (my translation).

Using this plain reading of the texts, Paul saw leadership as a community function rather than as a hierarchy. The goal of leadership was to equip believers for ministry (διακονία; *diakonia*). Paul uses the Greek *diakonia* (ministry) as much for what others were to do as for what he also did. He spoke about the *diakonia* of reconciliation in 2 Corinthians 5:18 and his *diakonia* to the Gentiles in Romans 11:13. The *diakonia* was not to make anyone stumble (2 Cor 6:3). Both Archippus (Col 4:17) and Timothy (2 Tim 4:5) were to fulfill their *diakonia*, and Mark was useful to Paul for *diakonia* (2 Tim 4:11).

What we sometimes fail to see in Paul is his desire to include everyone in *diakonia*. Each disciple was to be a part of *diakonia*, just as he was. Paul seems to love to place himself alongside of others in *diakonia*. We have already seen him include himself with Timothy, Apollos, Epaphras, Tychicus, and Phoebe. We have seen him coauthor seven of his thirteen epistles with Silvanus (1 Thess 1:1; 2 Thess 1:1), Timothy (2 Cor 1:1; Phil 1:1; Col 1:1; 1 Thess 1:1; 2 Thess 1:1; Phlm 1), and Sosthenes (1 Cor 1:1). Perhaps nowhere is Paul's shared leadership highlighted better than in Romans 16:3–16:

> Greet Prisca and Aquila, my fellow workers in Christ Jesus, who risked their necks for my life, to whom not only I give thanks but all the churches of the Gentiles give thanks as well. Greet also the church in their house. Greet my beloved Epaenetus, who was the first convert to Christ in Asia. Greet Mary, who has worked hard for you. Greet Andronicus and Junia, my kinsmen and my fellow prisoners. They are well known to the apostles, and they were in Christ before me. Greet Ampliatus, my beloved in the Lord. Greet Urbanus, our fellow worker in Christ, and my beloved Stachys. Greet Apelles, who is approved in Christ. Greet those who belong to the family of Aristobulus. Greet my kinsman Herodion. Greet those in the Lord who belong to the family of Narcissus. Greet those workers in the Lord, Tryphaena and Tryphosa. Greet the beloved Persis, who has worked hard in the Lord. Greet Rufus, chosen in the Lord; also his mother, who has been a mother to me as well. Greet Asyncritus, Phlegon, Hermes, Patrobas, Hermas, and the brothers who are with them. Greet Philologus, Julia, Nereus and his sister, and Olympas, and all the saints who are with them. Greet one another with a holy kiss. All the churches of Christ greet you.

What a remarkable example of community leadership. Just consider the terms: "fellow workers," "my kinsmen," "my fellow prisoners," "my beloved"— terms of affection from one movement leader to other movement leaders. Paul's leadership focused on equipping more leaders, and he believed that all disciples—those who had been adopted into the family of God (Eph 1:5)— were also responsible for *diakonia* just as he was responsible for *diakonia*.

This in no way diminishes Paul's leadership. On the contrary, Paul's leadership is set apart as that which motivated others to continue on God's mission of seeing more people worship him. It is a leadership that distinguishes a movement from an institution.

There is a clear danger when a movement becomes focused on a single leader. The number of heresies that grow out of Asia, beginning in the second century, testifies to the danger of elevating individuals to prominent places in the Christian community. Many of those heresies are remembered because of the name of the heretic: Marcion and Arius, to name two. The popularity of their beliefs led many astray and serves as a reminder that movement leaders must be aware of the difference between them and charismatic leaders.

## Movement Leadership versus Charismatic Leadership

Leadership sets the tone for the direction of a movement. In fact, one might argue that a movement will rise or fall largely on its leadership. To understand the effective movement leadership that we see in the New Testament is to understand the theocentric focus of the leaders. This leadership imbues a profound sense of humility, as it looks at Jesus as the chief cornerstone upon which the entire foundation of the household of God is built (Eph 2:19–22). Without him, everything crumbles under the weight of our inadequacies. It seems like we see contemporary movements regularly crumble, as leaders become enthralled with their own abilities and personalities. We see this most clearly in new religious movements (NRMs), but increasingly in the evangelical institution.

In the study of new religious movements, which are often pejoratively referred to as cults, leaders clearly take on a savior role, as followers are attracted to their charismatic personalities that often communicate their connection to God, or some supernatural force, which gave them special abilities or a position as a divine authority (Wessinger 2012; Dawson 2006). These personality cults— such as Jim Jones of the People's Temple, David Koresh of the Branch Davidians, or David Berg of the Children of God/the Family—exhibit extraordinary influence over their followers. While these extreme examples resulted in abuse and death, others have exhibited a spiritual abuse couched in Christian language that appears legitimate for a while, but they are often exposed by disillusioned followers. In recent times, one may recall Jimmy Swaggert, Jim Bakker, Ted Haggard, Mark Driscoll, Bill Hybels, and James MacDonald as well-known examples of charismatic personalities within the evangelical world who held an extreme influence over followers, thus permitting their deviant behaviors and moral failures.

We also see such examples in other places. One brother recently told me,

There is a guru-shishya concept in Indian faith. Guru is the teacher or master, and shishya is the disciple. Guru is the medium to reach a god. And he is equivalent to a god. And that's why we have so many human gods they call BABA in India, and there is a new one coming up each day. So this has crept inside the church too. There are certain people coming from Hindu faith, just exchanging the person and some church leaders taking advantage of it. Rather than directing the glory to God, they take credit to themselves and thus starting a new cult through them.

The characteristics of these leadership figures, whether in evangelicalism or in NRMs, are similar: they have an ability to form a charismatic bond with followers; they demonstrate "extraordinary" abilities to communicate with authority; and they have "extraordinary" experiences that have confirmed a divine calling. Where this type of charismatic leadership departs from movement leadership is in its anthropocentric focus, rather than the theocentric focus we see in the leaders of the New Testament movement. A cursory study of the Apostle Paul reveals multiple characteristics that are an antithesis to charismatic leaders: his self-identification as a *doulos* ("bond servant;" servant in ESV) of Christ (Rom 1:1); his self-identification as the chief of all sinners (1 Tim 1:15); his self-identification as a *diakonos* of the church (1 Cor 3:5). For Paul, this was not self-deprecation or a false humility, but the reality and realization of a life so focused on God that everything else, including himself, faded in the shadow of his glory. While Paul could rightly claim an authority over people (2 Cor 10:8), he would much rather identify himself with his co-laborers (2 Tim 1:7) and call others to join him on God's mission (1 Cor 11:1). This is the type of leadership that propels a movement into the future, as it is tied to God's mission and not their own.

There always seems to be a tendency to elevate religious personalities to such a height that the pressure and attention results in abuse. This was no different during the first century. There were many messianic figures proclaiming salvation for Israel and philosophers who amassed followings all over the Roman Empire. We have seen that Heraclitus' philosophy impacted Asia for nearly six hundred years. However, what we see in movement leaders is their deliberate focus on making Jesus famous among people—one of the reasons why Heraclitus wanes from influence.

This theocentrism is apparent in Paul, who, as we saw, mentions the three persons of the Trinity 133 times in his short circular letter to the churches of Asia. John's anonymity as the author of the Fourth Gospel is evidence that he wanted to draw his readers and listeners to Jesus and not to himself. Movement leaders are unwaveringly theocentric as they inspire Jesus' followers to join in God's mission as co-laborers—not in a hierarchical system that promotes their leadership, but rather in a community leadership among equals. These leaders knew that there was only one head of the church, and he is the only one worthy to follow.

So far we have seen movement leadership characterized by love and selflessness. Certainly movement leaders led others, and in large measure their leadership was lived out in a community. This community leadership is critical to the ongoing growth of a theocentric movement. Perhaps it was an organized community of leaders, although early movement leaders had a clear understanding that only Christ was the head of the church and everyone else served the head with the gifts he had given them (1 Cor 12). It is also apparent that movement leaders in Ephesus pointed people to God (Eph 4:13). As we know, however, movements need structure, and the manner in which a movement is structured also factors into whether it becomes an institution or continues expanding its influence more broadly.

## Movement Structures

If there is a chronology to leadership development of the New Testament church movement, then we would conclude that elders were the first leadership position established prior to the death of James, the brother of John, in AD 44 (Acts 12:1–2), when they are first mentioned (Acts 11:30). Most likely a Jewish synagogue influence, Paul and Barnabas continued this tradition and appointed elders in the new churches of Galatia around AD 49. We see this tradition confirmed in Ephesus as well, around AD 57, as we consider Paul's meeting with the elders in Acts 20. David Hesselgrave summarizes this succinctly:

> New Testament believers, therefore, had a model for church leadership and organization. It is not to be inferred that they followed this synagogue pattern rigidly, however. The point is that the early believers were aware of basic ways and means for conducting corporate spiritual life and business. (1980, 351)

Since I have suggested an early date for 1 Timothy, the positions of deacon and overseer must have been established around AD 55 or 56. This is later confirmed in Philippi, when Paul and Timothy wrote to the bishops and deacons in AD 63. It appears that the only churches that established a threefold leadership were those in Ephesus and presumably others in Asia (overseer [1 Tim 3:1–7], elders [Acts 20:17] and deacons [1 Tim 3:8–13]). However, were such structures Paul's intention? Even more so, how did such a structure propel growth in the early church? These are the questions a movement thinker must ask.

The form of leadership emerging out of the movement in Ephesus focused on propelling the gospel to the nations so that more people would worship God. There would be no place for a monarchial episcopate. There was no place for any type of hierarchical structure of leadership in the movement, whether elder-ruled or congregation-ruled ecclesiastical polities. Such a leadership was neither observed in first-century Christianity nor taught by Jesus. Instead, what we see in the early movement is a form of leadership that functioned as a community engaged in maturing disciples and evangelizing the lost. It was not a community bogged down with endless staff meetings. It did not form committees for building campaigns. It wasn't even concerned with having the latest training material for children's ministry. This leadership fully engaged in God's mission of more people coming before his throne and following its only leader, Christ himself.

## Leadership Structure in the Early Church

As you will recall, stage two of the life cycle of a movement concentrates on training qualified people to lead the movement, and Paul clearly has leadership in mind as he ensures the ongoing maturation of saints in Asia. By the end of his tenure in Ephesus, multiple elders had been appointed to care for the church (Acts 20:17). However, as the movement grew, it appears that new positions of leadership emerged. By the time Paul writes his first letter to Timothy, it is clear that three types of leaders are distinguished in the movement of Ephesus: bishop, or overseer; elders; and deacons, or ministers.

In the living memory of Paul, that is, the period of time when the next generations were alive at the same time as Paul, several letters were written by early church leaders who noticeably indicated that the churches in Asia and Achaia exhibited this threefold leadership. Clement of Rome writes about the leadership structure in the church in Corinth (1 Clement). Ignatius of Antioch alludes to this structure in his letters to the churches in Philadelphia, Ephesus, Magnesia, Tralles, and Smyrna. Polycarp is well aware of the threefold leadership in the churches of Asia also. The bishops-elders-deacons leadership model no doubt developed to accommodate the phenomenal growth of the church in the Roman Empire. By the time of Clement, Ignatius, and Polycarp, Christianity made up nearly 2 percent of the entire empire—approximately 861,000 people gathering in homes to hear God's Word, worship, pray, fellowship, and continue to extend the gospel through their social networks (see table 10).

The church needed a leadership structure that would accommodate such growth and help thrust it to new levels. Important to note, Paul did not create this structure in a vacuum. Just like the form of leadership emerging in the

Jewish church, that which emerged in the Gentile church reflected leadership structures observed in the culture. The bishop, or overseer (ἐπίσκοπος; *"episkopos"*), for example, emerged in the church out of a context where such a title was given to leaders who held positions in the city or in private associations or volunteer organizations in the Greco-Roman world (Zamfir 2012). For example, in Athenian Constitution written around 325 BC, Aristotle notes that the Council of the Areopagus functioned as an *episkopos,*

> And he made a Council of four hundred members, a hundred from each tribe, but appointed the Council of the Areopagus to the duty of guarding the laws, just as it had existed even before as overseer [ἐπίσκοπος] of the constitution, and it was this Council that kept watch over the greatest and the most important of the affairs of state, in particular correcting offenders with sovereign powers both to fine and punish, and making returns of its expenditure to the Acropolis without adding a statement of the reason for the outlay, and trying persons that conspired to put down the democracy, Solon having laid down a law of impeachment in regard to them. (8.4)

Similarly, Appian of Alexandria (AD 95–165), writing about the Mithridatic wars that took place in the first century BC, uses episkopos to describe someone who held authority over a particular region. He writes, "Eumenes was afterward adjudged an enemy of Macedonia and put to death, and Antipater, who succeeded Perdiccas as overseer [ἐπίσκοπος] of the territory of Alexander, appointed Nicanor satrap of Cappadocia." (Mithridatic Wars 2.8)

It would only be natural that Paul sought a structure that reflected leadership of the culture, yet, as we will see, it becomes a leadership infused with the moral character concomitant with being a follower of Christ.

Outside of the New Testament, we have our first glimpse of this structure in the letters of Ignatius of Antioch. In his letter to the church in Magnesia, he writes:

> Since, then, in the persons mentioned before I have with the eyes of the faith looked upon your whole community and have come to love it, I exhort you to strive to do all things in harmony with God: the bishop is to preside in the place of God, while the presbyters are to function as the council of the Apostles, and the deacons, who are most dear to me, are entrusted with the ministry of Jesus Christ who before time began was with the Father and has at last appeared. (*Magnesiums* 6)

Ignatius believed that the bishop, presbyters (i.e., elders), and deacons were responsible for keeping the unity in the church (*Philadelphians* 7). Of deacons, Ignatius writes, "It is further necessary that the deacons, the dispensers of the mysteries of Jesus Christ, should win approval of all in every way; for they are not dispensers of food and drink, but ministers of a church of God. Hence, they must be on their guard against criticism, as against fire" (*Trallians* 2.3). By Ignatius' time, the church appears to be institutionalizing around leadership positions, as he also begins to delineate between clergy and laity,[47] something completely foreign to the New Testament authors, yet permissible as an ecclesiological opinion.

We should fully expect some sort of institutionalizing of leadership, and that is what we see going into the second century of the church. Before too much longer, schools to prepare people to teach sound doctrine begin to emerge, such as the Alexandrian School and the Antiochian School, each with their distinctive theological opinions. People in ministry now would be recognized by formal education as well as ordination. By the fourth century, church councils laid down rules for the clergy and exercised formal disciplinary actions against those whose lives did not adhere to the apostles' teaching.

Over the course of four centuries, leadership took on human structures that would have been unrecognizable to Paul and his community of movement leaders. So, it is to 1 Timothy that we turn to see a type of movement leadership that inspired believers to follow Christ and join in God's mission.

## The Movement Leaders of Ephesus

First Timothy, which is commonly referred to as the first pastoral epistle, is a letter of instructions from one *diakonos* to another. The nomenclature of "pastoral epistle" is misleading, as the word pastor does not appear in the three Pauline epistles—1 Timothy, 2 Timothy, and Titus—bearing that anachronistic moniker. As we have discussed, cultural bias often informs our interpretation of texts; and 1 and 2 Timothy, as well as Titus, were not immune to such bias. This "pastoral epistle" reference first appears in the eighteenth century in the writings of D. N. Berdot and Paul Anton (*Guthrie* 1990, 17). Perhaps such a view might have emerged out of the notion that the pastoral epistles were considered "church manuals" to guide leaders in structuring the church's governance and ministry.

Instead of focusing on the leadership of a movement that continued on God's mission to unite all things in Christ, scholars have treated the "pastorals" as instructions for ordering the church's prayer life, the position of women, leaders, and models for ministry (Fee 1985, 142). However, Gordon Fee asserts that 1 Timothy is directed as much to the young leader as to the house churches

---

47. Ignatius writes, "Let all things therefore be done by you with good order in Christ. Let the laity be subject to the deacons; the deacons to the presbyters; the presbyters to the bishop; the bishop to Christ, even as He is to the Father" (*Smyrnaeans 9*).

and their elders in Ephesus who were struggling with the growing number of false teachers (ibid., 141–51).[48] This purpose cannot be lost, for a movement, as mentioned, will rise or fall on the movement's leadership. When that leadership deviates from the original cause, then the movement eventually declines toward death. The church in Ephesus seemed to be on its way to decline, as several known to Paul and Timothy, perhaps even some who were elders, were straying from the truth. Their names have faded from history as a mere footnote to the movement that continued to spread successfully across the world.[49]

At the core of understanding 1 Timothy as a letter focused on leading a movement is understanding Paul and Timothy's friendship. Friendship might be too light of a word to describe what is one of the most inspiring relationships in the Bible. For Paul, Timothy was not simply a friend, not even a mere colleague or coworker, but he was like a son (Phil 2:22; 1 Tim 1:2). We do not have much detail of their first meeting, but we can certainly fill in the gaps as we read the accounts of their travels, as well as the six epistles they coauthored.

Timothy came to Christ during Paul and Barnabas' first missionary journey through the region of Galatia. His family was ethnically diverse, with a Greek father and Hebrew mother. The faith of his father is unclear. He could have been a God-fearing Greek, perhaps a soldier or farmer (2 Tim 2:3–4, 6), but due to a lack of reference to him, it is difficult to maintain such suggestions. He certainly must have been either sympathetic to Christianity or deceased; otherwise it seems unlikely that he would have allowed his son to travel with Paul. The fact that Timothy was not circumcised (Acts 16:3) might point to his father's unbelief and the probability that Timothy did not take part in education at a synagogue. No doubt, as Paul alludes, Timothy grew up learning the Hebrew Scriptures (2 Tim 3:14–16), most likely from his Hebrew mother and grandmother (2 Tim 1:5) rather than in a formal synagogue setting where most children would learn the Jewish faith.

It seems probable that Timothy was an athlete and valued physical fitness of some sort (1 Tim 4:8; 2 Tim 2:5). Unquestionably, this would have been important, if not necessary, for all his travel and responsibility—and what responsibility he had! As a young fellow worker, Paul left him, together with Silas, to continue the work in Thessalonica (Acts 17:14–15) and seemed to lean heavily on him to help mature disciples there (1 Thess 3:2). Paul sent Timothy to Corinth to remind the believers to follow Paul's example (1 Cor 4:16–17), and Paul might have sent him to Philippi so that he could learn how the church was doing (Phil 2:19–22). Paul left Timothy in charge of an extremely difficult

---

48. Note the first-person plural pronoun used in the final greeting in 1 Tim 6:20.

49. Paul lists those leaders who had gone astray: Phygelus and Hermogenes (2 Tim 1:15); Hymenaeus (1 Tim 1:20) and Philetus (2 Tim 2:17); Demas (2 Tim 4:10); Alexander (1 Tim 1:20; 2 Tim 4:14).

situation in Ephesus (1 Tim 1:3), and he called him to come see him one last time during his imprisonment in Rome (2 Tim 4:9), where Timothy himself would eventually be imprisoned (Heb 13:23).[50] Paul recognized Timothy's gifts and empowered him to use them for the extension of God's mission in the world. There was a level of mutual trust that can only come from the realization that the Holy Spirit indwelled each of them equally.

Trusting the leading of the Holy Spirit is of paramount importance, not so much in terms of the leader's life, as this is naturally assumed, but in the lives of those he or she is leading. If a movement leader cannot trust that the same Holy Spirit who guides him or her to also guide others, then the movement will devolve into an institution. Such a leader quickly professionalizes leadership, resulting in the exchange of biblical authority for ecclesial authority.

As a wise mentor, Paul wrote 1 Timothy to his younger, spiritual son and co-laborer of many years, giving instructions about how to lead the work in Ephesus on its movement trajectory. It appears that Ephesus had turned out to be a difficult environment for the younger *diakonos*, with many false teachers leading believers astray. Timothy is confronting them and those who do not respect the position that he holds as Paul's co-laborer. Paul shares his personal testimony as a reminder to Timothy that if Christ can work through him, the chief of sinners, then he can work through anybody.

The letter is a personal note of instruction and encouragement to Timothy and the disciples. Paul instructs him in the manner in which believers should live: how they conduct themselves in a Christian community; selection of an overseer and deacons; and ministry to different groups in the church. He warns Timothy against the false teachers and instructs him to keep the truth of sound doctrine as a responsible servant of the church. Paul encourages Timothy to fight the good fight, to live godly, and he reminds him that he is a gifted and faithful servant of the Lord.

All of Paul's instructions are in the context of what Timothy already knows about being a follower of Christ. He is to be on God's mission. He is to "wage the good warfare" (1 Tim 1:18), undeniably a reference to the spiritual battle of advancing God's kingdom in Ephesians 6. Timothy is to pray with purpose and call people from all of the house churches to pray knowing that God desires all—Jews, Gentiles, kings—to come to the knowledge of the truth (1 Tim 2:1–8). This was Paul's calling and it is to be Timothy's as well. In fact, it is to be the calling of every movement leader and those they disciple. Then Paul's

---

50. There are at least three reasons I believe Timothy was imprisoned in Rome: 1) he ostensibly visited Paul while he was imprisoned in Rome; 2) the anonymity of Hebrews might suggest Priscilla as the author, which would further suggest it was written from Rome (Rom 16:3); 3) Timothy was apparently in the same location as the author.

missiologically theocentric focus on God's mission is beautifully described: "[Jesus] was manifested in the flesh, vindicated by the Spirit, seen by angels, proclaimed among the nations, believed on in the world, taken up in glory" (1 Tim 3:16).

## Leadership Structure of a Movement

The leader of a movement must have the capacity to assess the most effective structure for ongoing growth. In 1 Timothy 3, Paul introduces Timothy to what appears to be a new level of leadership: the overseer (Greek ἐπίσκοπος; "*episkopos*"). The ESV translates the Greek τις ἐπισκοπῆς (*tis episkopes*) in 1 Timothy 3:1 as "the office of overseer." Zamfir notes that this position in the Greco-Roman world represents "a person who supervises the observance of laws or ethical norms, the order of the city, the life of a religious community, or the course of certain activities" (2012, 206). Indeed, the *episkopos* could have been the one charged with the "menial tasks" so often attributed to deacons as they gave oversight to such matters—even financial—of the city (ibid., 218). Paul's reference to the *episkopos* being free from the love of money lends credence to such an assertion. Yet it is apparent that Paul is much more concerned about this individual's character than the title, as he is with other leaders in the church, such as deacons and elders. In other words, the character of a leader was far more important to Paul than the positional title and function.

| Overseer | Deacons |
|---|---|
| 1 Timothy 3:1-7 | 1 Timothy 3:8-13 |
| Aspires to office of overseer | Dignified |
| Above reproach | Not double-tongued |
| Husband of one wife | Not addicted to much wine |
| Sober-minded | Not greedy |
| Self-controlled | Hold to the mystery of the faith |
| Respectable | Tested |
| Hospitable | Blameless |
| Able to teach | Not slanderous |
| Not a drunkard | Sober-minded |
| Not violent | Faithful in all things |
| Gentle | Husband of one wife |
| Not quarrelsome | Managing children and household well |

| Not a lover of money | |
|---|---|
| Manage own household well | |
| Not a recent convert | |
| Well thought of by outsiders | |

TABLE 20: OVERSEER AND DEACONS

Since we have already discussed the role of deacons, all that remains to be said is in reference to what some have suggested were the original "deacons" in Acts 6, as well as the role of women as deacons. First, most of the conversation regarding the role of the deacon emanates from the speculation that the first deacons were the seven chosen by the church in Jerusalem (Acts 6:1–6). While this was a long-held belief in the first three centuries of the church, many New Testament scholars today see a distinction between the deacons of 1 Timothy 3 and those of Acts 6. These prominent figures in Acts 6 were men full of the Holy Spirit and of wisdom, and we see two of them actively engaging people with the gospel. Whether they were deacons in the sense of 1 Timothy 3 is doubtful. In the first place, Luke never refers to them with that title. He does refer to their ministry of serving tables with the word *diakonia*, but he uses the same word to refer to the apostles in their ministry (*diakonia*) of the word and prayer. As McGiffert put it in the late 1800s, "There is just as much reason, therefore, on linguistic grounds, for calling the apostles 'deacons' as for giving that name to the Seven" (1890, 103). In fact, if Paul and Timothy, as well as Phoebe, bore the function of an apostle and were called deacons, then it might make more sense to see the apostles of Act 6 as deacons and the Seven as overseers or elders who cared for the flock.

The idea of the roles of the seven so-called deacons in Acts 6, however, persists. In the church today, the deacon is the one who "serves tables." As Anyabwile noted, "Therefore, you want to make sure that the potential deacon understands his role as an opportunity to free up the ministry of the Word and prayer, not to compete with it" (2012, 24). In spite of the biblical data clearly suggesting that the Acts 6 "deacon" evangelized and performed signs and wonders (Acts 6:8; 8:5), the perception that this individual waited on tables leads the contemporary church in the direction of institutionalization. There is no place in Scripture that suggests the *diakonos* held a position that took care of the menial tasks of a church.

Second, 1 Timothy 3:11 is another one of those verses where interpretation affected translation. The ESV renders the Greek γυναῖκας ὡσαύτως (*gynaikas hosautos*) as "Their wives likewise … " Due to the absence of the third-person plural possessive pronoun "their" in the Greek, there is no reason to equate γυναῖκας with the deacons' wives. Instead, *gynaikas* has the lexical range of "women" or "wives," indicating that either could be used in this instance. No matter which translation is used, though, it is clear that Paul expected women to be deacons equally with men.

Writing to Emperor Trajan (AD 98–117) about the early Christians, Pliny, the governor of Pontus and Bithynia, a region in Asia along the southern coast of the Black Sea, reported his encounter with the Christians he persecuted:

> Accordingly, I judged it all the more necessary to find out what the truth was by torturing two female slaves who were called deaconesses. But I discovered nothing else but depraved, excessive superstition. (*Letters* 10.96–97)

Clearly within the living memory of the early movement, even of those Christian and civic leaders going into the second century, women also served as deacons. As discussed above, Phoebe was one of the early examples (Rom 16:1). Euodia and Syntyche might also be included among the ranks of women deacons who "labored side by side with [Paul] in the gospel ..." (Phil 4:2). Junia, whom Paul identifies as among the apostles, would also qualify in the role of a deacon (Rom 16:7).[51] This was not a title of an ecclesial position, but a role that God used to mature disciples and spread the gospel.

The deacons, those men and women who served God, played a key role in preparing the church for ministry. Their character was just as important as their ability to equip believers. As we have seen with the overseer/bishop, the character of movement leaders is just as critical to the ongoing work of God's mission (see table 20). That character connected on every level of a movement leader's life: personal, marriage, family, relationships with employees or employers, and relationships with those in the community. We might use words like *integrity* and *authenticity* today; but in whatever way their lives were described, Paul expected them to live to a high standard.

From overseer and deacons, we move to a third leadership responsibility in the movement at Ephesus: that of the elders. We meet this group in Acts 20:28, as Paul was on his way to Jerusalem. Luke does not tell us how many there were, but we get a hint, as Paul appears to have taught them from house to house (Acts 20:20). Similar to the expected character of the overseer and deacons, elders cared for God's church by teaching correct doctrine and protecting her from false teaching. There was clearly a council or presbytery of elders, some of whom received some sort of remuneration for their service, something that we do not explicitly see for the position of an overseer.

---

51. The ESV translation of the Greek of Rom 16:7, οἵτινές εἰσιν ἐπίσημοι ἐν τοῖς ἀποστόλοις, makes it apparent that there is a bias against women in what is perceived to be a prominent position of ecclesial authority ("they are well known to the apostles"). The preposition ἐν is of place when connected to the dative τοῖς ἀποστόλοις, and should be translated "who are notable among the apostles." That is, they—Andronicus and Junia—are to be included among the other apostles.

If deacons are as I have laid out above, they were also remunerated in some manner as they served the church (Phil 4:14–16). For example, Paul clearly stated that while he was in Ephesus, he ensured his own personal needs, as well as those who worked with him (Acts 20:33–34). In Corinth, that was through a trade (Acts 18:1–3). The situation in Ephesus is less clear, yet it is not outside the realm of possibility to presume some sort of remuneration for Paul's hard work at the philosophical school of Tyrannus. Perhaps it is more likely that he continued in the tentmaking trade with Priscilla and Aquila, who were also in Ephesus, although it might have limited his ability to travel as much as he did in those years in Asia. Whatever the case, there were some elders and deacons who were compensated for their works of service in the church.

| Elders | |
|---|---|
| Acts 20:28-31 | Titus 1:5-9 |
| Pays careful attention to themselves | Above reproach |
| Pays careful attention to the flock | Husband of one wife |
| Is alert to false teaching | Children are believers |
| 1 Tim 4:14; 5:17-20 | Not arrogant |
| Council of elders | Not quick-tempered |
| Worthy of wages | Not a drunkard |
| | Not violent |
| | Not greedy |
| | Hospitable |
| | Lover of good |
| | Self-controlled |
| | Upright |
| | Holy |
| | Disciplined |
| | Hold firm to the word as taught |
| | Give instruction in sound doctrine |
| | Rebuke those who contradict it |

TABLE 21: CHARACTERISTICS AND DUTIES OF ELDERS

Again, as we see in tables 20 and 21, what appears to be clear in Paul's descriptions of the bishop, elders, and deacons is that character was far more important than title. Additionally, there is considerable overlap between the roles, as they all held similar responsibilities in preserving doctrine, discipling, and equipping the saints. However, many suggest that the bishop and elder are conflated into one type of leader, while the deacon remains distinct in his or her role as a servant who ensures that elders can teach and pray. I do not see this distinction in the New Testament, although I do see an allowance to make such a distinction based on an institutional model. Movements simply do not need a position that takes care of the menial tasks of a church, primarily because there are no menial tasks when all are called to be equipped for ministry and multiply disciples as they join in God's mission to bring more people to worship him.

People have a natural tendency to organize and systematize. Structures help provide order, and there is little doubt that the early church did likewise. How the church organized in the first century was a key determining factor to its ongoing growth. The leadership structure in Ephesus provides an example of a community of leaders charged with the continuing responsibility of partnering with God on his mission. This community of leaders held the responsibility to ensure the church stayed on track doctrinally, as they empowered believers in works of ministry while they declared the gospel from person to person, house to house, and in the marketplace. This leadership modeled what they observed in the lives of Paul, Timothy, John, and Peter. They loved the flock God placed in their charge. They selflessly cared for their needs. They also inspired them to be on God's mission, while not lording an ecclesial authority over them.

The most profound experience I have ever had in regard to leadership—and one of the greatest privileges I have had in ministry—occurred during my first years on staff with Cru. I joined Cru right out of college and was given an international assignment working in Eastern Europe and the Soviet Union, affectionately known as "Budzaria." Named after the Cru pioneer, Nelson "Bud" Hinkson, Budzaria was the "end of the world," where the missionary became a combination of Indiana Jones and James Bond. Or so we dreamed (perhaps *hallucinated* is a more accurate description)!

It was the Cold War era. Ronald Reagan had labeled the Soviet Union as the Evil Empire and boldly demanded that Mikhail Gorbachev tear down the Berlin Wall. For young, politically conservative, evangelical Americans, nothing could have been more exciting than to see Jesus Christ overthrow communism. And we did. What began in Czechoslovakia as the Velvet Revolution spread to

Hungary and Poland, then ended in a bloody battle on the streets of Timişoara and Bucureşti, Romania. The Soviet satellite countries were falling left and right, and we did not waste any time.

As a young twenty-something missionary, I totally felt like Timothy when Bud asked me to go with Daniel Sims to Romania to check on our brothers and sisters. It was as if Dan were Silas and we were traveling back to Thessalonica to check on the believers' progress. About ten days after Ceauşescu's execution on 25 December 1989, we drove from Starnberg, West Germany, to Timişoara, Romania. Along the way we stopped in Salzburg to pick up medical supplies and in Budapest to pick up Bibles. When we finally arrived at the border of Romania, we were welcomed as heroes; however, we also became targets of opportunity. But I digress.

I often think of the honor it was to serve with Bud during those days as something that Timothy must have felt while serving with Paul. Certainly many others who worked with Bud, as well as with Paul, felt the same way. There was something about Bud that made him a magnet for those of us who aspired to sacrifice everything for the gospel. We were ready to carry in our coffins and give our lives for the cause, just like those early missionaries to Africa.

Bud was a ball of fire who cared deeply for people and did not lord his position over them. His example of leadership demanded from us, but he also gave to us. He was always fast to listen and encourage. Bud took on God's mission with the same energy as an athlete competing at the top of his physical condition—and an athlete he was, as I have many fond memories of chasing him on his Czechoslovakian road bike up 4- and 5-percent grades in the foothills of the Alps. In his pursuit of joining with God on his mission, Bud's eyes were set on the prize of the upward call of God in Christ Jesus, and he set an example for us to follow. Bud was a movement leader who was largely responsible for starting movements on communist university campuses all over Eastern Europe and the Soviet Union. If ever there were an example of a movement leader similar to those in Ephesus, in my view it was Bud.

The best-known movement leaders in Ephesus were Paul and Timothy, but we might also talk about Priscilla and Aquila, who joined Paul on his first trip to Ephesus and remained there to continue the work (Acts 18:18–28), as well as Aristarchus and Gaius, who were held hostage until the intervention of the town clerk (Acts 19:29). And many other individuals, as we will see in the next chapter, exhibited the ability to lead a movement in continued growth. Their model was Paul, but they also saw the same qualities in John and Peter. It was a model that valued love of others and selflessness, as well as comradery, while they led as a community of equals who were empowered by the Holy Spirit to carry on the missiologically theocentric call of God and prepared others for the same task. They didn't have to squabble about strategy or ministry philosophy, because they all knew they were about fulfilling God's will to unite all things in Christ.

It was that type of inspiring leadership that compelled others to follow Christ and share his message with the world. Many of them gave their lives—willingly, as a sacrifice—just as they were called to do as imitators of God (Eph 5:1–2). It is no wonder that the disciples continued to multiply.

# CHAPTER 8

# *Multiplying a Movement*

Nearly every Thursday evening during my university days, I heard a long-time friend say something to this effect: "Welcome to Campus Crusade for Christ. Founded in 1951 on the campus of UCLA by Dr. Bill and Vonnette Bright, Campus Crusade works on university campuses in the United States and across the world." Amazingly, by the 1980s Campus Crusade for Christ (now known as Cru) had become one of the largest mission organizations in the world. Bright's simple model of "win, build, send" catalyzed thousands of university students to fulfill the Great Commission in this generation. The staff-directed, student-led movement multiplied disciples in a way that had not been seen for decades. It was not a unique approach, but rather one that began in the early days of Christianity.

Cru's multiplication strategy focused on preparing people to share their faith and disciple new believers in order to send them into the harvest field to share their faith and disciple others. Those student leaders motivated to win their campus for Christ typically took part in a discipleship group with one of the Cru staff. Weekly Bible studies, one-on-one discipleship, and regularly doing evangelism on campus were core aspects of our involvement and the model for our own discipleship.

When I arrived at A&M in 1983, I became a part of David Figari's small group. David and I both came to Christ at Northbrook High School in Houston, Texas, through the ministry of Mike Crandall and the staff of Student Venture. Mike faithfully discipled David and me, as well as many others, and helped build a foundation for the love of God that continues in both of our lives today. By my second year at A&M, I began leading a small group. Then, in my third year, I became a student leader and began to be discipled by the Cru campus director, Ray Anderson. A condition for being in Ray's group was that we were moving the people we were discipling in the direction of starting their own discipleship groups. As far as I can remember, my stream of discipleship only made it to the third generation, which was typical of those who were discipled by a Cru staff person. In the 1980s Cru at Texas A&M became one of the largest campus ministries in the world, with more than three hundred small groups in one of three types of Bible studies: Discovery Group, Discipleship Group, or Action Group.

I learned during those days with Ray that a movement, instead of a life cycle, involves a rhythm. A life cycle naturally comes to an end, and as we have seen historically, the decline of a movement is manifested in it becoming an institution or obsolete altogether (Addison 2019). A rhythm anticipates periods of growth and solidification and more growth. That was the beauty of the "win, build, send" model of Cru's ministry.

So at the start of each academic year, students and staff would plan this rhythm, which often incorporated major outreach events like Josh McDowell, who loved coming to Texas A&M, or the magician Andre Kole, in order for us to amass a pool of individuals to follow up on during the course of the semester. Discipleship Groups, then, would commit to reaching out to the hundreds of contacts we gathered, and each small group participant was equipped to begin a new Discovery Group with these new disciples. The rhythm would continue the following semester, with a greater focus on discipleship and engaging those who were a part of a Discovery Group in weekly evangelism. This rhythm only slowed during the summers, when literally thousands of students would travel the world on short-term missions trips to apply what they had learned on their respective campuses in other countries with other university students.

Today, with twenty-five thousand missionaries working in 190 countries, impacting more than two thousand universities, as well as other segments of society, Cru's global impact is nothing short of spectacular. Bright's vision to reach the world for Christ through college students is still the core of Cru's work. It was that vision which inspired many of us to leave our potentially lucrative careers for the sake of fulfilling the Great Commission in our generation. This is still my vision, and it is the vision of thousands of others, but it can only be accomplished through a ministry of spiritual multiplication.

## Spiritual Multiplication

Spiritual multiplication is not difficult. In fact, it is astonishingly simple. The idea, of course, comes from 2 Timothy 2:2: "What you [G2] have heard from me [G1] entrust to faithful men [G3], who will be able to teach others also [G4]." Spiritual multiplication, an anachronistic term for sure, is a principle of exponential growth to four generations. Paul represents a first-generation disciple (G1) who continues to make more disciples, one of whom was Timothy (G2). In Ephesus, Paul had at least eight additional named disciples (G2), who presumably applied the same spiritual multiplication asked of Timothy. These G2 disciples were then expected to make more disciples (G3), who would, in turn, make even more disciples (G4).

This is not simply adding people who identify as Christians, but it is multiplying the number of Christians who are disciple-makers. It is the difference between the reproductive growth of most mammals and the exponential cellular growth that constitutes the mammal or any cellular structure. It is the growth of disciples who continue to make disciples over time. This type of disciple-making represents a movement of individuals who have committed everything to see that more and more people worship God.

Mathematically speaking, the exponential growth of spiritual multiplication can be formulated as follows: $y=ab^x$, where $y$ equals the number of disciples made over time ($x$); $a$ equals the number of disciples making disciples; $b$ equals the number of disciples who will make more disciples; and $x$ equals the number of years disciples are being made.

If we apply this formula to Ephesus and use 2 Timothy 2:2 as the expectation for disciple-making, then the number of disciples making disciples would have been remarkable. So the number of named disciples working with Paul (G1) in Ephesus was at least 9 (G2). If Paul and these 9 (G2) each made 10 disciples annually (G3), who made 10 more disciples each (G4), then the exponential growth over the approximate three years Paul was in Ephesus would be $y=10(10^3)$, or 10,000 disciples. Granted, there were false teachers who adversely impacted the movement and led people astray. Nevertheless, we easily see that a movement occurred through spiritual multiplication.

| Disciples Working in Ephesus | Disciples Working in Asia |
|---|---|
| Priscilla and Aquila (Acts 18:18–19) | Lydia of Lydia (Acts 16:11–15) |
| Timothy (Acts 19:22) | Luke of Troas (Acts 16:10; Col 4:14) |
| Erastus (Acts 19:22) | Phoebe of Cenchreae (Rom 16:1) |
| Gaius (Acts 19:29) | Epaenetus (Rom 16:5) |
| Aristarchus (Acts 19:29) | Trophimus (Acts 20:4) |
| Alexander (Acts 19:33) | Mark (Col 4:10) |
| Tychicus (Acts 20:4; Eph 6:21; 2 Tim 4:12) | Epaphras (Col 4:12) |
| Stephanas (1 Cor 16:17) | Demas (Col 4:14) |

*Table continues on next page.*

| Disciples Working in Ephesus | Disciples Working in Asia |
|---|---|
| Fortunatus (1 Cor 16:17) | Nympha (Col 4:15) |
| Achaicus (1 Cor 16:17) | Archippus (Col 4:17) |
| Onesiphorus (2 Tim 1:16) | Philemon (Phlm 1) |
| | Apphia (Phlm 1) |
| | Archippus (Phlm 1) |
| | Onesimus (Phlm 10; Col 4:9) |

TABLE 22: NAMED DISCIPLES IN EPHESUS AND ASIA

In an ideal scenario, the growth of the movement in Ephesus, or any other place in the world, would have been phenomenal. Certainly this is overly simplistic and assumes that all disciples are making more disciples. If that actually happened, then the whole world would have been evangelized in the second century. The estimated global population in the first century was 330 million. It would have taken Paul and his nine disciples less than eight years to reach the entire planet with the gospel.[52] In fact, if 2 Timothy 2:2 was actually practiced in the church today, the task of world evangelization could be finished tomorrow.[53] All that is necessary is for each of us to lead three people to Christ in the next twenty-four hours. With more than 2,500 plans for world evangelization, why should this not be possible (Johnson and Zurlo 2020)?

In reality, there are many factors that hinder 2 Timothy 2:2 type of exponential growth:

1. **Geography**—although certainly not as much of a factor as it was in the first century, the difficulty to reach those who have not heard about Christ continues to present a challenge for world evangelization. Many unengaged unreached people groups (UUPGs) are unengaged simply because they live in remote areas that are practically and logistically difficult to reach.

2. **Level of commitment of disciples**—the World Christian Encyclopedia estimates the population of nominal Christians at 1.76 billion. The number of Christians who ostensibly believe in the necessity of gospel proclamation and would most likely be the ones to take the gospel to those who have never heard is 1.98 billion. Additionally, there are an estimated four hundred thousand full-time missionaries, representing 0.002 percent of this Christian population, with less than 2 percent of these missionaries actually going where they are needed most (Johnson and Zurlo 2020).

---

52. $y = 10(10^8) = 1,000,000,000$
53. $y = 3 \text{ billion } (3^1) = 9,000,000,000$

3. **Financial and organizational**—modern missions has created a financial and organizational system based on a business model that focuses on the personal well-being of the missionary, among other things. Today, in addition to a missionary's salary, missionaries raise money for health care, education, and retirement, as well as an administrative percentage to pay for organizational structures needed to support missionaries while they are deployed on the field (personnel in Human Resources, Accounting, Marketing, Communications, Security, Member Care, Development).

4. **Use of God's resources**—the global church spends more money on itself than it does on reaching those in need of the gospel. For instance, for every $588,000 spent by the global church, only one person is baptized (ibid.).

5. **Fear of persecution**—government seizure of church property, payment of bounties for Christians, as well as social pressures act as deterrents to the continued growth of Christianity in areas where Christian faith is nominal. At times, persecution can be self-inflicted if we lack respect for others (Acts 19:37). Even so, the *World Christian Encyclopedia* estimates that 487 Christians die every day from martyrdom (ibid.).

6. **False teachers and syncretism**—one does not have to look far to see the growing number of false teachers propagating a theology of personal well-being, wealth and prosperity, or the soon arrival of the apocalypse. In addition, evangelistic efforts lacking in discipleship are creating syncretistic churches that are confused about the call of Christ to renounce former allegiances.

7. **Immorality and hypocrisy**—the moral failure of Christian leaders and the hypocrisy of the church actually repel people from listening to the gospel, as well as act as a catalyst for Christians to leave the church, if not also to walk away from the faith (Packard 2015).

8. **Risk aversion**—churches are afraid to rock the boat. Due in part to the concern for sustaining the infrastructure that has formed to advance the ministries of church staff, taking the risk to multiply disciples places staff positions in jeopardy as more and more people are engaged in the ministry and are equipped to make more disciples.

These obstacles do not necessarily have to be roadblocks, but they have created challenges that the Christian movement faces every day. In the first century, the list of obstacles might not have been as long; but nevertheless, there were still obstacles. We will see in the next chapter that false apostles and immorality could have derailed the movement in Ephesus if the church would have persisted to abandon the work of her first love. Thankfully, that did not

# EPHESIOLOGY

happen, and the lampstand of the church continued to shine in a culture that desperately searched for a god to worship.

So let us turn once again to those first three years of Paul's ministry to see how the disciples multiplied. Then we will look at four key aspects of Paul's instructions to Timothy that encouraged the multiplication of disciples.

## The Nascent Movement in Asia

Paul's instructions to Timothy in what we call his second epistle was the model for the growth of the early church. It is what propelled the church from a small band of 120 disciples between AD 27 and 29 to a movement of an estimated 95,000 by AD 67, approximately eight hundred times larger than when it started (table 23). In Ephesus, the movement began with zero and in three years, as I suggested, grew to at least 541 and likely even more. Then, by AD 67 it constituted 10 percent of the city's population (see table 9 on page 31). But what evidence is there for this exponential multiplication of the movement?

| Year | Est. Number of Christians | Est. Empire Population | % of Population |
|------|---------------------------|------------------------|-----------------|
| 30 | 14,000 | 45,000,000 | 0.03% |
| 67 | 95,710 | 51,160,500 | 0.19% |
| 100 | 861,124 | 54,945,000 | 1.57% |
| 150 | 1,925,132 | 65,000,000 | 2.96% |
| 170 | 2,389,019 | 40,000,000 | 5.97% |
| 300 | 5,500,000 | 55,000,000 | 10.00% |

TABLE 23: REVISION OF RODNEY STARK'S ESTIMATES (SEE DISCUSSION REGARDING TABLE 10)

As we have seen, the movement in Ephesus began in Acts 18:19 when Paul, Priscilla, and Aquila first landed on the banks of the city in the late summer of AD 51 (Schnabel 2004, 1219). As was Paul's custom, he entered the synagogue and began to dialogue with the Jews. Paul's message was so compelling that the Jews wanted him to delay his departure to Antioch. We don't know exactly why, but Paul was determined to visit the church that had originally sent him and Barnabas on their first missionary journey (Acts 13). So he left Priscilla and Aquila with the responsibility for the nascent movement.

This was not their first opportunity to lead a church, however. As we learned in Acts 18:2, Priscilla and Aquila arrived in Corinth as a result of Claudius' expulsion of Jews from Rome sometime between AD 41 and 47. When Paul arrived in Corinth from Athens in AD 48, he went to see them, implying that they could have been known by Paul, perhaps due to their work in Rome. We learn later that the couple returned to their home city, where a church met in their house, sometime around AD 56 or 57 (Rom 16:3–5). When that church actually started is unknown, but we know that there was a Christian presence in Rome, most likely due to Jewish Christians from Rome who were in Jerusalem on the day of Pentecost (Acts 2:10). Paul had an experienced couple as fellow laborers for the gospel, and they were well equipped for ministry and explaining Scripture. He entrusted the work into their capable hands, and it continued to grow.

We might assume that a church started as a result of Paul's activities in the synagogue (Acts 18:18) but the text isn't clear until we see οἱ ἀδελφοὶ (*oi adelphoi*; "the brothers") in Acts 18:27. Nevertheless, the first evidence of conversion growth in Ephesus occurred when Priscilla and Aquila engaged Apollos with the gospel (Acts 18:24–28). An eloquent teacher of Scripture who knew the way of the Lord, Apollos spoke boldly in the synagogue where Paul had taught. Priscilla and Aquila continued their ministry in the same synagogue and heard Apollos speak, only to realize that he only knew the baptism of John. After they explained the gospel more accurately to him, Apollos set off for Achaia. Before departing, however, Luke tells us that "the brothers encouraged him and wrote to the disciples to welcome him" (Acts 18:27).

These *adelphoi* ("brothers") a term that Eckhard Schnabel points out is used for Christians (ibid., 1218), represent the first disciples. No number of disciples is given, but it is clear that they are the fruit of Paul's initial engagement in the synagogue and Priscilla and Aquilla's continued ministry in Ephesus. Therefore, it is likely that a church began in AD 51, when Paul, Priscilla, and Aquilla presented the gospel in the synagogue of the city. That church continued to grow under the leadership of Paul's faithful co-laborers to such an extent that there was a recognized body of "brothers" who might have already been known by the disciples in Corinth, as they addressed a letter to the disciples of the Corinthian church on behalf of Apollos.

Eventually Paul returns to Ephesus, but not before traveling throughout Galatia and Phrygia to encourage the churches that had already formed (Acts 18:23). Once he "strengthened the disciples," Luke notes that Paul traveled throughout the inland country on his way to the city. He had been prevented from going to this area at the beginning of his second missionary journey (Acts 16:6), but now appeared to be the proper occasion. It seems unlikely that he was traveling alone, although the text makes no reference to his fellow peripatetics. Nevertheless, his trek could have taken him from Asia Phrygia to Laodicea, Philadelphia, Sardis, Smyrna, Thyatira, and Pergamum—the other six churches of Revelation 2–3. Others have suggested that Paul's route back to Ephesus went through the highland region from Apameia to the Kaystros Valley through sixteen cities and villages along the way to Ephesus (ibid., 1200).

No matter the route to Ephesus, there is little doubt that Paul evangelized along the way and more disciples were made. It also afforded Paul an opportunity to learn about the culture of the Roman province of Asia as well as other parts of Asia as he dialogued with people, observed their practices and customs, and learned their history. He passed through regions where prominent temples were dedicated to the worship of Roman emperors and Greek gods and goddesses. In these regions the indigenous philosophy of Heraclitus was renowned, perhaps more than the philosophy of Socrates, Plato, and Aristotle. Occasionally Paul encountered a Jewish synagogue where he would, most assuredly, be invited to give testimony about Christ. After nearly two months of travel, beginning in Antioch and covering an estimated 810 miles, Paul finally arrived in Ephesus in the late spring or summer of AD 52, well prepared to engage people with the story of God.

## Multiplying the Movement in Ephesus

As we have seen, during Paul's initial visit to Ephesus, a church started among the Jews, and Paul's faithful companions, Priscilla and Aquilla, nurtured the new disciples in their faith. It is reasonable to expect that the small community of Jewish Christians continued to grow during Paul's absence. These faithful people now understood that their Messiah had come. God was indeed with them, just as they expected ever since Isaiah prophesied, "Therefore the Lord himself will give you a sign. Behold, the virgin shall conceive and bear a son, and shall call his name Immanuel" (Isaiah 7:14).

The Hebrew University demographer, Sergio Della Pergola, estimates that there were as many as 4.5 million Jews in the Roman Empire in the first century, representing about 10 percent of the total Roman population. An estimated 2.5 million Jews lived in Palestine, leaving the remaining 2 million spread throughout the conquered lands (Botticini and Eckstein 2012, 16–17). If these estimates are accurate, it would be reasonable to suggest a Jewish population for cities with a synagogue at between 2 and 4 percent. During Paul's tenure in Ephesus, there could have been between 1,000 and 2,000 Jews.[54]

No matter how many Jews lived in the city, people continued to respond to the good news of great joy, as the sons and daughters of Abraham learned of the long-awaited blessing. In chapter 2, I suggested a 1.06 percent response rate to the gospel during the first few months of the new church in Jerusalem. If the same were true in Ephesus, then we might expect that the new church began with ten to twenty disciples from the synagogue who responded positively to Paul's story of the Messiah (Acts 18:19–21, 27).

---

54. Josephus relates a decree written in 43 BC that recognized a Jewish presence in Ephesus (Antiquities 14.225-28).

Once Paul returned to the city (Acts 19:1), he encountered twelve men who Luke calls "disciples." These men were possibly companions of Apollos, but, like Apollos, they were believers who only knew John's baptism. Paul shared about the arrival of the Holy Spirit and they were baptized in the name of Lord Jesus (Acts 19:5). In approximately five months' time, the number of disciples in Ephesus at least doubled, and the Jews continued to show interest in learning more, as Luke tells us, "[Paul] entered the synagogue and for three months spoke boldly, reasoning (διαλέγομαι; *dialegomai*) and persuading them about the kingdom of God" (Acts 19:8). His persuasion must have been successful, as he dialogued with the exact people group who expected a Messiah. Nevertheless, there were some who, as Luke says, "became stubborn and continued in unbelief, speaking evil of the Way before the congregation" (Acts 19:9).

It should not escape our notice that the movement's identity was not with Paul or any other named disciple. The movement was identified with the moniker "the Way," first used in Acts 9:2 as the movement Saul (aka Paul) persecuted. Paul uses the moniker as well in his testimony before the Jews in Jerusalem (Acts 22:4). Even though Luke focuses his history of the early church on Paul, it is the Way that is persecuted. This movement's identity firmly focused on a missiologically theocentric understanding that it was not the people of the movement who were persecuted, but rather Jesus himself (Acts 9:5).

As we have seen, persecution, no matter how great or small, is often a sign that a cause is impacting a society. The mounting tensions resulting from the dissonance between Judaism and "the Way" hit a tipping point that threatened the status quo of the synagogue. Now, with perhaps as many as one hundred or two hundred disciples, Paul withdrew from the Jews and turned to the Gentiles, "reasoning [*dialegomai*] daily in the hall of Tyrannus" (Acts 19:9). Well equipped with his study of Heraclitus and observations of temple practices associated with Artemis and the sundry gods and goddesses worshipped in the city, the movement prospered, "so that all the residents of Asia heard the word of the Lord, both Jews and Greeks" (Acts 19:10).

The progress of the gospel was so extraordinary that people were being healed of diseases and demonic oppression. Practitioners of the magical arts, which contributed to the renown of Ephesus, were burning their books; "so the word of the Lord continued to increase and prevail mightily" (Acts 19:20). Luke tells us that the cost of the magical texts amounted to fifty thousand pieces of silver, nearly 137 years of wages, if these were silver drachmas (Schnabel 2004, 1221). While there is no way to estimate the number of magicians this might represent, it is safe to assume that there were many who converted to Christ. The events that transpired through the faithful witness of Paul and the disciples became known to all of the estimated 51,000 residents of Ephesus, so that the church grew to an estimated five hundred disciples over the next few months.

The growth was not abated or deterred in spite of mounting opposition to "the Way," beginning first from the Jews and now from the Greeks. The increasing number of disciples had an economic impact on the worship of Artemis (Acts 19:24). Such an impact suggests that a significant number of those who rejected the idols made of human hands had turned to the living λόγος (*logos*), who was foretold by Ephesus' most renowned philosopher. Six hundred years prior to Paul's arrival, he wrote:

> Although this λόγος ever exists, men are ignorant both before they hear and after they have once heard. For even though all things happen in accordance with this λόγος, they are like men of no experience when they experience words and deeds such as these, when I distinguish each thing according to its nature and explain how it is. Other men are as unaware of what they do when awake as they forget what they do when asleep. (Heraclitus, *On Nature*, Frag 1)[55]

These words, once veiled in a text housed in the temple of Artemis, were now revealed in the word of the Lord proclaimed by Paul and the disciples. Students of philosophy, practitioners of the magical arts, worshippers of the goddesses and gods imagined in temples dotting the landscape—in fact, all the residents of the great city who were as proud of the massive structure perched on the hill as they were of their own philosopher, whose book was in the temple—heard the true meaning of the *logos*, and it turned the city upside down. The disciples were multiplying. It was not accomplished perfectly, but the impact on the socioeconomic fabric of the city is undeniable, as "a wide door for effective work has opened to [Paul], and there are many adversaries" (1 Cor 16:8). In spite of the adversaries, by AD 53 there were likely hundreds of disciples meeting in houses all over Asia and Ephesus (1 Cor 16:19). The house churches prospered as a result of spiritual multiplication, the natural result of disciples fully engaged in a missiologically theocentric passion for God's mission and committed to more people worshipping him.

## Timothy's Multiplication of Disciples

The idea of spiritual multiplication did not begin when Paul wrote 2 Timothy 2:2.[56] It was the principle for growth in the early church modeled by Paul and reiterated throughout his epistles. From Corinth, in AD 50 or 51, he wrote to the church in Thessalonica, "For not only has the word of the Lord sounded forth from you in Macedonia and Achaia, but your faith in God has gone forth everywhere, so that

---

55. In regard to λόγος (*logos*), Edward Hussey points out, "This shows that the *logos* exists and has authority independently of what Heraclitus may happen to say; so that it is not in virtue of being Heraclitus' account that it has the properties mentioned" (1982, 57).

56. It would be safe to say that the principle of spiritual multiplication begins with Christ's commission to make disciples (Matt 28:18-20). This is the normal expectation for those who call themselves a disciple of Christ. Simply stated, disciples make disciples.

we need not say anything" (1 Thess 1:8). Again from Corinth, in AD 58, he told the growing movement in Rome that "your faith is proclaimed in all the world" (Rom 1:8). Perhaps from a Roman imprisonment in AD 61, Paul and Timothy wrote to encourage the Philippians in their partnership in the gospel (Phil 1:5). Similarly, to the Colossians, the two wrote, "Let your speech always be gracious, seasoned with salt, so that you may know how you ought to answer each person" (Col 4:6). The proclamation of the gospel and the making of disciples were paramount in the movement, and Timothy was smack in the middle as a co-laborer.

However, Timothy faced a particularly difficult situation in Ephesus. The church was rocked with false teaching. Several key leaders who had worked with Paul had been led astray in heresy (2 Tim 1:15). Quarrels about silly myths, as well as sexual immorality, threatened the growing influence of the disciples on the region (2 Tim 2:16, 22). Now Timothy was charged to continue the multiplication of the movement and ensure its fidelity to the Christian faith (2 Tim 3:14–16). To do so, Paul reminded him to remain strong in Christ's grace and entrust what he has learned to faithful people who will continue to pass it on to others (2 Tim 2:1–2).

What we observed in 1 Timothy we also see here: A leader who is taking time to equip his disciples to lead a movement is a leader committed to the long-term maturation of those he disciples and to the development of more leaders. The result is simply the church that Christ promised to build. Paul is this type of leader. He is not an organizational leader. He did not write vision or mission statements. Instead, he accepted the mission of God and inspired others to follow his example of utilizing the gift he had been entrusted with to unite all things in Christ. Successful multiplication of disciples is achieved to the degree that disciples see their disciple-maker just as engaged in making disciples as he has called them to be. This is a movement leader, who, like Paul, can call his disciples to "do all to the glory of God. Give no offense to Jews or to Greeks or to the church of God, just as I try to please everyone in everything I do, not seeking my own advantage, but that of many, that they may be saved. Be imitators of me, as I am of Christ" (1 Cor 10:31–11:1).

Second Timothy, the most personal and intimate of all of Paul's letters, finds him back in prison awaiting his execution. The apostle is feeling alone, but maintains a wonderful perspective of being Christ's prisoner rather than a prisoner of the Roman government. Only Luke is by Paul's side as he writes to his longtime friend and movement partner, Timothy. All in Asia have left him: one disciple became attached to worldly things, another close friend is dead, and other friends are in different parts of the world.

In this most personal letter, we read of Paul's passion for the movement of God and the movement leader's life. We get a sense of his pain because many had fallen away from the faith. We also sense his great love and affection for Timothy. They had been co-laborers for nearly twenty years when Paul writes. Timothy is discouraged at the plight of the church, and Paul encourages him with a timely letter of appreciation and commitment for his son in the faith. In the midst of these challenges, Paul clearly calls Timothy to continue building the movement by making disciples.

Unlike his first letter, which focused attention on specific cultural, doctrinal, and ecclesiastical issues, his second letter focused on the personal and ministry life of a movement leader. These two aspects of a movement leader's life were not bifurcated; rather, they were integrated. For Paul, a movement leader's identity was solely based on the fact that he was adopted into God's family. His entire life was united in God's mission. It is what woke him in the morning and allowed him to rest at night. It paid no attention to the number of hours worked per week. It was not a job that ensured a comfortable life and financial security. It gave all and it risked all for the sake of God's mission, and it did so with a clear conscience before God and people (2 Tim 1:3).

We see four key areas in Paul's instructions that ensure the ongoing multiplication of a movement. These are not strategic initiatives. They are not evaluating current trends to determine the direction for God's mission. They do not have goals and target numbers to reach. Instead, they are focused on a movement leader's individual competencies at their intersection with God's will of uniting all things in Christ (Eph 1:10). So we see Paul's leadership expressed in 1) empowering Timothy to use his gifts; 2) inspiring Timothy to join in suffering; 3) entrusting Timothy to teach others; and 4) reminding Timothy to preach the Word.

### Empower Movement Leaders to Use Their Gifts

After Paul ensured Timothy of his continual prayers and deep desire to see him again, he encouraged him in his faith and reminded him of his giftedness (2 Tim 1:3–7). In three of Paul's letters, he writes about spiritual gifting as a grace given to the believer by the Holy Spirit (Rom 12:3–8; 1 Cor 12:1–11; Eph 4:11). Spiritual gifts were not personality traits or talents, but special abilities instilled in the believer by God and recognized in the church as a means to build the body of Christ.

While we are clear on Paul's gift as a preacher, apostle, and teacher (2 Tim 1:11), Timothy's gift is less defined. Traditionally, we have thought of Timothy as being timid, and so Paul states, "for God gave us a spirit not of fear but of power and love and self-control" (2 Tim 1:7). However, this seems peculiar, as we have seen Timothy charged with leadership tasks in the most challenging places in the Roman Empire. Additionally, Timothy was with Paul and Silas in Philippi when they were thrown in jail (Acts 16:19–24). In Thessalonica, Timothy was present when the Jews raided the house of Jason (Acts 17:5). In Corinth, Timothy witnessed Sosthenes' beating before Gallio (Acts 18:17). Finally, Timothy himself was imprisoned (Heb 13:23), perhaps in the same dungeon in Rome after he visited Paul. "Timid" would not be the word I would chose to describe this movement leader!

Perhaps Timothy was an evangelist, since Paul encourages him to "do the work of an evangelist, fulfill your ministry [διακονίαν; *diakonian*]" (2 Tim 4:5). As we discussed in the last chapter, a movement leader's responsibility is to prepare the saints for works of ministry (Eph 4:12). So Paul might have equipped Timothy for the work of an evangelist, or the work of an evangelist was Timothy's ministry (*diakonian*) and therefore his gifting. Timothy was also an encourager and teacher, as Paul entrusted him to visit the church in Thessalonica in order "to establish and exhort you in your faith" (1 Thess 3:2). Throughout his second letter, Paul reminds Timothy to teach those in Ephesus (2 Tim 2:2, 14, 24–25; 3:16; 4:2). No matter Timothy's God-gifted ability, a movement leader is to use his or her gift for the building up of the saints in a manner that leads to the multiplication of disciples.

Over the years there has been a trend in Christian leadership development to focus on personality profiles—Myers-Briggs, DiSC, Style of Influence indicators, or the nine Enneagram types—for determining a person's place in ministry. This was absolutely foreign to the early movement leaders—not because personality profiles did not exist. They did exist. The earliest recorded attempt to understand human temperaments were by Hippocrates and Galen in the fourth century BC (Ruch 1992). For the early movement leaders, God was the one who gifted people, and the expectation was that all people would use their gifts in accordance with their purpose—as much for works of ministry (*diakonia*) as for service to one another (Eph 4:12; 1 Peter 4:10).

If a movement is going to multiply effectively, movement leaders must be using their gift to empower others to use their gift. Movement leaders are not concerned about a personal or organizational agenda, because their only agenda is God's mission of more and more people worshipping him. They are not building a brand that attracts clients. They are concerned with making disciples who are equipped in their giftedness to join in God's mission; and then they turn them loose, trusting their disciples as Paul did Timothy, when he wrote, "For this reason I remind you to fan into flame the gift of God, which is in you through the laying on of my hands" (2 Tim 1:6).

We should not misunderstand the distribution of the gift as something passed from one person to another. Paul knew that God the Holy Spirit distributed gifts as he deemed necessary (1 Cor 12:11). In Timothy's case, confirmation of the gift came by a prophecy through the council of elders (1 Tim 4:14), as Paul affirmed through the laying on of his hands that God indeed gifted Timothy (2 Tim 1:6b). The gifting of movement leaders is recognized and confirmed by others. The gift is not determined by an assessment, but demonstrated in the context of God's mission.

**Inspire Movement Leaders to Join in Suffering**

In the previous chapter, we observed a community of leaders inspired by the beautiful relationships Paul had with people all over the Roman Empire. Paul had an ability to include others in the partnership of the gospel, thus inspiring them to go the distance in their service to God. Obviously, some did not finish the race. Early on in his missionary travels, Paul lost Mark for some unknown reason (Acts 13:13), only later to be reunited, as Paul recognized Mark's contribution to God's mission (Col 4:10; 2 Tim 4:11). Demas was another who put his hand to the plough, only to turn back to the world (2 Tim 4:10).

There is no way for us to know what exactly transpired, but it would be altogether presumptuous of us to think that Paul's style of ministry or personality was at fault, even though many suspect as much. It seems to me that this is beyond what the biblical text allows, since we have numerous instances of positive relationships between Paul and others, not to mention the fact that the unity of believers was a prominent theme in his epistles.

Paul's relationship with Timothy was not atypical, as Paul had the same affection for others (Rom 12:10; Phil 1:8). However, at this moment when Timothy seems the most discouraged, Paul reminds him that they are in this movement together:

> Therefore do not be ashamed of the testimony about our Lord, nor of me his prisoner, but share in suffering [together] for the gospel by the power of God, who saved *us* and called *us* to a holy calling, not because of *our* works but because of his own purpose and grace, which he gave *us* in Christ Jesus before the ages began, and which now has been manifested through the appearing of *our* Savior Christ Jesus, who abolished death and brought life and immortality to light through the gospel, for which I was appointed a preacher and apostle and teacher, which is why I suffer as I do. But I am not ashamed, for I know whom I have believed, and I am convinced that he is able to guard until that day what has been entrusted to me. (2 Tim 1:8–12; emphasis added)

In true Pauline fashion, Timothy's closest friend launches out with exuberance in a string of 105 Greek words with no punctuation, perhaps the second-longest sentence in the New Testament next to Ephesians 1:3–14, and the point is clear. Paul and Timothy are intrinsically tied together as brothers in Christ on God's mission. Timothy clearly heard Paul's reminder that Jesus is their Lord, and that he is to join in suffering with Paul. It is God who saved them and called them. Throughout the 105 words, Paul lets Timothy know that he is not alone.

Movement leaders face challenging situations. As we sat with three movement leaders who were multiplying disciples all over their country, Tapan looked at me with total seriousness and said, "Dr. Michael, I am not satisfied with you." We had spent the previous day looking at 2 Timothy and the encouragement we see in contexts where the disciples were suffering. Our brothers needed encouragement, as we sought the Holy Spirit's leading in how to proceed in a country where the threat of persecution and imprisonment are real. We had heard stories of disciples going into churchless villages and being beaten for sharing the gospel. In spite of the challenges, the men were discipling eighteen leaders, who were discipling ninety-five others, who were leading 183 house churches.

I felt a pit in my stomach when I heard Tapan's words, but I got it—so I thought. I live in a country where there is no threat of being imprisoned or beaten for sharing my faith. How in the world could I come to his country thinking I might be able to show them something from the Bible that they are not already living? With his eyes trained on mine, he continued, "We need to hear more from you."

At that moment I realized that movement leaders need to know that they are not alone. To Tapan, I took a risk, albeit nominal, to come to his country to be with him and the others. It refreshed him to see my willingness to stand alongside him and his fellow leaders and to share God's Word together.

I am no Paul, or even a Timothy. More than likely, you aren't either. Nevertheless, letting our brothers and sisters who live and work in difficult places know that we join them in their struggle inspires them to continue on God's mission to multiply disciples where there currently are none. These are movement leaders who value others, not as a commodity to achieve a goal, but as brothers and sisters adopted to fulfill God's mission.

### Entrust Movement Leaders to Teach Others

As we have noted, one aspect of Timothy's gift was teaching—no doubt one of the reasons he coauthored 1 and 2 Thessalonians in AD 50–51, 2 Corinthians in

AD 57, and Philippians, Colossians, and Philemon in AD 62–63. Paul recognized early in Timothy's spiritual development that God gifted him to communicate the Word. In this final letter, however, Paul reaffirms the necessity of not only teaching others but of following that teaching in his personal life: "Follow the pattern of the sound words that you have heard from me, in the faith and love that are in Christ Jesus" (2 Tim 1:13). Paul reiterates this importance: "But as for you, continue in what you have learned and have firmly believed, knowing from who you learned it" (2 Tim 3:14). The ability to teach begins with the application in a movement leader's own life: "By the Holy Spirit who dwells within us, guard the good deposit entrusted to you" (2 Tim 1:14).

Timothy learned from Paul, but his childhood was founded on the "sacred writings" he had heard from his mother and grandmother (2 Tim 1:5; 3:15). His example demonstrated that he not only taught the Christian life, but lived it as well. The apostle Paul sums up the life of the teacher and the responsibility of teaching God's Word best: "Do your best to present yourself to God as one approved, a worker who has no need to be ashamed, rightly handling the word of truth" (2 Tim 2:15). These were the things Paul charged him to entrust to the disciples, who would then "be able to teach others" (2 Tim 2:2).

Multiplying disciples is the responsibility of the movement leader. Instead, we often tend to outsource our discipleship. We look for the latest book or video by a well-known author who can teach us how to make disciples effectively, or plant churches, or create programs that will attract more people to our buildings. We tend to outsource our theological education as well. We need commentators to tell us what the Bible says, and we are approaching a time when we need additional commentators to tell us what the commentators are saying. It does not escape me to realize that what I just stated also applies to this book. My hope, however, is that a study of a New Testament movement will inspire a new movement focused on a missiologically theocentric reading of Scripture with the eyes of those in the first century who took part in the most fantastic outpouring of the Holy Spirit ever witnessed.

The content of what is taught is as important as the person who teaches it, and we need not look any further for it than what Paul taught the churches in Asia. If we were to use Western theological categories for Paul's Ephesian epistle, then an outline of what was taught might look like the following:

I. Salutation (1:1–2)

II. Theology Proper (1:3–23)
   A. Father (1:3–6)
   B. Christology (1:7–12)
   C. Pneumatology (1:13–14)
   D. Paul's prayer (1:15–23)

III. Theological Anthropology (2:1–22)
  A.  Hamartiology (2:1–3)
  B.  Soteriology (2:4–10)
  C.  Ecclesiology (2:11–22)
IV. Missiology (3:1–21)
V.  Practical Theology (4:1–6:20)
  A.  Ecclesiology II (4:1–10)
  B.  Charismata (4:11–16)
  C.  Christian Conduct (4:17–5:20)
  D.  Christian Submission (5:21–6:9)
  E.  Christian Battle (6:10–20)
VI. Final Salutation (6:21–24)

The danger of Western theological categories is that our study of God's Word can become a system of silos isolated from God's mission. Our systematic theology can most certainly benefit from the study of Ephesians, but that was not the author's original intent. As we have discussed, Paul was a missiological theologian in search of the connecting point between God's story and the story of people. In his missiologically theocentric grounding of the saints in Asia, Paul is most interested in the church's understanding of God's will to unite all things in Christ and how our identity as adopted children compels us to unite in God's mission to tell his story to all nations. Instead of a typical Western linear outline, a missiologically theocentric framework of Ephesians might look like the following:

FIGURE 4: GOD'S WILL

This missiologically theocentric approach to the content we teach and entrust to others to pass along produces multiplication. It is solely concerned with God's glory and the fact that he is most glorified when more people worship him. It directs us to the completion of his mission as the myopic preoccupation of our daily lives. Everything we are, our very identity, aligns with his will, and we understand the events that transpire in our lives—good ones and bad ones—through the perspective of the completion of God's mission and his glorification. A missiologically theocentric framework compels us to exclaim, "Now to him who is able to do far more abundantly than all we ask or think, according to the power at work within us, to him be glory in the church and in Christ Jesus throughout all generations, forever and ever. Amen" (Eph 3:20–21).

## Remind Movement Leaders to Preach the Word

It should go without saying, but nonetheless—for multiplication to happen, the gospel must be shared. It really is that simple. If we are not sharing the good news of great joy that is intended for all nations and reminding our disciples to do the same, then we will never see multiplication nor a movement. As we have seen, this was not the case in the movement in Ephesus. Proclamation of the gospel, by necessity, is the product of a missological theology. It connected God's story with the story of the Ephesians, and it was a story that was shared all across Asia. So Paul reminds Timothy,

> Remember Jesus Christ, risen from the dead, the offspring of David, as preached in my gospel, for which I am suffering, bound with chains as a criminal. But the word of God is not bound! Therefore I endure everything for the sake of the elect, that they also may obtain the salvation that is in Christ Jesus with eternal glory. The saying is trustworthy, for: If we have died with him, we will also live with him; if we endure, we will also reign with him; if we deny him, he also will deny us; if we are faithless, he remains faithful—for he cannot deny himself. (2 Tim 2:8–13)

I love traveling with our brothers and sisters in their countries. Their love for the Lord and for people is stimulating. Whether it is Justus in Uganda, traveling the dusty roads to Karamojong; Beni in Nepal, trekking on the Great Himalayan Trail; Reyansh in India, walking a path along the railroad track; or Juan in Colombia, hiking through the jungles—these are brothers who take every opportunity to share the gospel with everyone they encounter, no matter the risk. These are disciples who genuinely demonstrate what it means to be "all in." They model what Paul told Timothy, "Preach the word, be ready in season and out of season" (2 Tim 4:2).

These brothers remind me that whether I am in a cycling accident near Johnson Park, playing a pickup game of basketball at Hughes Park, seeing the cardiologist in Zeeland, having blood drawn at Spectrum, or working out in a fitness center at the Holiday Inn Express, I am also to "Preach the word, be ready in season and out of season." A movement leader, one whose focus is in on the completion of God's mission, has no excuse not to share the gospel wherever he encounters people. This is not an act of obedience, but rather one of identity. This person, like Paul, will exclaim at the end of his life: "For I am already being poured out as a drink offering, and the time of my departure has come. I have fought the good fight, I have finished the race, I have kept the faith" (2 Tim 4:6–7).

There is no guarantee that people will come to Christ. We do not know when someone will respond to God's call on his or her life. That is a work of the Holy Spirit. We simply need to be faithful family members participating in the family business. Bill Bright taught that successful witnessing was merely sharing the gospel in the power of the Holy Spirit and leaving the results to God. Ultimately, God is more desirous for his glory than we are, and he is at work for that glory.

Paul laid out four key areas that help ensure the ongoing multiplication of a movement: 1) empower movement leaders to use their gifts; 2) inspire movement leaders to join in suffering; 3) entrust movement leaders to teach others; and 4) encouraged movement leaders to preach the Word. I wish I could promise that if you are faithful in these areas that your church would grow or that a movement would start, but I cannot. What I can say is that Timothy was faithful in these areas, and the movement in Ephesus continued to spread throughout the city, the surrounding towns and villages, and the entire region of Asia. History testifies to the significance of this movement, whose missiologically theocentric engagement of its world with God's story continues to impact us today.

❦

One summer day in Kathmandu we sat on the carpet-covered dirt floor in a small corrugated tin structure constructed beside one brother's home. A small group of eight pastors came together for encouragement from God's Word, as we were just learning about the government's crackdown on short-term missionaries coming into the country for evangelistic purposes. The penalty for expatriates, if caught, was expulsion from the country. If a Nepali were with the group, the penalty for him would be five years in prison.

The resolve on the faces of our brothers was resolute. Nothing was going to stop them from multiplying disciples. Just a century ago there was only one known evangelical pastor in the country. Now, in a nation made up of more than 139 distinct ethnic groups, disciples have multiplied among every tribe. Still there are hundreds of villages dotting the landscape of the mountainous country that have not heard the name of Jesus, and the desperate attempt of the government to restrict the work of God's Spirit was not going to dissuade these men.

Movement leaders must have this kind of resolve to inspire the disciples to stay focused on God's mission. Paul was such a leader, and he motivated his disciples by empowering them to use their gifts, inspiring them to join in suffering, entrusting them to teach others, and reminding them to preach the Word. Such movement leadership propelled the church in Ephesus to become the most successful movement in the New Testament. The impact of the gospel across Asia was directly connected to what Paul, Priscilla, and Aquilla started in AD 51. It was not easy, and over the next couple of decades the movement continued to face challenges that threatened its witness. At a critical juncture in her history, Jesus intervened to ensure that the church stayed focused on the work of her first love. That is the subject of the penultimate chapter about this movement.

# CHAPTER 9

# Sustaining a Movement

Reverend Judy Mbugua is a towering figure in Nairobi, Kenya. Her rise as a prominent religious personality is only as significant as her heart for the poor. She may not be quite the Mother Teresa of her country, but she is certainly close. Her untiring efforts to help those in the most dreadful conditions of any world-class city is as unwavering as her faith that God can do amazing things in the lives of those living in extreme poverty.

A few years ago, I had the wonderful privilege of working with Reverend Judy on her initiatives to bring the gospel to one of the largest urban slums in Africa, if not the world. Kibera is home to thousands of families who, in many cases, left their rural homes in hopes of finding prosperity in the capital city. The rapid urbanization of Nairobi placed incredible stress on an infrastructure that was ill-prepared for such growth. The unfortunate result has been the emergence of multiple slum areas constructed on land that was allocated to Nubian soldiers serving as a British regiment in the early 1900s. The farmers and their families essentially squat on parcels wherever they find space. Electricity is virtually nonexistent. Clean water and proper sanitation present enormous problems for exacerbating preventable water-borne diseases.

It does not take long for one to recognize the appalling conditions people suffer through in an attempt to achieve a better position in life. There are no sidewalks and no sewage drains. The hand-dug trenches lining the dirt pathways between the sheet metal houses are filled with human excrement, as most do not have a toilet in their homes. The smell is oppressive. Flies landing in the places of open defecation carry filth and disease from one unsuspecting child to another.

There are many INGOs (international nongovernmental organizations) and churches working in the slums. Their well-envisioned intentions have made little difference as the population continues to swell. Nevertheless, a number of clean-water projects are providing an important resource for human well-being. Alongside of hygiene projects, clinics are treating cholera, typhoid, malaria, and dysentery. Public latrines are constructed in an attempt to discourage open defecation, yet old habits are hard to break, as you learn when your foot lands in a pile of human waste lying on a path. Educational programs largely operated by volunteers and faith-based organizers hold promise that through education people might be lifted out of extreme poverty, especially girls and women.

In a day when the social justice issues confronting the church could paralyze her, Reverend Judy stands tall as one who has not forgotten the primacy of the gospel. In an address to a group of Christian leaders representing twenty-six countries, Reverend Judy applauded their efforts to combat extreme poverty. The bravery of these leaders to unselfishly place themselves and their organizations in the proximity of injustice when others would not is an action representing the hands and feet of Christ himself. In that context, Reverend Judy reminded all of us, "It would be a terrible tragedy to help those living in deplorable condition to escape poverty only to see them miss the streets of gold."

Reverend Judy keeps the main thing the main thing. Unwaveringly committed to gospel proclamation, she sees that true hope comes only from a relationship with Jesus Christ—when one day people from every nation, tribe, and language will worship God on the new earth, where the injustices we see, and many experience, will no longer exist. It is that hope which promises a prosperous future. While addressing the needs of the poor has always been important to the church (Gal 2:10), it is not the main thing. Hope, true hope, does not come when poverty is alleviated or when everyone has clean water and proper sanitation. True hope, as Reverend Judy testifies, comes from faith in an Almighty God who alone lifts us out of the mire of our spiritual poverty whose end is far worse than the Kibera slums.

Sustaining a movement presents unique challenges. What might start as a genuine movement of the Holy Spirit, resulting in hundreds of thousands of people coming to Christ, can easily wind up as a stagnate institution maintaining a legacy only in word. It is a loss of vision for God's mission, a distraction from the original cause that will turn a movement into an ideology or philosophy. These distractions aren't necessarily bad things. In fact, they are often good things. They just aren't the main thing. They might be important to sustaining a ministry, but they could also threaten a movement.

Our focus here is to examine two ways the movement in Ephesus continued to grow and how a loss of vision nearly cost it the testimony it had shared all over Asia. Between Paul's presumed execution by decapitation around AD 67 and Timothy's imprisonment (Heb 13:23), the church continued its ministry, albeit not without struggles. Several years later, Jesus intervenes not only to encourage the church for the works she was doing, but also to admonish her for forgetting the works of her first love (Rev 2:1–7). This chapter will examine the good things the church in Asia did, and how good things can distract from the main thing—the proclamation of the good news that the nations are included in the plan of God. Throughout the rest of the book of Revelation, the Apostle John communicates the vision that all people, nations, tribes, and languages will one day worship before the throne.

Most interpretations of Revelation focus on Christianity in relationship to the second coming of Christ. Evangelicals have typically held one of four views in interpreting Revelation: futurist, idealist, historicist, or preterist (Pate 2010). While there is certainly merit in studying a system of interpreting the events in Revelation, in this chapter I will argue that John's primary focus was to continue to prophesy about the completion of God's mission, as it is the ultimate vision of God's will as expressed by Paul (Eph 1:11), John (John 20:19–23), and Peter (1 Peter 3:15). It was this vision of the completion of God's mission that Timothy worked hard to fulfill (2 Tim 4:2). That vision is the one critical key to sustaining a movement. If we squander the vision of God's mission, the movement will decline. And Ephesus was on the brink of losing that vision— the very heart of God.

## The Missiology of Revelation

The experience must have been incredible. Here they were, the eleven apostles gathered with Jesus and a number of other disciples. It would be the last time they were physically present with the resurrected Christ. Jesus, in his radiant glory, is about to ascend to the throne, where one day every knee will bow and every tongue will confess that he is Lord. There, in a field, the disciples had one last opportunity to interact with Jesus. So naturally they asked the question burning on all their minds: "Lord, will you at this time restore the kingdom of Israel?" (Acts 1:6).

It was not the first time they wondered about the answer to that question. Yet Jesus clearly taught them before his death and resurrection that no one but the Father knows the time (Matt 24:36; 25:13). They still didn't get it. I love Jesus' patience as he replies, "It is not for you to know times or seasons that the Father has fixed by his own authority. But you will receive power when the Holy Spirit has come upon you, and you will be my witnesses in Jerusalem and in all

Judea and Samaria, and to the end of the earth" (Acts 1:7–8). When the Holy Spirit came fifty days after Jesus' resurrection, they finally understood—or at least they began to understand more clearly (Acts 2:1–4).

The disciples' question continues to mesmerize many Christians today. In the nineteenth and twentieth centuries, a movement focused on eschatology (the study of the end times) arose, as dispensational premillennialism increased in popularity. The so-called Bible and prophecy conferences represented the latest theological fascination to capture the hearts and minds of those who, like the disciples, desired to know when the kingdom would be restored. Growing out of a number of historic events and developments—the Scopes trial, the Social Gospel movement, the Modernist versus Fundamentalist debates, World Wars I and II—evangelical Christians were fascinated with questions regarding Jesus' second coming and his reign during the millennial age (Sandeen 1970).

The puzzling issue, however, when considering the message of Revelation and the penchant evangelicals have for the study of the end times is what exactly changed since Jesus told his disciples, "It is not for you to know times or seasons that the Father has fixed by his own authority" (Acts 1:7). It seems to me that to interpret Revelation exclusively as a book of eschatology is to misunderstand the grand narrative of the Bible. Granted, the end will come, and the Apostle John reassures the seven churches in Asia that God is sovereign. Nothing, not even the present persecution the churches suffer, will stop God from completing what he had originally set out to do. John's charge from the angel was to keep this vision before the churches, as he was told, "You must again prophesy about many peoples and nations and languages and kings" (Rev 10:11).

So John begins his revelation to the seven churches—Ephesus, Smyrna, Pergamum, Thyatira, Sardis, Philadelphia, and Laodicea—with the reminder that they are a kingdom of priests set apart by Jesus to his God and Father (Rev 1:6). Within the churches' living memory, they would have recalled Peter's similar encouragement during a different period of persecution, or perhaps even the same period:[57] "But you are a chosen race, a royal priesthood, a holy nation, a people for his own possession, that you may proclaim the excellencies of him who called you out of darkness into his marvelous light" (1 Peter 2:9).

---

57. Irenaeus confirms that Revelation was written almost during his day, after the reign of Domitian from AD 81 to 96 (*Against Heresies* 5.30.3). There is some debate about whether there was a persecution during Domitian's period. See Brian W. Jones, *The Emperor Domitian* (New York: Routledge, 1992). If a persecution occurred, then Revelation could be dated to the reign of Nero (AD 54–68) and the first persecution of Christians. However, if Irenaeus and Jones are correct, then the *Sitz im Leben* of Revelation must be revisited.

The believers' purpose, as they had learned from Paul, Timothy, Peter, and now John, is to be on God's mission of uniting all things in Christ—or, as Peter phrased it, to "proclaim the excellencies of him who called you." Just as Jesus is the faithful witness (Rev 1:5), so the churches are to be faithful witnesses of the risen Christ, the Alpha and Omega, who will be worshipped by every nation, tribe, and language—a prophecy John declares five times (Rev 5:9; 7:9; 10:11; 14:6; 15:4).

Our desire to know the story of the end times is often clouded in the particular scenes John describes—the seven bowls, the seven seals, the seven trumpets, the horsemen, the lake of fire, the battle of Armageddon—rather than in the prophecy that God's mission will be completed (Rev 10:11). John, who stood with Jesus before his ascension and heard him say once again that he is not to be concerned about when the Father will restore the kingdom, reminds the churches, "Blessed is the one who reads aloud the words of this prophecy, and blessed are those who hear, and who keep what is written in it, for the time is near" (Rev 1:3). Yes, signs are all around, suffering and persecution are acute, yet the focus is on the prophetic voice, the voice of God's priests, that proclaims, "Worthy are you to take the scroll and to open its seals, for you were slain, and by your blood you ransomed people for God from every tribe and language and people and nation, and you made them a kingdom and priests to our God, and they shall reign on the earth" (Rev 5:9).

It is a missiologically theocentric understanding of Revelation that points us to the proclamation of the gospel to every ethnic group on the planet so that more and more people will be at God's throne in worship. However, our anthropocentric tendencies in reading Revelation focuses our attention on what will happen to us rather than on the prophecy that God's mission will be complete and on his call for us to join that mission. The great joy that awaits the Christian is not that our suffering will be alleviated, but that we will be eternally glorifying our Creator on the new earth with people from all over the globe. As John put it, "No longer will there be anything accursed, but the throne of God and of the Lamb will be in it, and his servants will worship him" (Rev 22:3).

Reverend Judy knows that the gospel proclamation that leads to professions of faith in the one true God is the only hope for a suffering and dying world. She understood what took Jesus' disciples years to understand. It was not about ushering in the kingdom of God, and it was not about the poor. It was about making more kingdom citizens who will worship their God for eternity. The church of Ephesus and the six other churches in Asia heard this message, and God's Word spread in remarkable ways through the faithful testimony of the saints. However, by the time John records his revelation, it seems that some of the churches were losing their focus, and the angel charged John to keep the vision before them.

## Jesus' Letter to the Ephesians

Ephesus was clearly the seat of Christianity during the last five decades of the first century. Paul and Timothy, as well as Priscilla and Aquila, join God on his mission of self-revelation, which began six hundred years prior to their arrival, to make explicit what Heraclitus understood implicitly. Eventually, Peter and John emerge on the scene to encourage the believers to stay on God's mission. Ultimately, Jesus himself intervenes in the life of the church and those other churches which began as a result of the effort that saw all of Asia impacted by the λόγος (*logos*) of the Lord (Acts 19:10). Jesus' letter is nothing short of amazing:

> I know your works, your toil and your patient endurance, and how you cannot bear with those who are evil, but have tested those who call themselves apostles and are not, and found them to be false. I know you are enduring patiently and bearing up for my name's sake, and you have not grown weary. But I have this against you, that you have abandoned the love you had at first. Remember therefore from where you have fallen; repent, and do the works you did at first. If not, I will come to you and remove your lampstand from its place, unless you repent. Yet this you have: you hate the works of the Nicolaitans, which I also hate. He who has an ear, let him hear what the Spirit says to the churches. To the one who conquers I will grant to eat of the tree of life, which is in the paradise of God. (Rev 2:2–7)

The people of the church in Ephesus actively engaged their community. It seems like they had a dynamic apologetic ministry combatting false teaching prevalent since the time Paul wrote his first letter to Timothy. It appears the church suffered persecution from people in the community but remained faithful through it, as Peter indicates in his first letter. The church's sense of justice for women also led her to stand against sexual immorality. We know the pagan practices associated with the temple of Artemis, as well as other cultural practices, were the epitome of self-indulgence and narcissism and that the church did not tolerate such acts of evil in their society or among the believers.

Even with the various good ministries in the church, Jesus had this one thing against them: "You have abandoned the love you had at first." That first love, I believe, is the key to sustaining a movement. It is a love so deep that it emanates from our identity as adopted children of God (Eph 1:5) who bear not only his image but his heart to see every people group worshipping their

Creator (Rev 7:9). First, however, we will examine what the church did right, the good ministry that engaged theological and social issues in the community, and then move to the first love they abandoned—the main ministry of joining God's mission to unite all things in Christ.

| Church | Commendation | Admonition | Warning | Reward |
|---|---|---|---|---|
| Ephesus (Rev 2:1-7) | Patient endurance; stands against false apostles; hates the works the Nicolaitans (i.e. the works of those who exploit women) | Repent from abandoning the works of their first love | Removal of lampstand | Eat of the tree of life in paradise |
| Smyrna (Rev 2:8-11) | Do not fear suffering; be faithful until death | | | Crown of life; not hurt by the second death |
| Pergamum (Rev 2:12-17) | Hold fast to Jesus' name; did not deny faith | Some who continue to practice magic; eating food sacrificed to idols; sexual immorality; hold the teaching of the Nicolaitans | Jesus will come and war against those who do not repent | Hidden manna; white stone with a new name |
| Thyatira (Rev 2:18-29) | Love, faith, service, endurance, greater works; hold fast the faith | Tolerance of sexual immorality; eating food sacrificed to idols; learning the deep things of Satan | Throw practitioners into great tribulation; children struck dead | Authority over the nations; the morning star |
| Sardis (Rev 3:1-6) | A few who continue to walk with Christ | Dead, incomplete works | Jesus will come against them like a thief | Clothed in white garments; never blot name from book of life |

| | | | | |
|---|---|---|---|---|
| Philadelphia (Rev 3:7-13) | Kept Christ's word; not denied Christ's name; hold fast | | | Keep them from the hour of trial; make a pillar in God's temple; write God's name, God's city, and Jesus' new name on him |
| Laodicea (Rev 3:14-22) | | Complacency; not recognizing true state; be zealous and repent | Jesus disciplines those he loves | Christ will dine with those who repent; sit with Christ on his throne |

TABLE 24: THE SEVEN CHURCHES OF REVELATION 2-3

## The Good Ministry in Ephesus

There are many good ministries that can be accomplished in a church: children, youth, prayer, small groups, benevolence, and more. The issue a movement thinker will constantly confront is which of the good ministries potentially distract from the main ministry. It does not mean that these good ministries are unimportant. In fact, as we see in Jesus' letter, there are those that must be important, since he commended the church for her good works. Indeed, the church most definitely heeded Peter's words, "Keep your conduct among the Gentiles honorable, so that when they speak against you as evildoers, they may see your good deeds and glorify God on the day of visitation" (1 Peter 2:12). So we will look a bit more closely at the good ministries that led Jesus to commend the church in Ephesus.

### Sustaining Correct Doctrine

From very early on in the movement in Ephesus, addressing false teaching played a prominent role in the lives of the churches' elders, as well as for Timothy. In fact, as Paul writes to Timothy, this is of major importance. "As I urged you when I was going to Macedonia, remain at Ephesus so that you may charge certain persons not to teach any different doctrine" (1 Tim 1:3). Those divergent doctrines seem to have pertained to "myths and endless genealogies" (1 Tim 1:4).[58]

---

58. Early apologists, such as Irenaeus and Justin, identified the false teaching with the term Gnosticism. Gnosticism is a moniker representing a broad, unorganized, dualistic belief that religious *gnosis*, i.e., a superior spiritual knowledge, is of greater benefit than the physical/material world. There is no indication in church history of an organized *Gnosticism* with a

On his way to Jerusalem, Paul knew that false teachers would arise in Ephesus, even among the elders themselves: "I know that after my departure fierce wolves will come in among you, not sparing the flock; and from among your own selves will arise men speaking twisted things, to draw away the disciples after them" (Acts 20:29–30). Time and again the church heard warnings from the apostles. A few years later, Peter would caution, "But false prophets also arose among the people, just as there will be false teachers among you, who will secretly bring in destructive heresies, even denying the Master who bought them, bringing upon themselves swift destruction" (2 Peter 2:1).[59]

These false teachings were persistent, as Paul later readdresses them (2 Tim 4:4) and as Peter again tackles the problem in his second letter to the churches of Asia (2 Peter 1:16). By the time John addresses the church, it appears that the myths are much more defined: denial of the incarnation (1 John 1:2); declaration that the Father is unknown (1 John 2:23–25); belief that the Holy Spirit came on Jesus after baptism and left before the crucifixion (1 John 5:6). By the second and third centuries, there are clear heterodoxical theologies emerging in Asia through the false teacher Marcion (i.e., Docetism) and others. In the fourth century, these heresies took shape in Arianism, Sabellianism, and Nestorianism, which denied the Trinity and became formidable opponents to the apostolic tradition.

There is no reason why we might suspect that the church today is immune to such false teachers. I was quite surprised when I heard something like this from a top-line leader in a church planting movement (CPM). Our regional equipping director and I were conducting a training session with a group of forty or so pastors from twelve of the twenty-nine states of one South Asian country. A part of the training included short, biblical, and reproducible sermons using a method adopted from the International Mission Board. The passage for the morning was Acts 2:37–47:

> Now when they heard this they were cut to the heart, and said to Peter and the rest of the apostles, "Brothers, what shall we do?" And Peter said to them, "Repent and be baptized every one of you in the name of Jesus Christ for the forgiveness of your sins, and you will receive the gift of the Holy Spirit. For the promise is for you and for your children and for all who are far off, everyone whom the Lord our God calls to himself." And with many other words he bore witness and continued to exhort them, saying, "Save yourselves from this crooked generation." So those who received his word were baptized, and there were added that day about three thousand souls.

unified system of beliefs. *Gnosticism* is best described as a sundry of beliefs in a special form of knowledge accessible to all and distinct from the apostolic tradition.

59. Second Peter 3:1 indicates that the audience for this letter is the same as for Peter's first letter–namely, the churches in Asia.

And they devoted themselves to the apostles' teaching and the fellowship, to the breaking of bread and the prayers. And awe came upon every soul, and many wonders and signs were being done through the apostles. And all who believed were together and had all things in common. And they were selling their possessions and belongings and distributing the proceeds to all, as any had need. And day by day, attending the temple together and breaking bread in their homes, they received their food with glad and generous hearts, praising God and having favor with all the people. And the Lord added to their number day by day those who were being saved.

Arjun, a dynamic communicator, sat on the edge of his seat waiting to volunteer to preach his mini-sermon. The day before, he impressed everyone with his passion for God's Word. This day, as he rose out of his seat anxious to share with the same zeal as before, he boldly declared that we are to be baptized only in the name of Jesus, as he espoused the non-Trinitarian modalistic Christology of Oneness Pentecostalism—known as the Jesus Only movement—that is growing across his country.

As he concluded, another brother invited me to address the heresy we had just heard. My mind immediately turned to Paul's words: "The Lord's servant must not be quarrelsome but kind to everyone, able to teach, patiently enduring evil, correcting his opponents with gentleness. God may perhaps grant them repentance leading to a knowledge of the truth, and they may come to their senses and escape from the snare of the devil, after being captured by him to do his will" (2 Tim 2:24–26). Through a process of discovery, the group of pastors doing theology in community looked at the whole counsel of God to determine that baptism should be conducted in the name of the triune God as taught by Jesus himself (Matt 28:18–20). They did not condemn our brother in the Lord, but gently brought him back to correct doctrine.

Unlike Paul's instructions to Timothy (2 Tim 2:24–26), false teachers in our world are typically exposed publicly in dramatic declarations of heresy, not all that dissimilar from what we encountered in the open theism debate, but more often in the public square through social media. Church planting movements, as we see in the New Testament and around the globe, are even more susceptible to heresy, due in part to the fact that they grow so quickly. It is not unlikely that new Christians coming out of distinct religious practices will incorporate aspects of their former religious lives into their new Christian life. In some notable examples—African Initiated Churches, Zionism in southern Africa, Santeria in the Caribbean, Umbanda in Brasil, and American nationalistic religion—a syncretism of two belief systems creates an expression of a new faith that is altogether unrecognizable from the original.[60] Paul makes it clear. The responsibility of those leading the movement is to address false teaching: the overseer is to teach (1 Tim 3:2), the elders are to protect (Acts 20:28–29), and the deacons are to equip (Eph 4:12–14). It was a team effort by those who followed Christ as the only head of the church.

False teaching, even in the church today, is a reality and should rightly concern those of us who are seeing exponential growth of disciples. These new believers are acutely susceptible to being led astray by those who propagate a similar, but clearly heterodoxical, gospel. There are many instances of an unsuspecting and unequipped person who professes faith in Christ being persuaded by the teaching of the Jesus Only movement, Jehovah's Witnesses, or Mormons who sweep in after the well-intentioned evangelistic efforts of a church, short-term missions team, or missions organization. Unlike the situation of the church in Ephesus, unfortunately, leaders of these new believers are ill-prepared to confront heresy and sometimes fall victim themselves.

Vinod has worked hard to ensure this does not happen on his watch. He leads a movement in South Asia of twenty established churches, two hundred house churches, and many others just beginning. He recently shared this with me:

> [CPMs] are very much vulnerable to such cults. One of the major drawbacks with the CPMs is that the strong foundations are not being laid for the next appointed leaders. So [the Christian] is easily convinced if something new is taught, because he does not have a strong biblical foundation.

The movement in Ephesus matured disciples and developed leaders. However that happened, they seemed to have gotten it right. Jesus indicates that the false apostles were tested and found deviant from the faith (Rev 2:2). Timothy's disciple-making, as well as Paul, Peter, and John's admonitions, all seem to point to the faithfulness of the church in Ephesus to maintain correct doctrine, which is fundamental to sustaining a movement. Paul writes to Timothy, "If you put these things before the brothers, you will be a good servant [διάκονος; *diakonos*] of Christ Jesus, being trained in the words of the faith and of the good doctrine that you have followed" (1 Tim 4:6).

It should go without saying that the false teaching in the early church focused primarily on various understandings of God. These were not philosophical differences of ministry, as there is certainly evidence of such differences (Acts 15:36–41; 1 Cor 3:10–15; Phil 1:15–18). Those philosophy of ministry disparities, although divisive, did not result in heresy. They were most definitely

---

60. For an excellent discussion on syncretism, see the Evangelical Missiological Society volume *Contextualization and Syncretism: Navigating Cultural Currents* (Pasadena, CA: William Carey Library, 2006).

hurtful, but not theologically harmful. Similarly, the false teachings were not theological opinions or *theologoumenon*, as we discussed in chapters 4 and 5.

*Theologoumenon* more often relates to theological development other than theology proper—i.e., the study of God. For example, three prominent opinions of the Eucharist are held by those who fall within the boundaries of orthodox Christianity: transubstantiation, consubstantiation, and symbolic. There are two basic opinions of baptism: pedobaptism and adult baptism, as well as many views on the method of baptism. Similarly, there are two differing opinions of the role of women in the church: complementarian and egalitarian. Both are held by both men and women who are solidly evangelical. While these theological positions can be equally as divisive, and have been through the decades, they remain opinions rather than authoritative doctrine.[61]

As we discussed in chapter 4, part of the missiological theologian's challenge is to be aware of theological developments and then to discern whether they are beliefs that might deviate from our understanding of God or are simply *theologoumenon*. Western missionaries must be especially vigilant. Even though we bring theological presuppositions to the mission field that are often rooted in Western theological traditions, missiological theologians understand how Western theology has been influenced by Western cultures and how these opinions potentially impact non-Western cultures. This is not a value statement, but rather an observation that our cultural background—even our particular Christian background—influences the manner in which we think and formulate our theology. We have to be cognizant of how our positions might judge another's as false, when in fact our positions are merely theological opinions or ministry philosophy.

During the newly established freedom in Romania in the 1990s, evangelicals flooded the country on short-term trips. Some were focused on evangelism and others were focused on training, as Romanian pastors were hungry to learn God's Word from American pastors. It was not uncommon on these "training" trips for sharp debates to arise between Western pastors, who typically held to the doctrine of the eternal security of the believer, and Romanian pastors,

---

61. Care must be taken that our theological opinions do not affect our theology proper. For example, a neo-subordinationism can emerge from a complementarian view of the roles of men and women. Such a view threatens the doctrine of the Trinity by arguing that the Trinity is a hierarchy, meaning that the Son and Holy Spirit are subordinated to the Father. In the fourth century, a heretical form of subordinationism led Arius to deny the two natures of Christ, which was condemned in the first ecumenical council of Nicaea in AD 325. Jesus is eternally and ontologically God and human, and coequal with God the Father and God the Holy Spirit in authority. There is no reason why our views of men and women should be assumed on the Trinity. Complementarians can argue their position without anthropomorphizing the Godhead as evidence of subordination in human relationships. See Kevin Giles, *The Trinity and Subordinationism: The Doctrine of God and the Contemporary Gender Debate* (Downers Grove, IL: InterVarsity, 2002); and Bruce A. Ware, *One God in Three Persons: Unity of Essence, Distinction of Person, Implications for Life* (Grand Rapids: Crossway, 2015).

who typically held to the position that believers can lose their salvation. The arguments were often distracting and resulted in little change, as the cultural milieus in which these views were held were dramatically different. In Romania, being a disciple came with a great cost, and many believers suffered the price of following Christ. Those who gave up their faith to escape persecution were considered to have lost their salvation. In the United States, there is very little, if any, cost to being a Christian. It is as if our "born again" right is eternal security, just as our American right is eternal freedom.

In contexts in which there are distinct doctrinal differences, Western missionaries should defer to our national brothers and sisters unless there is a clear case of doctrinal heresy. In the example of the doctrine of eternal security in Romania, there were competing views that fell within the bounds of orthodox theology, so bracketing belief is important for the ongoing work of God's mission.

Maintaining correct doctrine—standing against the false teaching that might arise in a movement—is critical to its ongoing fidelity to Scripture and the well-being of believers. As Paul makes clear to the church in Ephesus, the movement leaders, that community of individuals charged with equipping the saints, are responsible for the health of the church—"so that we may no longer be children, tossed to and fro by the waves and carried about by every wind of doctrine, by human cunning, by craftiness in deceitful schemes" (Eph 4:14). Movement leaders—overseers, elders, and deacons—served the church in a community of theologizers, ensuring that disciples matured and God's mission continued to be the main focus.

## Sustaining Moral Integrity

Just as Jesus commended the church in Ephesus for its stance against false apostles, so he commended the church as it stood against the Nicolaitans (Rev 2:6). Very little is known of this obscure group; nonetheless, Jesus denounced their practices, which appear to be associated with divination practices along the lines of Balaam (Num 22:5–7; Rev 2:14–15). The magical practices taking place in Ephesus are well noted in Luke's history (Acts 19:19), and it is reasonable to suspect that some Christians either reverted back to those practices or Christianity syncretized with the magical practices. John also mentions those who acted like Jezebel, who supported the work of Balaam (Rev 2:20). Ostensibly, these were women who had the reputation of being prophetesses, likely associated with the temples and symposia—Greek parties in which intellectual conversations were combined with sexual promiscuity.

Whatever the case, while John uses Balaam and Jezebel as examples of what was happening in Pergamum (Rev 2:14) and Thyatira (Rev 2:20), the same might be said for the Nicolaitans. That is, something was going on in Ephesus, Pergamum, and Thyatira that looked similar to what John knew as the practices of the Nicolaitans. These three churches wrestled with the ongoing religious practices that incorporated sexual immorality (specifically adultery), divination, and theophagy. It is notable that of the three churches wrestling with these ongoing practices, only Ephesus is commended, while Pergamum and Thyatira are warned.

The first we learn any details about the Nicolaitans was in AD 180, when Irenaeus noted:

> The Nicolaitanes are the followers of that Nicolas who was one of the seven first ordained to the diaconate by the apostles. They lead lives of unrestrained indulgence. The character of these men is very plainly pointed out in the Apocalypse of John, [when they are represented] as teaching that it is a matter of indifference to practice adultery, and to eat things sacrificed to idols. (*Against Heresies* 1.26)

There are several other references to the Nicolaitans within the early church, but they mostly draw upon Irenaeus.[62] If we take what we can discern from John's Revelation—as well as references from Paul (1 Tim 1:10; 3:2) and Peter (2 Peter 2:14) regarding the issues of sexual immorality and adultery—and assume a grain of truth from Irenaeus, then the situation we see in Asia fits with what we know about the worship of Artemis, Dionysus, and Greek symposia in relationship to the prominence of women in the region.[63] It also lends color to how we might understand Paul's direction to Timothy with regard to women (1 Tim 2:8–15) and Peter's specific instructions to women (1 Peter 3:1–6).

While there are those who characterize Paul as a misogynist, others have taken a softer position and claim that his instructions concerning women emerged due to the practice of temple prostitution in Ephesus. However, prostitution was not associated with the temple of Artemis, yet the misunderstanding persisted based on a misapplication of Strabo's observation of temple prostitution in Corinth (Baugh 1999, 446). Instead, the prominence of women at Ephesus came in the fact that Artemis was the goddess of childbearing and of maidens. In the third century BC, the poet Callimachus wrote this in Artemis' voice:

> On the mountains will I dwell and the cities of men I will visit only when women vexed by the sharp pang of childbirth call me to their aid even in the hour when

---

62. For instance, Clement of Alexandria, *Stromota* 3.4.25-26; Tertullian, *Prescriptions Against Heresies* 33; Hippolytus, *Refutations* 7:24; and Eusebius of Caesarea, *Church History* 3:29.

63. There were, in fact, temples to many gods and goddesses all across Asia.

I was born the Fates ordained that I should be their helper, forasmuch as my mother suffered no pain either when she gave me birth or when she carried me in her womb, but without travail put me from her body. (*Hymn III to Artemis*, 1)

Artemis, the lady of maidenhood, as Callimachus wrote, ensured the salvation of all creatures in childbearing, including women (ibid., 109).

There aren't many ancient references to courtesans—the women who accompanied men in a symposium—in Ephesus, but they certainly were a part of the culture of Asia. For instance, after the death of Attalus III in 133 BC, Asia was ceded to Rome. Attalus' supposed half-brother, Aristonicus, whose mother was an Ephesian courtesan, attempted to lay claim to their father's kingdom, yet failed (Head 1880, 65).

Similarly, Plutarch (AD 46–120) tells us of a prominent courtesan, Aspasia, from Asia, whose house in Athens attracted influential Greek poets and philosophers, including Socrates. In *Life of Pericles*, Plutarch observes, "This may be a fitting place to raise the query what great art or power this woman had, that she managed as she pleased the foremost men of the state, and afforded the philosophers occasion to discuss her in exalted terms and at great length" (*Life of Pericles*, 24). Plutarch continues,

And so Aspasia, as some say, was held in high favour by Pericles because of her rare political wisdom. Socrates sometimes came to see her with his disciples, and his intimate friends brought their wives to her to hear her discourse, although she presided over a business that was anything but honest or even reputable, since she kept a house of young courtesans. (Ibid.)

These courtesans had tremendous influence in their communities. Lucian, the second-century AD author of *Dialogues of the Courtesans*, describes these companions of the participants of symposia:

In the first place, she dresses attractively and looks neat; she's gay with all the men, without being so ready to cackle as you are, but smiles in a sweet bewitching way; later on, she's very clever when they're together, never cheats a visitor or an escort, and never throws herself at the men. If ever she takes a fee for going out to dinner, she doesn't drink too much—that's ridiculous, and men hate women who do—she doesn't gorge herself—that's ill-bred, my dear—but picks up the food with her finger-tips, eating quietly and not stuffing both cheeks full, and, when she drinks, she doesn't gulp, but sips slowly from time to time... . Also, she doesn't talk too much or make fun of any of the company, and has eyes only for her customer. These are the things that make her popular with the men. Again, when it's time for bed, she'll never do anything coarse or slovenly, but her only aim is to attract the man and make him love her; these are the things they all praise in her. (xx)

In Alciphron's *Letters of Courtesans*, written in the third century AD, Thais, the courtesan of Alexander the Great, recounts the influence of women on the education of men by contrasting them with sophists:

> But possibly we seem to you inferior to the sophists because we don't know where the clouds come from or what the atoms are like. I myself have gone to school to see them and have talked with many of them. No one, when he's with a courtesan, dreams of a tyrant's power or raises sedition in the state; on the contrary, he drains his early-morning beaker and then prolongs his drunken rest until the third or fourth hour. We teach young men just as well as they do. Judge, if you will, between Aspasia the courtesan and Socrates the sophist, and consider which of them trained the better men. You will find Pericles the pupil of one and Critias the pupil of the other. (4.7.5–7)

The influence of women in Asia and in Greek society in general directly contradicted the expectation of "women who profess godliness" (1 Tim 2:10). However, the influence was strong, as was the response of the early Christian leaders. In this context, Paul writes that "women should adorn themselves in respectable apparel, with modesty and self-control, not with braided hair and gold or pearls or costly attire" (1 Tim 2:9), reminiscent of the apparel described by Lucian. In distinction from a courtesan, Paul states, "I do not permit a woman to teach or to exercise authority over a man; rather, she is to remain quiet" (1 Tim 2:12). This was as much an admonition to Christian women to not be like the courtesans as it was for Christian men who enjoyed their company. In other words, it represented a cultural paradigm shift impacting the social fabric of both men and women in Ephesus.

It is no wonder that Paul required the overseer and deacons to be the husband of one wife. Rather than addressing polygamy, which did not play a prominent place in Greek culture, 1 Timothy 3:2 and 3:12 address divorce and adulterous relationships, which were more common. This is not to say that the New Testament promotes plural marriage; it just simply is not addressing it. The point that Jesus was raising in Revelation with the church in Ephesus was that they didn't settle for the culturally acceptable practices leading to sexual immorality and promiscuity. In fact, they combated it and raised the dignity of women by rescuing them from the immoral pleasures of men. Just as correct doctrine is critical to the health of a movement, so is the moral integrity of those in the movement. Movement leaders were held to a high standard.

In a recent conversation about the early days of his ministry in the highlands of an Indo-Chinese country, "Uncle Monnie," as he is known around the world, shared about the time they learned that an acceptable cultural practice among a tribal people also impacted Christianity. At the point when married women reached menopause, their husbands had the cultural right to take on a mistress, since sexual relations with their wives were not culturally appropriate. As Christianity entered this environment, Monnie discovered that the practices continued among pastors. Through a study of biblical marriage, they were able to successfully eradicate the practice from the church and bring church leaders back in line with proper moral behavior. When Christianity enters a religious context that devalues women, it is not uncommon for cultural practices to continue if they are not explicitly addressed.

In Ephesus, the practices were addressed soon after the start of the movement. As I have argued, Paul wrote Timothy just three years after the movement began to ensure that he took proper measures to address the moral integrity of the church. While some surely continued in promiscuous relationships, the church was largely successful in living to a high moral standard. For a movement to sustain its growth, it must take moral integrity seriously. The devaluing of women, as we see in the cultural practices of Ephesus and around the world today, will be a clear deterrent to growth if for no other reason than the fact that women make up the majority of many societies. If a movement does not lift the dignity of women, then it simply becomes a pawn in propagating a misogynic culture foreign to the New Testament church.

The longer immoral issues and false teaching are not addressed, the more likely they will be accepted as proper practices. If they are not dealt with quickly, Jesus might say, as he did to the church at Pergamum, "Therefore repent. If not, I will come to you soon and war against [those who hold false teaching] with the sword of my mouth" (Rev 2:16); or to the church in Thyatira, "Behold, I will throw [Jezebel] onto a sickbed, and those who commit adultery with her I will throw into great tribulation, unless they repent of her works" (Rev 2:22). This is absolutely serious. Jesus does not tolerate immorality or heresy in his church, and movement leaders are to ensure they do not occur.

## Sustaining Our First Love

The movement in Ephesus is a wonderful example of house churches and movement leaders who took doctrine and morality seriously. Addressing the house churches in Ephesus less than four decades after the movement began, Jesus applauded them for the good ministry they were doing. However, as he said, "But I have this against you, that you have abandoned the love you had at first" (Rev 2:4). It is a perplexing comment, especially since we have seen the church diligently work to combat false doctrine and sexual immorality. In the context of the book of Revelation, false prophets (16:13; 19:20; 20:10) and sexual immorality (9:21; 14:8; 17:2, 4; 18:3, 9; 19:2; 21:8; 22:15) factor prominently. It would be reasonable to suggest that demonstrating an aversion to such issues and even addressing them straight up in the church would indicate the believers' love for Christ. According to Jesus, however, the difference between what they were doing and what he expected them to do stood significantly distinct from one another.

One thing, though, is clear: Whatever their first love was, Jesus demanded that they get it back. "Remember therefore from where you have fallen; repent, and do the works you did at first. If not, I will come to you and remove your lampstand from its place, unless you repent" (Rev 2:5). The good works for which Christ commends them are qualitatively different than the good works that is the love of Christ.

As I suggested above, if a missiological understanding of Revelation is at the core of understanding John's prophecy, and that prophecy is focused on every tribe, nation, people, and language worshipping God, then the Ephesians' first love must somehow be tied to the work of uniting all things in Christ (Eph 1:10). As we saw in chapter 6, God's will is singular and clear, and the church is chosen and predestined in love to share in the responsibility of his will by declaring the mystery of Christ (Eph 1:4–5; 3:9–10). It is also clear that Jesus' warning of taking away the church's lampstand is a euphemism for the removal of the church's witness in the society, as it would no longer be permitted to represent the light of the world.

The apostle of love is unambiguous that the church's first priority is to love Christ. A repeated theme throughout his Gospel, he obviously understands what Jesus intends for the Ephesians. As John told those in Ephesus in the Fourth Gospel, "God so loved the world, that he gave his only Son, that whoever believes in him should not perish but have eternal life" (John 3:16). In fact, the love of Christ for us is the model by which we are to love. That sacrificial love which focused on God's glorification is a love that compels us to tell his story to others so that they see how God relentlessly pursues them. The love that Christ speaks about, the love that the Ephesians abandoned, is a work by which we—just as John heard from Jesus in Peter's restoration—are called to tend and feed those who are his, both those present and those future members of the flock (John 21:15–17).

It is to this purpose, the fulfillment of God's mission as the manifestation of our love for Christ, that Paul prays for the saints, and an appropriate place to conclude this chapter:

> For this reason I bow my knees before the Father, from whom every family in heaven and on earth is named, that according to the riches of his glory he may grant you to be strengthened with power through his Spirit in your inner being,

so that Christ may dwell in your hearts through faith—that you, being rooted and grounded in love, may have strength to comprehend with all the saints what is the breadth and length and height and depth, and to know the love of Christ that surpasses knowledge, that you may be filled with all the fullness of God.

Now to him who is able to do far more abundantly than all that we ask or think, according to the power at work within us, to him be glory in the church and in Christ Jesus throughout all generations, forever and ever. Amen. (Eph 3:14–21)

❦

As is common in many endeavors, the tendency to institutionalize seeps into the movement in Ephesus somewhere between AD 66 and 96, as Jesus reprimands the Ephesians for abandoning their first love (Rev 2:4). Over this period of time, the church's passion for doing good things is commended: a vibrant apologetics ministry that stood against false teaching and a justice ministry condemning sexual immorality and adultery while raising the dignity of women. Along the way, however, the good things overcame the main thing: proclaiming the mystery that God was reconciling both Jews and Gentiles through Jesus Christ. With a missiological reading, Revelation ceases to be primarily focused on the *eschaton*, something that distracted even Jesus' disciples from their mission (Acts 1:6). Instead, Revelation focuses on the participation of the seven churches of Asia in bringing all nations, tribes, and languages before the throne of God (Rev 7:9; 10:11). It is a call to all the churches to complete the mission of God for the praise of his glory.

The ability for a movement to sustain growth over time is directly connected to its passion for God's mission. Just as Reverend Judy understood, all the good ministry we might do—the educational programs, clean-water initiatives, hygiene and sanitation projects, health care, and even combating human trafficking and deviant doctrines—can be a distraction from helping people to the streets of gold that John so beautifully reveals (Rev 21:9–27). It is a place where "[God] will wipe away every tear from their eyes, and death shall be no more, neither shall there be mourning, nor crying, nor pain anymore, for the former things have passed away" (Rev 21:4).

Our daughter Michaela and I were having another one of our great theological conversations. They are getting increasingly rare, not due to a lack of desire, but rather to her life work as a social worker, currently in the Baltimore public school system. Nevertheless, as I was concluding this chapter she had just begun to attend a Bible study on the book of Revelation. As she shared with me that evening, her words seem to ring true: "Daddy, I believe the tears that

God will wipe away are due to the fact that we will recognize all the people we did not share Christ with and realize that they will be eternally separated from us and God."

An absolutely tragic thought. Can you imagine a world without those loved ones—family, friends, even neighbors and colleagues—knowing that we had a sacred duty to share the gospel with them and did not?

We are getting closer to those streets of gold as the church continues on her mission. Today, as near as we can tell, two-thirds of the global population does not know Christ and 2.1 billion people are completely outside the reach of the gospel—a number that is increasing daily as the population continues to swell. Additionally, nearly 6 million people, representing 269 distinct ethnic groups living in their homelands, have never been contacted by a missionary. We estimate that it will take another 311 missionary units to risk all for the gospel to engage these people with the love of Christ. These people have stories of searching for a God they do not know. The Holy Spirit is at work among them, yet they do not see him.

Now the church must fulfill her responsibility to make God's story known. A movement of God is happening in the world today. He will accomplish his mission, as John prophesied. The question for us is this: Will we demonstrate our love for Christ by joining God in his mission to see every tribe, nation, language, and people worship him?

# CHAPTER 10

## The Anatomy of a Movement

In the 1990s, the gospel made unprecedented inroads into former communist countries. Masses of Christians on short-term missions teams (STMTs) came to the formerly closed countries and shared their faith with an openness that had never been witnessed. Stadiums were packed with people who desired to hear the good news of a liberating Christ, and reports indicated that thousands upon thousands of people responded to the gospel by going forward in answer to a call to salvation.

During the summer of 1990, an STMT assigned to one of the most oppressed of the former communist countries began a new engagement strategy by focusing their efforts on a single location for two weeks. During the reign of communism, short-term missions teams typically traveled from location to location throughout a country in order to not be detected by the authorities or risk exposing national partners. All that changed with new avenues of ministry, which included public showings of *The Jesus Film*, open street evangelism, and stadium crusades.

This particular STMT was the first to ever show *The Jesus Film* in a public setting in that country. The unairconditioned auditorium was packed on that warm summer evening, as nearly six hundred people from the city crowded in to see the movie. At the conclusion of the film, a clear presentation of the gospel was made and an estimated three hundred people indicated decisions for Christ by raising their hands. The response was so incredible that the team was compelled to continue the work in that city and begin to disciple the new believers. Of the three hundred people who indicated decisions for Christ, only sixty were successfully followed up, and they eventually formed the core group of a new church. That church was started a year later, during the summer of 1991, and more and more people came to Christ.

In the first year, the church grew to over one hundred. Small groups of adults, as well as university and high school students, met regularly. People in the church were leading others to Christ, and the church engaged the community through a university ministry and outreach at an orphanage, while emerging leaders shared the responsibility for the spiritual well-being of the new believers. With the optimism of what the Lord was doing, the strategy launched in other cities. Eventually the movement grew to seven church planting streams in the least reached and spiritually darkest areas of the country.

Over time, however, it became clear that the impact was not as great as what had been hoped. Even though the churches were growing, they eventually learned that the Mormons, Jehovah's Witnesses, and Bahai were also growing, as they often came on the coattails of evangelistic crusades to draw those whose spiritual appetites were whetted to a different spiritual path. While the Jehovah's Witnesses have had a long existence in Eastern Europe, today they have more than 40,000 Bible teachers and 551 congregations in this Eastern European country. Since 1993, the Latter-day Saints have grown to 16 congregations with over 3,000 members, while Bahai has 183 congregation with an unknown number of adherents.

Meanwhile, the evangelical population of this specific country has not grown significantly since its liberation from communism. That first church that started in 1991 would eventually grow to about 150 people, start a new church plant in their city, and send teams to help start other church plants in two different cities. But the church has now dwindled to 30. They have a national pastor and a beautiful church building, but no vision for multiplying disciples. In a very real sense, they abandoned the works of their first love and fell victim to an institutional model of ministry.

Other factors certainly contributed to the stagnation of the movement. The young pioneer missionary church planter leading the new movement was no doubt overly idealistic and anxious to see the gospel spread throughout the country. New missionaries came from traditional American churches—full of zeal to make an impact, but without any cross-cultural or movement experience. An important missions lesson was learned: If the people recruited to missions are not making an impact at home, it will be difficult for them to make an impact on the mission field.

The vibrancy of a young church engaged in her community soon gave way to a pastoral care model for the congregation. The movement became anthropocentric, as the needs of the saints overcame the proclamation of the gospel. Some of the new churches began to become attractional; after all, "attractional church" was the new fad that seemed to be working in the States in the 1990s. Soon national leaders were no longer leading small groups, as the missionary staff took those responsibilities. And rarely did people share their faith. What had started as a dynamic movement, with passion for joining in God's mission, devolved into an institution whose concern was inward. Today they wonder if they will be able to afford the expenses of maintaining their church building constructed with donations from well-meaning Westerners.

At the beginning of the book, I discussed the idea that movements have life cycles. What we learn in the study of the Ephesian movement demonstrates something different. As I argued in chapter eight, a movement has a rhythm: growth, solidification, expansion. To put this in ephesiological terms: launching, grounding, leading, multiplying, sustaining. What I learned in the 1990s in Romania is that causes, not movements, have a life cycle. At first people are excited about what they hear and want others to know about it as well. Then they become more strategic, as they attempt to solidify their vision and train people to propagate the cause. Soon the cause grows in need of a bureaucracy and formalizes training. Along the way, it becomes increasingly difficult to mobilize people to the cause, and the movement becomes an institution. It happens everywhere, but it does not have to (Addison, 2019). When it does, it is often due to the fact that what began as a movement had lost its vision for the works of their first love.

In this final chapter, we will synthesize what we have observed in the Ephesian movement. The central focus of *Ephesiology* has been the characteristics that define a disciple of a movement, albeit implicit, and the framework that contributes to a movement's health. If our ministries or movements lack these, then we might soon face a similar demise as the movement in this former communist country.

## Characteristics of the Disciples in the Ephesian Movement

It should be clear that when we are talking about the Ephesian movement we are talking about a group of people who are passionate for God's will to unite all things in Christ (Eph 1:10). In fact, this was not only Paul's expectation of disciples, it was the norm. Certainly not everyone who professed faith in Christ became a Timothy, Epaphras, or Gaius. However, those early movement leaders expected the Holy Spirit to radically change individuals from seeking their own glorification to seeking God's glorification in everything they did.

It isn't uncommon to find myself in conversations with church leaders about the definition of a disciple. I will often scratch my head and wonder what kind of a leader struggles with coming up with such a definition. The difficulty and confusion, however, seems clear. It cannot be due to a lack of education or Bible knowledge, or at least that is what I want to believe—although there might very well be a systemic problem in the way we prepare church leaders in our Bible colleges and seminaries. Rather, it is due to the dichotomy between the disciples we read about in the New Testament and the people sitting in the pews who we believe are disciples.[64] The fault for this dichotomy falls squarely on the shoulders of church leaders: pastors and staff, elders and deacons. The solution for this dichotomy also falls on these same leaders.

Throughout *Ephesiology*, we have seen at least eleven characteristics of a disciple. A movement leader is crystal clear about these characteristics. First, disciples surrender to God's will and maintain the works of their first love (Eph 1; Eph 5:18–19; Rev 2:4). On the occasion when disciples ask, "What is God's will for my life?" they are asking the wrong question. A disciple's will is completely submitted to God's will, and there is no choice but to do the works of their first love and glorify him who sits on the throne.

Second, disciples declare the mystery of Christ to the nations (Eph 3:4–10, 1 Tim 2:1–4). The work of Christ in his ministry, suffering, death, resurrection, ascension, and session broke the barrier and united a new people for God's kingdom. Disciples have eyes that see every person they encounter as a person God is pursuing. They understand that they might very well be the instrument that God uses to draw this person to be a new worshipper. However, it is not only those they might encounter in their social network. Disciples have a vision for the 2.1 billion people who do not have access to the gospel.

Third, disciples are equipped by movement leaders for ministry (*diakonia*; Eph 4:12; 1 Timothy). Every disciple, through the gifts God has given, is qualified for ministry. Movement leaders must trust that the Holy Spirit who is leading them will also lead the disciples. So, their responsibility is to ensure that the disciples have every opportunity to use those gifts in the context of the church and especially in the context of completing God's mission.

Fourth, disciples exhibit the fruit of the Spirit (Eph 4–5). The unity and peace among disciples can only be explained by the Holy Spirit. Disciples do not compete with one another or jockey for positions of influence. After all, they understand that they already have a position of influence in their identity with Christ. They are ambassadors who are given the great responsibility of representing their Father. This is only possible in a life full of the Holy Spirit.

Fifth, disciples are empowered by the Holy Spirit to be witnesses (Eph 5:18–19; 2 Tim 1:7). Jesus came to declare God's glory. Paul, Timothy, John, and Peter modeled what that looks like in a movement. There is no wiggle room here. Disciples share the gospel in the power of the Holy Spirit with those

---

64. I'm fully aware of the fact that Paul never uses the term "disciple" in his writing. In fact, the word disappears from the New Testament writers in Acts 21:16. Instead, it is more common for Paul to use the term "saints" (Eph 1:1) or simply "brothers" (1 Thess 3:7) as a moniker for Christ-followers and various metaphors to illustrate discipleship: parenting (1 Thess 2:7); farming (1 Cor 3:6); soldiering (2 Tim 2:4); exercising (1 Cor 9:24-27). Since "disciple" is so common in our parlance, I'll continue to use it.

they encounter no matter where they are. Yes, that includes the nations, but it also includes the home, office, grocery story, or any other place where people need the good news.

Sixth, disciples are godly men and women, employees and employers, husbands and wives, and parents (Eph 5:21–6:9). The New Testament expects a complete disciple; that is, a discipleship that impacts every facet of an individual's life including the family and the workplace.

Seventh, disciples pray for opportunities to share the gospel, because they know God is most glorified when more people are worshipping him (Eph 6:18–20; 1 Tim 2:1–4). It certainly is not the only thing disciples pray for, but it is a preoccupation of theirs.

Eighth, disciples are respectful of people and culture when they do evangelism (Acts 19:8, 37). They understand that all people are created in the image of God, and that very fact demands that people are respected. This does not mean that disciples agree with the belief system or worldview of every person they meet, but they understand that God is in pursuit of them. A disciple helps remove the scales from peoples' eyes so they too can see plainly the God who is in front of them.

Ninth, disciples learn sound doctrine from movement leaders who are able to teach (1 Tim 4:7). We have some of the most remarkable teachers in our pulpits today. Yet these dynamic, powerful expositors more frequently tickle the ears of Christians and fail to produce disciples fully committed to God's will. If the sermons you preach, the small groups you lead, or the time you spend with individuals do not result in people making more disciples who are worshipping God, then you are contributing to an anthropocentric theology that further deepens the institutionalizing of the church.

Tenth, disciples are willing to suffer for the sake of the gospel (2 Tim 1:8). Suffering will look differently across the world. The persecution that disciples are willing to endure pales in comparison to the crown of righteousness that is laid up for all those who love the appearing of Christ (2 Tim 4:8).

Finally, disciples are committed to multiplying more disciples (2 Tim 2:2). If you have a church of one hundred people, there is no reason why it cannot be a church of two hundred people next year. This doesn't require new programs, Facebook ads or more staff, although it might require that you reexamine the staff you have to be sure they are the right team of movement leaders. It will require you to make disciples who will make more disciples. They will not be content sitting in the pew listening to sermons or volunteering for the church's programs. Pure and simple, disciples multiply while volunteers stay busy. Disciples are engaged in their Father's business. A movement leader ensures that they have every opportunity to do so.

## Framework of the Ephesian Movement

Just as there are characteristics of a disciple implicit in the Ephesian movement, there is also a framework emerging from our study of the movement in Ephesus. First, the early missionaries launched a movement that is missiologically theocentric, with the heart to connect God's story with the story of culture. This feature of the framework assumes that the missionaries are theologically and missiologically prepared to launch a movement. It is a critical mistake, as noted in the anecdote above, to send missionaries or to staff churches with people who are not properly equipped to work within a movement. It is equally a mistake to appoint elders and deacons or to hire pastors that are not movement oriented. These missiological theologians need to have the skills to effectively connect God's story to the story of a culture. In order to do that, movement leaders must dialogue with people, observe the culture, and study its history— what I call missiological exegesis. That exegesis is foundational to developing a missiological theology that communicates God's story in such a way that a culture sees their story.

Second, Paul grounded the movement with the vision to fulfill God's will of uniting all things in Christ. If a movement cannot answer the question of God's will, then it is bound to an anthropocentric exercise of developing its own vision and mission and risks missing the joy of joining in God's mission of more people worshipping him and seeing his vision of the nations before his throne. When grounded, the movement sees the church as God's instrument in advancing the gospel, not a structure that congregates spectators. It has a vision for the nations in their community and in the world that unifies the believers as brothers and sisters of the same family working in peace to complete God's mission. These saints are equipped for the ministry of engaging the world.

Third, Paul and Timothy led the movement as a community of brothers and sisters determined to equip the saints for ministry. A movement is able to identify leaders with good reputations in the community who are well respected and able to teach sound doctrine. Their focus is not on their agenda, but on equipping the saints for God's mission. They do not lord their leadership over others. Instead, they work in a community of leaders committed to the same cause.

Fourth, the disciples multiplied a movement by empowering leaders to use their gifts, inspiring them to join in suffering, entrusting them to teach others, and reminding them to preach the Word. The movement successfully multiplied disciples who willingly risked all for the gospel. These disciples were not content with a Bible study, but were intent on making more disciples who made even more. They were striving for exponential growth, as they focused on more people worshipping God.

Finally, the church in Ephesus sustained the movement by reengaging the works of her first love. The movement was active in the community and stood for what was right. Its leaders ensured that false teachers were corrected, and they upheld the dignity of all people. Most of all, the church focused on the completion of God's mission of more people worshipping him. This was their first love, and it was demonstrated by mobilizing the movement to engage its Jerusalem, Judea, Samaria, and the rest of the world. The disciples in Ephesus multiplied disciples, resulting in multiple communities of more disciples everywhere in Asia.

These five features of a framework are not guarantees, but I dare you to try them. The Holy Spirit moved in extraordinary ways through the lives of people in the New Testament, and he did it as they launched new movements, grounded them in a missiologically theocentric mission, led them to see more and more people worshipping God, multiplied the disciples around the world, and sustained the works of their first love to see God's mission completed. It happened two thousand years ago. We see it happening around the world today. I believe it can also happen in the West if we are unyielding in our identity as family members on our Father's business.

As these characteristics of a disciple and framework for the growth of a movement are applied by Western missionaries overseas, we face an additional challenge to ensure the movement becomes indigenous. This is a persistent problem, as churches in various cultures around the world tend to take on the identity of the missionary's home country. A proper missiological theologian will allow the identity of a movement to evolve from within a culture. For that to happen, we need to be aware of five salient features of an indigenous movement. When we keep these in mind, we will ensure a culturally appropriate expression of Christianity.

## Features of an Indigenous Movement

About an hour outside of the capital city of one Asian country, I sat in a bamboo-walled church on a cool Saturday in November. To help keep the warmth inside, the walls were packed with mud and the dirt floors were covered with thick carpets. Since they had no chairs, we sat on the ground, men on one side and women on the other. The church obviously used its own resources to construct a structure that expressed its culture, and the atmosphere was certainly colorful and expressive.

As I continued to make observations, though, things began to become confused. Here in this village church, in a country that clearly rejects Christianity as a Western religion, there was a Christmas tree decorated at the front, complete with lights, tinsel, and a star on the top, with a banner written in English:

"Merry Christmas." The worship leaders were leading the small congregation in songs that had been translated from English, with a drum set, electric guitar, and keyboard, along with microphones, speakers, and amplification. The style was not at all what I had imagined to be an indigenous worship service, but rather an attempt to reproduce a Western form of church left by well-meaning missionaries.

This is not a unique story, but one that is repeated all around the world. The influence of Western forms of the church, particularly in countries that are hostile to Christianity, can place an undesired stumbling block in the paths of those we are trying to reach, as well as produce unnecessary persecution provoked by what is believed to be a foreign religion. Along with the entrapments of nonindigenous musical instruments and linear pedagogical methods, it seems difficult for Christianity to shed its Western garb in order to become genuinely indigenous. This new form of colonialism risks not only the witness of Christ, but also the lives of believers, who are often viewed as servants of a Western religious agenda. Our need is for a model of the church that is respectful of both the culture and Scripture.

## The Threat of Neocolonialism

Most would agree that the colonial era in South America, Africa, and Asia did see remarkable change (Ferguson 2003). However, such change was often at the expense of the cultures where colonial powers settled. The hallmarks of colonialism were summarized with three Cs: Commerce, Civilization, and Christianity (Cooper 2005). The historian Stephen Neill equated the colonial agenda with the view that Europeans impoverished and exploited indigenous people, who were believed to be inferior and weak (Neill 1966). In a very real sense, colonialism saw the need to help a people who were deficient in their abilities to help themselves in ways consonant with a colonial worldview.

Due to the desire of colonial powers to expand their wealth, commerce became a key means of securing future financial sustainability. As the British missionary statesman Thomas Fowell Buxton believed, the Bible should go hand in hand with commerce. His watchword, "The Bible and Plow," set an expectation that along with the gospel came a concomitant financial advantage. The colonial agenda was very much about seeing commercial gain, more for the respective colonial power, but also to a lesser degree for some who became the elite in the cultures that were colonized.

Civilization during the colonial powers' tenure in South America, Africa, and Asia was naturally defined by European civil society. Educational and health institutions were classic examples of the definition of civilization, in addition to governmental systems and geopolitical boundaries.

An ethno-graphic map of these regions would illustrate the stark difference between what we have come to know as the geopolitical boundaries and the boundaries of the various people groups.

For the people of a colonial power to be civilized, it meant that they would look like Europeans. This often materialized in shedding cultural particularities and replacing them with those of Europe. Instead of unique cultural expressions of ethnic groups, people took on the European systems and styles. Most evident in dress, people abandoned their ethnic garb for trousers, shirts, and dresses. Also, education focused on the liberal arts and away from traditional knowledge, which was considered inferior to science and technology.

In addition, health care relied on medicine rather than traditional healing. While not all bad, it left continents with systems that were not indigenous and difficult to maintain once colonial powers left. In the case of education, for example, the colonial systems continued with typical rote methods of teaching, in spite of the fact that Western teaching methods have progressed due to a greater understanding of effective learning. With a new awareness of oral learning for the majority of the world, attention is rightly redirected to the most effective ways of learning based on cultural preferences.

The unfortunate consequence of commerce and civilization was a view that Christianity is a Western religion imposed on communities by colonial powers. Christianity, in many former colonial countries, is a foreigner's faith, as it also had its own ideas of how Christianity should be expressed. Proper Christianity for Protestants was European or American, and although Protestant churches were more often conducted in the vernacular, liturgically the church was expressed as any service one might walk into in Europe or the United States. In spite of the three-self church idea that emerged in the late nineteenth century, churches still looked Western. While leadership, ministry, and finances would eventually be indigenous in some cases, worship expressions of Christianity remained foreign, as well as expressions of systems of theology. Traditional music and instruments, mistakenly thought to be connected to the "heathen" religions, were replaced by organs. In the contemporary climate, organs have now been replaced with drum sets, electric guitars, pianos, and amplification systems, similar to what I observed in Asia.

In a Ugandan village near Lake Victoria, I stood in wonder inside a red brick church as three men played three different types of indigenous drums. The worship was expressive and dynamic, as the congregation danced around the building in praise to God. It was an emotionally moving experience to see a people express their love for God in a way that was clearly a part of their cultural heritage. After the service, the pastor came to me and apologized. To him, and to many clergy around the world, a worship service needed amplification, along with a drum set, guitars, and electric keyboard. He was hopeful that they would soon have electricity so that they could have a "proper" church service.

Even though we have long passed the colonial period, remnants of those past days still threaten the advancement of the gospel. In place of colonialism, globalization, as well as Western systems (political, commercial, ecclesiastical), have been established, and while the systems are led by nationals, the new national systems act in similar ways as the colonial powers. This neocolonialism continues to advance its own contemporary ideas of commerce, civilization, and Christianity. One of the beauties of the New Testament movement was its ability to connect with cultural forms, while remaining faithful to the apostolic tradition.

## Indigenous Church of the New Testament

It appears that in God's providential wisdom, the New Testament church did not have to struggle through the development of a system that would facilitate the believers in worshipping God. The Jewish culture of the day provided an applicable model for the church, and ultimately this model was implemented wherever the community of Christ engaged Jewish culture. The similarities of the synagogue to the church are striking. It is evident throughout the Jewish mission in the book of Acts (2:42–47; 14:23; 20:17–28) that the church appointed elders, held services of prayer, and provided for the daily needs of widows, as did the synagogue.

Nearly four decades ago, Ralph Winter related the implications of this for church planters in his day, and it is still applicable in ours.

> In fact, the profound missiological implication of all this is that the New Testament is trying to show us how to borrow effective patterns; it is trying to free all future missionaries from the need to follow the precise forms of the Jewish synagogue and Jewish missionary band, and yet to allow them to choose comparable indigenous structures in the countless new situations across history and around the world—structures which will correspond faithfully to the function of patterns Paul employed, if not their form! (Winter and Hawthorne 1981, 180)

In addition to the synagogue model, Gentiles formed a different church structure that expressed their particular cultural background. The *oikos* model was based on a socioeconomic system in which the head of the household was also the spiritual leader of those under his patronage. When Christ was proclaimed to the Gentiles and congregations were formed, they formed around the *oikos* of a leader. As we learned in chapter 7, even the leadership of the church took on the cultural leadership form of overseer-elders-deacons. Clearly the New Testament demonstrates the indigenous nature of the church, and this, no doubt, contributed to the rapid expansion of a movement of house churches throughout the Roman Empire.

We have also observed an indigenous expression of a system of theology in the early church. This missiological theology focused on connecting stories, and it was most evident in the understanding that God is working in cultures to make himself known—the core of missiological theism. In Athens, it manifested through the philosophy of Aratus. In Ephesus, we see it from Heraclitus. The early missiological theologians made explicit that which was implicit in the culture. As we have observed, Paul expresses a missiological theology in Ephesians and John in his Gospel. It was their ability to connect the story of God to the story of the culture that ensured an indigenous Christianity. This was not contextualization, nor was it a redemptive analogy. It was not a missionary's ingenuity in expressing Jesus to a culture. It was the observation of what God was already doing in the culture and effectively declaring what the culture was searching for.

Whereas we can celebrate the demise of colonialism, the threat of a neocolonial power, particularly on indigenous people groups and rural villages, is just as real as it was two hundred years ago. Even though we clearly see how first-century movement leaders adapted to culture, the tendency of missionaries is to replicate the traditions of the missionary's culture. National church leaders naturally believe the missionary has their best interests in mind, yet the reality—as expressed in the title of Roland Allen's first book, *Missionary Methods: Saint Paul's or Ours?*—is that the missionaries tend to reproduce the methods of an institutional approach that is no longer working in the West, rather than the missiologically theocentric method of Paul. To make a missiologically appropriate adjustment, the five-self indigenous model provides criteria that places a buffer between the Western expression of Christianity and a non-Western community.

### Measuring Indigeneity

Indigeneity can be measured in many ways. Traditionally, the three-self model was touted as an early attempt to express the characteristics of an indigenous church. Around the turn of the twentieth century, Rufus Anderson and Henry Venn argued that a church would identify with a culture when it had its own leadership (self-governing), reached out to the community (self-propagating), and provided for its own financial needs (self-funding). While the three-self church structure helped new churches become sustainable, it did not effectively address the issues of expression and theology. Later in the twentieth century, the South African missiologist David Bosch suggested that the church needed a fourth self: *self-theologizing* (Bosch 1991). It was when a national church began to develop its own theology, according to Bosch, that it would genuinely become indigenous.

However, as we continue into the twenty-first century, churches around the world—no matter if they are Catholic, Orthodox, Coptic, or Protestant—carry on their own particular liturgical and worship traditions to such a degree that the churches do not express their own rich cultural heritage. To adjust for this global observation, a fifth self—self-expression—is focused on adapting cultural forms in biblical ways that identify the church with the culture.

The goal of a church planting movement is indigeneity. A church is indigenous when it becomes self-sustaining in five areas: leadership, multiplication, teaching, financing, and expression. The five-self framework encourages a congregation to rely upon its own resources to become sustainable. Having a clear sustainability plan at the beginning of a new church plant provides a greater sense of creating a movement of evangelism and discipleship that will grow exponentially over time, without relying on Western resources. It also requires us to think about systems that are culturally consonant with and conducive to the longevity of the work. The five-self model prevents missionaries from setting up structures that cannot be sustained by the resources of the new church.

The church indigeneity matrix (CIM) is one tool to help determine a church's level of indigeneity. The matrix is a self-assessment tool for churches to evaluate their progress from being a new church plant to becoming a reproducing church that is a leader in a church planting movement. See Table 25 on the next page.

The Western conformity of the global church runs the risk of creating a church that is homogenous and without distinct cultural expressions. The beautiful picture that the Apostle John paints for us in Revelation is a church that is identified by sundry cultures and expressions of worship to the one true Creator and God. Distinct languages will be used to worship the King, with the implication that every ethnic group will bring something unique to the throne. As John wrote, "Who will not fear, O Lord, and glorify your name? For you alone are holy. All nations will come and worship you, for your righteous acts have been revealed" (Rev 15:4).

There is a risk of continued resistance to the gospel, as ethnic groups desire to preserve their own cultures and view Christianity as a threat because of its Western baggage. The gospel—and by extension, the church—is not a Western creation. They are both given by a creative God who has determined the boundaries for all people groups, so that they might seek after God and even find him (Acts 17:26–27). To deny a unique expression of the church in a particular culture is to deny the very uniqueness of people as created in God's image.

| | CIM0 | CIM1 | CIM2 | CIM3 | CIM4 | CIM5 | Total |
|---|---|---|---|---|---|---|---|
| Self-Propagating | No ministry initiatives | Evangelism | Short-Term discipleship | Leadership multiplication | Long-Term discipleship | Church multiplication | |
| Self-Governing | No indigenous ecclesiastical structure | Indigenous ecclesiastical structure | Indigenous leadership development | Leaders appointed by church | Leaders are multiplying churches | Leaders leading movements | |
| Self-Funded | Church receives outside support | Church gives | Church supports its own ministry | Church supports its pastor | Church gives to missions | Church supports missionaries | |
| Self-Theologizing | No Bible interpretation | Proper understanding of basic Bible interpretation | Doing theology in community | Indigenous discipleship program | Cultural relevant theological topics | Teaching culturally relevant theological topics | |
| Self-Expression | No indigenous worship | Indigenous instruments used in worship | Church service is culturally appropriate | Culturally relevant place of worship | Indigenous music written | Culturally appropriate ecclesiology | |

TABLE 25: CHURCH INDIGENEITY MATRIX

As we sat in a home in Chennai, India, listening to a group of Christian leaders talk about their experiences, a translator interrupted the conversation to share that this leader had been beaten five times and that another leader had been imprisoned three times. Each of the thirty or so leaders had their own stories to tell. The scene was vaguely reminiscent of my junior high school days, when all of us boys would gather together in the schoolyard to compare our scars. As we shared the exploits that marked our bodies, the memory of the pain was overshadowed by the fantastic stories in a childish game of one-upmanship.

What I was hearing in India, however, was qualitatively different. The joy that I saw on the faces of so many leaders who had suffered for the sake of Christ was testimony to the momentary light afflictions that pale in comparison to the glory of more people following Jesus every day. For them, the scars of persecution are worth the pleasure of knowing that the gospel is spreading, disciples are being made, and God is being worshipped.

If a missiologically theocentric movement is the heart of your church, ministry, or mission, you could do no better than to discover for yourself what motivates leaders like these and the others I have written about in *Ephesiology*, as well as what motivated the church in Ephesus to continue the works of her first love. It is one thing for me to lay out what I see and have experienced. It is something quite different for you to begin to see and experience it as well.

I hope I have at least inspired you to continue on this journey toward a New Testament movement. To be honest, I hope that I have inspired you to put on the glasses of those first-century movement leaders and see what they saw, learn what they learned, and put into action a missiologically theocentric pursuit for God's glory. To this end, I continue to pray for you as the Apostle Paul did for the churches in Asia. I hope you will also pray this for me.

> For this reason, because I have heard of your faith in the Lord Jesus and your love toward all the saints, I do not cease to give thanks for you, remembering you in my prayers, that the God of our Lord Jesus Christ, the Father of glory, may give you the Spirit of wisdom and of revelation in the knowledge of him, having the eyes of your hearts enlightened, that you may know what is the hope to which he has called you, what are the riches of his glorious inheritance in the saints, and what is the immeasurable greatness of his power toward us who believe, according to the working of his great might that he worked in Christ when he raised him from the dead and seated him at his right hand in the heavenly places, far above all rule and authority and power and dominion, and above every name that is named, not only in this age but also in the one to come. And he put all things under his feet and gave him as head over all things to the church, which is his body, the fullness of him who fills all in all. (Eph 1:15–23)

Every year, I tend to get the wonderful opportunity to go to a conference for church planting, discipleship, or the like. Inevitably, the information at these events is similar to what it must feel like to drink out of a fire hydrant—it's more than I can handle, it keeps on coming, and I am not too sure what to do with it all now that it's here.

Perhaps you feel the same way after reading this book. Perhaps you feel, though well-argued and nicely paced, the information in these pages was more than you can handle, it just kept coming and you aren't really sure what to do with it. You've now arrived at the Afterword wide-eyed, your heart likely burning, and this question rolling around in your mind: "Now what?"

"Now what?" This question has been nagging me since interacting with the many facets that this book addresses. I started on this journey with Michael before the book came out, and the increased exposure to these ideas heightened the need for an answer: *now what?* As a pastor in a legacy(ish) church, I've questioned everything that we do. *Is this reaching anyone? Am I fighting what God wants to do in America and worldwide? Am I entertaining and merely keeping this dying system alive for another year?* The thoughts presented through *Ephesiology* have caused me to go back to the theological drawing board. I've spent a great deal of time in prayer and thought. I've been reading, I've been prodding, I've been digging into all that we are a part of at Neartown Church and I've answered the "now what?" question in this way: *Restore.*

Why *restore?* Because I am desperate to restore my heart and the ministry that God has given me to his intended end; not mine, not my denomination's, not my culture's. Here's how that's impacting four areas for me.

Preaching: Are my words on Sundays simply stroking the intellectual ego of people who want to know more Bible knowledge? Are they giving folks an easy three-step self-help program? Or are they helping ignite within others a white-hot pursuit of God's will to unite all things in Him? *Am I playing my part in restoring God's intent for passionate worshippers through my ministry?*

Leadership Development: Are the leaders I am raising up encouraged to try harder, try different, or submit to the gracious God we serve? Phrased differently, am I modeling a leadership that has one authority (Jesus) and invites them to walk alongside me in calling ALL to worship of Him? *Am I growing leaders with a Godward focus?*

Personal Discipleship: Am I asking these new believers or potential believers to adopt new morals or to take on the life-altering identity of a child of the King? *Am I restoring others to God's intent for a world of reconcilers?*

Kingdom Impact: Am I involved in collaboration to prove how awesome we are to other churches or am I linking arms with others to see the name of Christ grow in fame and glory throughout Houston (and beyond)? Am I building God's Kingdom or my own? Am I putting all my energy behind the efforts that all may know peace in Christ or behind building a bigger brand (while claiming it is for Christ that we keep needing "more" out of people)? *Am I restoring Christ's vision for a unified church?*

But that's me. How might you go about answering this question of, "Now what?"

Can I offer the standard, near cliché Christian first step? *Pray.* Seriously! Take some time away today and carve out space over the next few days to pray. Some suggestions for that prayer time:

- God, where have I put anything (systems, denominations, institutions, figure-heads, leaders, theological systems, just to name a few) ahead of you? Please open my eyes to what I've been blind to.

- Repent! Leave behind your affection (that might have bordered on worship) of these other things and turn your eyes and heart back to this True King, Jesus Christ.

- Jesus, lead my heart back to you, my first love, in all things.

- God, draw my attention and efforts to your will—to unite all things in you through Jesus Christ (Eph 1:10).

- Holy Spirit, empower me to faithfully pursue a missiologically theocentric passion for your mission of bringing more people to worship you.

After doing the heart work of prayer, repentance and submission, step two is a baseline assessment. What I mean is not a long, drawn out, formalized assessment. Rather, look back over the book; where did you feel that your work, your ministry, your church, or your institution has begun (or continued) to be entrenched in simply surviving as opposed to pursuing God's will? Where did you feel totally undone and almost frustrated because of where things have gotten in your area of ministry?

Once you've been able to articulate some of these spots, go back to prayer.

Ask God how he'd like for you to respond to this awakening. Do you quit and move to Asia? Do you seek a higher position within your network/denomination to effectively raise your concerns? Do you redouble your efforts to see the people in the areas where God has placed you come to know him as Saviour? Do you increase your time in Jesus' presence because you know you're where you are because that's been lacking? Is there a work in the culture that you know God wants to have you bring the good news of His Son and you are uniquely gifted to speak into? Is there a personal, professional or public change that you need to embark on?

In this prayer, remember—God hasn't stopped working simply because you and his Bride in the West have been distracted or too easily satisfied in worthless things. Ask God where he *has been moving*. Ask God for the eyes to see his movement and the strength to join him in it.

Lastly, I want to state something that you may have noticed by now—*Ephesiology* is not attempting to provide a new system for you to put in place, a better model to pursue or even a new set of figure heads to look up to. The aim of this book has been dead set on God's glory and more people pursuing that unabashedly. A renewed focus here might lead you to walk away from "tried and true" playbooks from renowned organizations. It might propel you towards one of the many actions you just prayed for (or a countless number unlisted). Whatever it is, we invite you to embrace it with us. Join our Ephesiology Laboratory (scan the QR code for more information). We want to  encourage you in whatever steps you feel you or your church need to take to re-engage the culture and the place that God has put you. We want to connect you to other Laboratory partners who are also working in their unique cultures and places and asking some of these daring questions. Furthermore, we want to do all we can to develop the future of the Bride of Christ in whatever expression it takes to the glory of His name and the expansion of His kingdom.

And, if you've done *all* of this and still don't feel you know what to do, then join us on our podcast weekly as we wrestle through these steps as well. Whatever the case, you can just join us weekly, whether you've figured out what God's calling you to or not. We're all on common ground.

**ANDREW JOHNSON**
associate pastor of Neartown Church, Houston, TX
co-host, Ephesiology Podcast

*Movement Action Plan*

For video instructions on the Movement Action Plan, scan the QR code or go to our website at https://ephesiology.com/movement-action-plan/

## General Information

Target Area: _____

Address: _____

Estimated Total Lostness: _____

Estimated Response to the Gospel: _____

Estimated Number of House Churches/Small Groups Needed to Establish: _____

Potential Partners in Our Area: _____

## Vision

- What is God's vision for your target area? Let the Holy Spirit motivating your spirit to engage the lost in your community.

- Use a calendar to set up a regular time of prayer focusing on seeing your target area with God's eyes for the lost (daily personal prayer, weekly key leader prayer, monthly partner prayer, quarterly twenty-four-hour prayer).

|  | Week 1 | Week 2 | Week 3 | Week 4 |
|---|---|---|---|---|
| Sunday |  |  |  |  |
| Monday |  |  |  |  |
| Tuesday |  |  |  |  |
| Wednesday |  |  |  |  |
| Thursday |  |  |  |  |
| Friday |  |  |  |  |
| Saturday |  |  |  |  |

## Church Planting Movement Blueprint

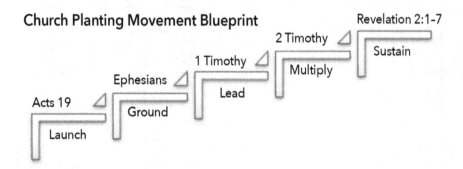

### Preparation to Launch a Movement

- How is the Holy Spirit motivating you to engage your community?
- What is the story of the people in your target area (culture, history, beliefs)?
- What stories in Jesus' life do you believe will connect with the stories of the target area?
- What is your compelling view of God?
- What is the connecting point between your compelling view of God and the people of the target area?
- Write out a brief gospel presentation that will resonate with the people in your target area:

### Preparation to Ground a Movement

- Articulate your understanding of a discipleship process:
- How many and who are the leaders equipped to disciple new believers and lead house churches/small groups?

### Preparation to Lead a Movement

- What steps have you taken to identify the right people who are capable of teaching correct doctrine and who live a life modeled after 1 Timothy 3?

### Preparation to Multiply a Movement

- How does your discipleship process multiply disciples?
- Is your model replicable, and if so, how?
- How long will it take for you to multiply small groups or house churches with your current plan?

### *Preparation to Sustain a Movement*

- What is your plan to keep people focused on the main ministry of engaging the lost and building up worshippers of God?

- Define "disciple":

## Action Steps

The Four Fields Cycle is a simple tool to help you think through an engagement, evangelism, equipping, and establishing strategy. For video instructions on the Four Fields Cycle, scan the QR code or visit our website at https://ephesiology.com/the-four-fields-cycle/

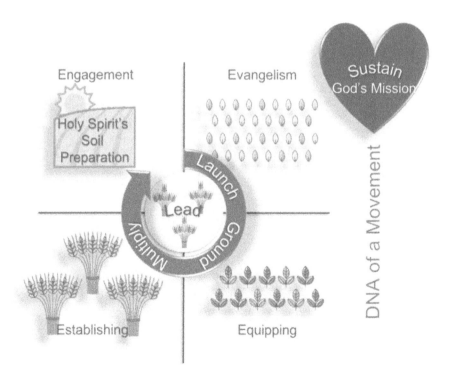

*Moving to Engagement*

1.  What have you identified that you can do today to begin engaging your community?

Start Date: _____/_____/_____

2.  What have you identified that you can do next week to begin engaging your community?

Start Date: _____/_____/_____

### *Moving to Evangelism*

1.  How will you be present in the community?

2.  How often will you be in the community? Describe what that will look like.

Start Date: _____/_____/_____

## *Moving to Equipping*

1. How have you prepared the team to equip new believers?

2. What are the first five studies that you will do to disciple new believers?

3. What is your long-term plan to disciple new believers?
   List the next twelve studies.

## *Moving to Establishing*

1.  What locations have you identified that will serve as the location of small groups/house churches?




2.  How will you continue your presence in the community?




3.  Are you prepared to contact new believers on a daily, weekly, monthly basis? What will this practically look like?

# EPHESIOLOGY

## Accountability Plan

*Launching a Movement*

Number of community visits:

Number of spiritual conversations:

Number of gospel conversations:

Number of new followers of Jesus:

*Grounding a Movement*

Number of follow-up meetings with new followers of Jesus:

Number of small groups/house churches started:

Number of new followers of Jesus attending Sunday morning:

*Leading a Movement*

Number of leaders equipped:

*Multiplying a Movement*

Number of new disciples engaging the lost:

Number of new disciples beginning small groups/house churches:

*Sustaining a Movement*

Number of disciples:

Number of people engaging people versus new programs:

# APPENDIX B

# Movement Maturity Matrix

The Movement Maturity Matrix (3M) is an evaluative tool designed to help you assess where your church has strengths and where it needs strengthened in relationship to becoming a movement. The evaluative statements making up the matrix are based on the movement at Ephesus and characteristics we see in the New Testament that propelled the gospel forward in all of Asia. Pastors, elders, staff, and key leaders can utilize the tool together and assess where they should concentrate their efforts in order to help the church mature into a movement in their community.

Each box in the matrix is given one value: true = 1; false = 0. The "Total" vertical column helps you see where you will want to give attention. Scores of three or less should stimulate discussion among your leadership related to reasons why the score is low and steps that should be taken to strengthen the respective area. The "Total" horizontal row gives you an overall score regarding where you are on the movement continuum. The score is weighted as you work across the continuum, indicating that the more weight given to a column, the closer you are to the characteristics of the Ephesian movement.

The evaluative statements are generally meant to build from one to the other. For example, it would be difficult to say that a church can communicate God's story if it is not grounded theologically. Similarly, you would not say that a church can connect theology and culture if the church has not first exegeted the culture. However, a hard line is not drawn between each statement. For example, you might have APES-T leaders (apostles, prophets, evangelists, shepherd-teachers) who are equipping the saints for ministry, but struggle to maintain unity and peace in the congregation. Mostly I hope that these statements represent common sense as you evaluate your church in the context of how the Ephesian movement exploded all over Asia.

| | M1 | M2 | M3 | M4 | M5 | Total |
|---|---|---|---|---|---|---|
| Launching a Movement | Church is grounded theologically | Church can effectively communicate God's story | Church has exegeted the culture | Church has connected theology and culture | The community's story is seen as a part of God's story | __/5 |
| Grounding a Movement | Can answer the question "What is God's will?" | Sees the church as God's instrument in advancing the gospel | Church has a vision for the nations in their community and in the world | Church strives together for unity and peace | APES-T are equipping the saints for ministry | __/5 |
| Leading a Movement | Church can identify leaders with good reputations in the community | Leaders are able to manage their oikos well | Leaders are equipped to teach sound doctrine | Leaders focus on equipping the church for ministry | Leaders are multiplying more leaders | __/5 |
| Leading a Movement | Church is successful in making disciples who willingly risk for the gospel | Disciples are equipped to make more disciples | Disciples are discipling more disciples | Disciples are seeing G3 growth | Disciples are seeing G4 growth | __/5 |
| Sustaining a Movement | Church has an apologetics ministry that is gracious in addressing community issues | Church has a social justice ministry focused on addressing issues in the community | Church is focused on the completion of God's mission of more people worshipping Him as their first love | The church's mission activity is focused on Jerusalem, Judea, Samaria, and the end of the world | The church is planting more churches in their community and world | __/5 |
| Total | __/5 | __x2= __/10 | __x3= __/15 | __x4= __/20 | __x5= __/25 | __/75 |

TABLE 26: MOVEMENT MATURITY MATRIX

# REFERENCES

Addison, Steve. 2019. *The Rise and Fall of Movements: A Road Map for Leaders.* 100Movements Publishing.

Alexander, Loveday. 1995. "Paul and the Hellenistic Schools: The Evidence of Galen." In *Paul in His Hellenistic Context*, edited by Troels Engberg-Pedersen. Minneapolis: Fortress.

Allen, Roland. 1912 (1962). *Missionary Methods: Saint Paul's or Ours?* Grand Rapids: Eerdmans.

Anson, Edward M. 2010. "The Introduction of the 'Sarisa' in Macedonian Warfare." *Ancient Society*, vol. 40: 51–68.

Anyabwile, Thabiti M. 2012. *Finding Faithful Elders and Deacons.* Wheaton, IL: Crossway.

Barkhuizen, J. H. 1990. "The Strophic Structure of the Eulogy of Ephesians 1:3–14." *HTS Teologiese Studies* 46, no. 3: 390–413.

Barna Group. 2019. "Almost Half of Practicing Christian Millennials Say Evangelism Is Wrong." Barna Group website. February 5, 2019. https://www.barna.com/research/millennials-oppose-evangelism/.

Baugh, S. M. 1999. "Cult Prostitution in New Testament Ephesus: A Reappraisal." *Journal of the Evangelical Theological Society* 42, no. 3: 443–60.

Betz, H. D., ed. 1986. *The Greek Magical Papyri in Translation, Including the Demotic Spells.* Chicago: University of Chicago Press.

Blumer, Herbert. 1969. "Collective Behavior." In *Principles of Sociology.* 3rd ed., edited by A. M. Lee. New York: Barnes and Noble.

Bosch, David. 1991. *Transforming Missions: Paradigm Shifts in Theology of Missions.* Maryknoll, NY: Orbis Press.

Botticini, Maristella, and Zvi Eckstein. 2012. *The Chosen Few: How Education Shaped Jewish History, 70–1492.* Princeton, NJ: Princeton University Press.

Bright, Bill. n.d. "Catch the Excitement for the Great Commission." Accessed October 25, 2017. https://www.cru.org/train-and-grow/transferable-concepts/help-fulfill-the-great-commission.html.

Brinks, C. L. 2009. "'Great is Artemis of the Ephesians': Acts 19:23–41 in Light of Goddess Worship in Ephesus." *The Catholic Biblical Quarterly* 71.

Cambier, J. 1963. "La Benediction d'Eph 1,3–14." *ZNW* 54: 58–104.

Carson, Donald A. 1990. *The Gospel According to John*. Grand Rapids: Eerdmans.

Charanis, Peter. 1975. "Cultural Diversity and the Breakdown of the Byzantine Power in Asia." *Dumbarton Oaks Papers* vol. 29:1–20.

Cooper, Michael T. 2005. "Colonialism, Neo-Colonialism and Forgotten Missiological Lessons." *Global Missiology 2*, no. 2. http://ojs.globalmissiology.org/index.php/english/article/view/105

———. 2009. "The Role of Nature, Deities, and Ancestors in Constructing Religious Identity in Contemporary Druidry." *Pomegranate: The International Journal of Pagan Studies* 11, no. 1.

———. 2010. *Contemporary Druidry: An Ethnographic and Historiographic Study*. Salt Lake City: Sacred Tribes Press.

———. 2018. "Toward a Biblical Understanding of Finishing the Task." *Global Missiology* 2, no. 2, No. 15. http://ojs.globalmissiology.org/index.php/english/article/view/2079

———. 2019. *God's Mission in the World: A Simple Study of the Bible's Grand Narrative for Oral Learners*. Ephesiology Press.

Dale, Robert William. 1897. *The Epistle to the Ephesians*. London: Butler and Tanner.

Dawson, Lorne L. 2006. "Psychopathologies and the Attribution of Charisma: A Critical Introduction to the Psychology of Charisma and the Explanation of Violence in New Religious Movements." *Nova Religio: The Journal of Alternative and Emergent Religions* 10, no. 2: 2–28.

Erickson, Millard. 1984. *Christian Theology*. Grand Rapids: Baker.

Fee, Gordon D. 1985. "Reflections on Church Order in the Pastoral Epistles, with Further Reflections on the Hermeneutics of Ad Hoc Documents." *JETS* 28, no. 2: 141–51.

Ferguson, Niall. 2003. *Empire: How Britain Made the Modern World*. London: Penguin Books.

Florovsky, George. 1995. "The Authority of the Ancient Councils and the Tradition of the Fathers." In *Eastern Orthodox Theology*, edited by Daniel B. Clendenin, 115–24. Grand Rapids: Baker.

Foulkes, Francis. 1989. *The Letter of Paul to the Ephesians: An Introduction and Commentary*. Grand Rapids: Eerdmans.

Frayer-Griggs, Daniel. 2013. "The Beasts at Ephesus and the Cult of Artemis." *Harvard Theological Review* 106, no. 4: 459–77.

Frend, W. H. C. 1984. *The Rise of Christianity*. Minneapolis: Fortress.

Fu, Jackson. 2016. "The Economics of Empire: Housing Size and Per-Capita Wealth in Asia." Proceedings of the National Conference on Undergraduate Research. University of North Carolina.

Garrison, David. 1999. *Church Planting Movements*. Richmond, VA: Office of Overseas Operations, International Mission Board of the Southern Baptist Convention.

———. 2004. *Church Planting Movements: How God Is Redeeming the World*. Monument, CO: WIGTake Resources.

Giles, Kevin. 2002. *The Trinity and Subordinationism: The Doctrine of God and the Contemporary Gender Debate*. Downers Grove, IL: InterVarsity.

Glover, Robert. 1931. *The Progress of World-Wide Missions*, 3rd ed. New York: Harper and Brothers.

Guthrie, Donald. 1990. *The Pastoral Epistles*. Grand Rapids: Eerdmans.

Harris, William. 1991. *Ancient Literacy*. Cambridge, MA: Harvard University Press.

Head, Barclay Vincent. 1880. *On the Chronological Sequence of the Coins of Ephesus*. Paris: Rollin and Feuardent.

Hesselgrave, David. J. 1980. *Planting Churches Cross-Culturally: A Guide for Home and Foreign Mission*. Grand Rapids: Baker.

Hiebert, Paul G. 1994. *Anthropological Reflections on Missiological Issues*. Grand Rapids: Baker.

Hill, Charles E. 1998. "What Papias Said About John (And Luke) A 'New' Papian Fragment." *Journal of Theological Studies*, NS, vol. 49, part 2: 582–629.

Hopkins, Keith. 1998. "Christian Number and Its Implication." *Journal of Early Christian Studies* 6, no. 2: 185–226.

Hussey, Edward. 1982. "Epistomology and Meaning in Heraclitus." In Language and Logos: Studies in *Ancient Greek Philosophy*, edited by Malcom Schofield and Martha Nussbaum, 33–60. New York: Cambridge University Press.

Johnson, Todd M., and Gina A. Zurlo, eds. 2020. *World Christian Database*. Leiden/Boston: Brill.

Jones, Brian W. 1992. *The Emperor Domitian*. New York: Routledge.

Kahn, Charles H. 1981. *The Art and Thought of Heraclitus: Fragments with Translation and Commentary*. Cambridge: Cambridge University Press.

Keener, Craig S. 2010. *The Gospel of John: A Commentary, Vol. 1*. Grand Rapids: Baker Academic, 2010.

Kemmler, Dieter W. 1975. *Faith and Human Reason: A Study of Paul's Method of Preaching as Illustrated by 1–2 Thessalonians and Acts 17, 2–4*. Leiden: Brill.

Klauck, Hans-Josef. 2003. *Magic and Paganism in Early Christianity*. Minneapolis: Fortress.

Kostenberger, Andreas. 2005. "The Destruction of the Second Temple and the Composition of the Fourth Gospel," *Trinity Journal* 26: 205–42.

Kramer, H. 1967. "Zur sprachlichen Form der Eulogie Eph 1, 3–14." *Wort und Dients* Vol. 9: 34–46.

Larkin, William J. 1995. *Acts*. Downers Grove, IL: InterVarsity.

Lewis, C. S. 1944. *Theology as Poetry?* Oxford Socratic Club. Samizdat: Samizdat University Press.

———. 1952. *Mere Christianity*. New York: Harper Collins.

LiDonnici, L. R. 1992. "The Images of Artemis Ephesia and Greco-Roman Worship: A Reconsideration." *The Harvard Theological Review* 85, no. 4: 389–415.

Lindsay, Hugh. 2011. "Adoption and Heirship in Greece and Rome." In *A Companion to Families in the Greek and Roman Worlds*, edited by Beryl Rawson. Hoboken, NJ: Blackwell.

Littman, R. J., and M. L. Littman. 1973. "Galen and the Antonine Plague." *The American Journal of Philology* 94, no. 3: 243–55.

Logan, Robert. 1990. *Beyond Church Growth: Actions Plans for Developing a Dynamic Church*. Grand Rapids: Revell.

Macionis, John J. 2001. *Sociology*. 8th ed. Upper Saddle River, NJ: Prentice Hall.

Marshall, Howard. 1980. *The Acts of the Apostles: An Introduction and Commentary*. Grand Rapids: Eerdmans.

Mason, Arthur James. 1899. *The Five Theological Orations of Gregory of Nazianzus*. Cambridge, MA: Cambridge University Press.

McClure, Jennifer M. 2016. "Introducing Jesus's Social Network: Support, Conflict, and Compassion." *Interdisciplinary Journal of Research on Religion* 12, no. 5: 2–21.

McGiffert, Arthur Cushman. 1890. *The Church History of Eusebius, Translated with Prolegomena and Notes*. Grand Rapids: Christian Classics Ethereal Library.

Miller, Fredrick D. 1999. "The end of SDS and the emergence of weatherman: Demise through success." In *Waves of Protest: Social Movements Since the Sixties*, edited by J. Freeman and V. Johnson, 303–24. Lanham, MD: Rowman & Littlefield.

Moltmann, Jürgen. 1977. *The Church in the Power of the Spirit: A Contribution to Messianic Ecclesiology*. London: SCM Press

Monfort, Cesar Carreras. 1996. "A New Perspective for the Demographic Study of Roman Spain." *Revista de Historia da Arte e Arqueologia* no. 2, 59–82.

Morris, Rudolf E. 1949. "Vincent of Lérins: The Commonitories." In *The Fathers of the Church*. Edited by Ludwig Schopp. New York: The Fathers of the Church, Inc.

Neill, Stephen. 1966. *Colonialism and Christian Missions*. New York: McGraw-Hill.

Netland, Harold A. 2001. *Encountering Religious Pluralism: The Challenge to Christian Faith Mission*. Downers Grove, IL: InterVarsity.

Oden, Thomas. 1993. "Why We Believe in Heresy," *Christianity Today* 40, no. 3: 13.

Olson, Roger. 2008. "The Classical Free-Will Theist Model of God." In *Perspectives on the Doctrine of God: Four Views*, edited by Bruce Ware, 148–72. Nashville: B&H Academic.

Packard, Josh. 2015. *Exodus of the Religious Dones: Research Reveals the Size, Make-Up, and Motivations of the Formerly Churched Population*. Loveland, CO: Group Publishing.

Parks, Kent. 2017. "Finishing the Remaining 29 Percent of World Evangelization: Disciple-Making Movements as a Biblical, Holistic, and Radical Solution." *Lausanne Global Analysis*. Vol. 6, issue 3. May 2017. https://www.lausanne.org/content/lga/2017–05/finishing-the-remaining-29-of-world-evangelization.

Pate, C. Marvin. 2010. *Four Views of the Book of Revelation*. Grand Rapids: Zondervan.

Pinnock, Clark. 1994. "Systematic Theology." In *The Openness of God: A Biblical Challenge to the Traditional Understanding of God*, edited by Clark Pinnock, 101–25. Downers Grove, IL: InterVarsity.

Phipps, William E. 1980. "The Heresiarch: Pelagius or Augustine?" *Anglican Theological Review* 62:124–133.

Prill, Thorsten. 2017. "Martin Luther and Evangelical Mission: Father or Failure?" *Foundations* 73: 21–50.

Rainer, Thom E. 2018. "Hope for Dying Churches." Facts & Trends, LifeWay website. January 16, 2018. https://factsandtrends.net/2018/01/16/hope-for-dying-churches/.

Redman, Shawn. 2012. *Missiological Hermeneutics: Biblical Interpretation for the Global Church*. Eugene, OR: Wipf and Stock.

Richardson, Don. 1976. *Peace Child: An Unforgettable Story of Primitive Jungle Treachery in the Twentieth Century*. Ventura, CA: Regal.

Robbins, Charles J. 1980. "The Rhetorical Structure of Philippians 2:6–11." *CBQ* 42: 73–82.

Robinson, Benjamin W. 1910. "An Ephesian Imprisonment of Paul." *Journal of Biblical Literature* 29, no. 2: 181–89.

Ruch, Willibald. 1992. "Pavlov's Types of Nervous Systems, Eysenck's Typology and the Hippocrates-Galen Temperaments: An Empirical Examination of the Asserted Correspondence of Three Temperament Typologies." *Personality and Individual Differences* 13, no. 12: 1259–71.

Runciman, Steven. 1982. *The Medieval Manichee*. Cambridge: Cambridge Univ. Press.

Russell, J. C. 1958. *Late Ancient and Medieval Population*. Philadelphia: The American Philosophical Society.

Sandeen, Ernest R. 1970. *The Roots of Fundamentalism: American and British Millenarianism, 1800–1930*. Chicago: University of Chicago Press.

Sanders, John. 2008. "Divine Providence and the Openness of God." In *Perspectives on the Doctrine of God: Four Views*, edited by Bruce Ware, 196–240. Nashville: B&H Academic.

Schnabel, Eckhard J. 2004. *Early Christian Mission*. Downers Grove, IL: InterVarsity.

Schuler, Kristen. N.d. *Unashamed Faith*. Plano, TX: East West Ministries International.

Sequeira, Aubrey. 2015. "A Plea for Gospel Sanity in Missions," *9Marks Journal*. December 21, 2015. https://www.9marks.org/article/a-plea-for-gospel-sanity-in-missions/.

Silver, Carly. 2010. "Dura-Europos: Crossroads of Cultures." *Archaeology*. Archaeological Institute of America. August 11, 2010. https://archive. archaeology.org/online/features/dura_europos/.

Smith, Steve, and Ying Kai. 2011. *T4T: A Discipleship Re-Revolution*. Monument, CO: WIGTake Resources.

Stark, Rodney. 1996. *The Rise of Christianity: A Sociologist Reconsiders History*. Princeton, NJ: Princeton University Press.

Stott, John R. W. 1979. *The Message of Ephesians: God's New Society*. Leicester: InterVarsity.

Van Rheenen, Gailyn, ed. 2006. *Contextualization and Syncretism: Navigating Cultural Currents*. Pasadena, CA: William Carey Library.

Von Campenhausen, Hans. 1998. *The Fathers of the Church*. Peabody, MA: Hendrickson.

———. 1969. *The Fathers of the Latin Church*. Stanford: Stanford University Press.

Ware, Bruce A. 2002. "Defining Evangelicalism's Boundaries Theologically: Is Open Theism Evangelical?" *The Journal of the Evangelical Theological Society* 45.2:193–212.

———. 2008. "A Modified Calvinist Doctrine of God." In *Perspectives on the Doctrine of God: Four Views*, edited by Bruce Ware, 76–120. Nashville: B&H Academic.

———. 2015. *One God in Three Persons: Unity of Essence, Distinction of Person, Implications for Life*. Grand Rapids: Crossway.

Weber, Jeremy. 2017. "Evangelical vs. Born Again: A Survey of What Americans Say and Believe Beyond Politics." *Christianity Today*, December 6, 2017. https:// www.christianitytoday.com/news/2017/december/you-must-be-born-again-evangelical-beliefs-politics-survey.html.

Wenham, David. 1995. *Paul: Follower of Christ or Founder of Christianity?* Grand Rapids: Eerdmans.

Wessinger, Catherine. 2012. "Charismatic Leaders in New Religions." In *Cambridge Companion to New Religious Movements*, edited by Olav Hammer and Mikael Rothstein, 80–96. Cambridge: Cambridge University Press.

Westhead, Nigel. 1995. "Adoption in the Thought of John Calvin," *Scottish Bulletin of Evangelical Theology* 13, no. 2:102–15.

Wilder, Terry L. 2014. "Missions Methods and Principles." Editorial. *Southwestern Journal of Theology* 57, no. 1:1–3. https://swbts.edu/sites/default/files/images/ content/docs/journal/57_1/57.1%20Editorial%20Wilder.pdf

Winter, Ralph D., and Steven C. Hawthorne. 1981. *Perspectives on the World Christian Movement, A Reader*. Pasadena, CA: William Carey Library.

Wu, Jackson. 2014. "There Are No Church Planting Movements in the Bible: Why Biblical Exegesis and Missiological Methods Cannot Be Separated." *Global Missiology* 1, no. 12.

Xie J., et al. 2011. "Social Consensus Through the Influence of Committed Minorities." *Physical Review* E 84, 011130: 1–8.

Zamfir, Korinna. 2012. "Once More About the Origins and Background of the New Testament Episkopos." *Sacra Scripta* 10, no. 2: 202–22.

Zylstra, Sarah Eekhoff. 2018. "The 8 People Americans Trust More Than Their Local Pastor." *Christianity Today*. January 5, 2018. https://www.christianitytoday.com/news/2018/january/8-people-americans-trust-more-than-their-local-pastor.html.

The following ancient sources were utilized throughout the text where noted. These texts are easily accessible via an Internet search.

Alciphron. *Letters of Courtesans.*

Ambrosiaster. *Epistle to the Ephesians.*

Appian of Alexandria, *Mithridatic Wars.*

Aratus. *Phaenomena.*

Aristotle, *Athenian Constitution.*

Augustine. *Epistle 93.*

Augustine. *The Literally Meaning of Genesis.*

Callimachus. *Hymn III to Artemis.*

Chrysostom, John. *Homilies on Ephesians.*

Clement of Alexandria. *Stromota.*

Clement of Rome. *First Epistle to the Corinthians.*

Cyprian. *On the Unity of the Church.*

Diogenes Laërtius. *Lives of Eminent Philosophers.*

Ephiphanius. *Panarion.*

Eusebius. *Church History.*

Gregory of Nazianzus. *Five Theological Orations.*

Heraclitus of Ephesus. *On Nature.*

Hippolytus. *Refutation of All Heresies.*

Homer. *Iliad.*

Ignatius of Antioch. *Letter to the Smyrnaeans.*

Ignatius of Antioch. *Letter to the Trallians.*

Ignatius of Antioch. *Letter to the Philadelphians.*

Ignatius of Antioch. *Letter to the Ephesians.*

Irenaeus. *Against Heresies.*

Jerome. *Commentary on Matthew.*

Josephus, Flavius. *The War of the Jews.*

Josephus, Flavius. *Antiquities.*

Justin. *Dialogue with Trypho.*

Justin. *First Apology.*

Lucian. *Dialogues of the Courtesans.*

Marius Victorinus. *Commentary on the Letter to the Ephesians.*

*Martyrdom of Polycarp*

Origen. *Against Celsus.*

Origen. *Letter to Gregory.*

Papius. *Exposition of the Sayings of the Lord.*

*Papyri Graecae Magicae*

Pausanias. *Descriptions of Greece.*

Pliny the Younger. *Letter to Emperor Trajan.*

Plutarch. *Life of Antony.*

Plutarch. *Life of Pericles.*

Strabo. *Geography.*

Tertullian. *Apology.*

Tertullian. *On the Prescriptions of Heretics.*

Theodoret. *Letter to John the Economus.*

Vincent of Lerins. *Commonitorium.*

Xenophon of Ephesus. *Ephesian Tales of Anthia and Habrokomas.*

**MICHAEL T. COOPER** currently serves as an executive for a missions agency, training national leaders in evangelism, discipleship, leadership development, and church planting. He is the former president and CEO of an international NGO. In 2010, he founded a Business as Mission initiative that focused on helping alleviate spiritual and economic poverty in the developing world. For a decade he equipped undergraduate and graduate students at Trinity International University with skills to engage culture. He has thirty years of ministry and missions experience, ten years as a pioneer church planter in Romania after the fall of communism. He holds a MA in Missions from Columbia International University and a PhD in Intercultural Studies from Trinity Evangelical Divinity School. Throughout his career, Michael has focused on creative ways to engage difficult-to-reach people with the gospel.

CPSIA information can be obtained
at www.ICGtesting.com
Printed in the USA
LVHW031935061220
673493LV00017B/2401

3 4711 00232 8245

9 781645 082767